OTC Derivatives: Bilateral Trading & Central Clearing

Global Financial Markets Series

Global Financial Markets is a series of practical guides to the latest financial market tools, techniques and strategies. Written for practitioners across a range of disciplines it provides comprehensive but practical coverage of key topics in finance covering strategy, markets, financial products, tools and techniques and their implementation. This series will appeal to a broad readership, from new entrants to experienced practitioners across the financial services industry, including areas such as institutional investment; financial derivatives; investment strategy; private banking; risk management; corporate finance and M&A, financial accounting and governance, and many more.

Titles include:

Daniel Capocci
THE COMPLETE GUIDE TO HEDGE FUNDS AND HEDGE FUND STRATEGIES

Guy Fraser-Sampson
INTELLIGENT INVESTING
A Guide to the Practical and Behavioural Aspects of Investment Strategy

Michael Hünseler
CREDIT PORTFOLIO MANAGEMENT
A Practitioner's Guide to the Active Management of Credit Risks

Ross K. McGill
US WITHHOLDING TAX
Practical Implications of QI and FATCA

David Murphy
OTC DERIVATIVES: BILATERAL TRADING & CENTRAL CLEARING
An Introduction to Regulatory Policy, Market Impact and Systemic Risk

Gianluca Oricchio
PRIVATE COMPANY VALUATION
How Credit Risk Reshaped Equity Markets and Corporate Finance Valuation Tools

Andrew Sutherland and Jason Court
THE FRONT OFFICE MANUAL
The Definitive Guide to Trading, Structuring and Sales

Michael C. S. Wong and Wilson F. C. Chan (*editors*)
INVESTING IN ASIAN OFFSHORE CURRENCY MARKETS
The Shift from Dollars to Renminbi

Global Financial Markets series
Series Standing Order ISBN: 978–1137–32734–5

You can receive future titles in this series as they are published by placing a standing order. Please contact your bookseller or, in case of difficulty, write to us at the address below with your name and address, the title of the series and the ISBN quoted above.

Customer Services Department, Macmillan Distribution Ltd, Houndmills, Basingstoke, Hampshire RG21 6XS, England

OTC Derivatives: Bilateral Trading & Central Clearing

An Introduction to Regulatory Policy, Market Impact and Systemic Risk

David Murphy

First published 2013 by
PALGRAVE MACMILLAN

Palgrave Macmillan in the UK is an imprint of Macmillan Publishers Limited,
registered in England, company number 785998, of Houndmills, Basingstoke,
Hampshire RG21 6XS.

Palgrave Macmillan in the US is a division of St Martin's Press LLC,
175 Fifth Avenue, New York, NY 10010.

Palgrave Macmillan is the global academic imprint of the above companies
and has companies and representatives throughout the world.

Palgrave® and Macmillan® are registered trademarks in the United States,
the United Kingdom, Europe and other countries

ISBN: 978–1–137–29385–5

This book was designed in Stone Serif and Stone Sans by the author.
It is printed on paper suitable for recycling and made from fully
managed and sustained forest sources. Logging, pulping and manufacturing
processes are expected to conform to the environmental regulations of the
country of origin

A catalogue record for this book is available from the British Library.

A catalog record for this book is available from the Library of Congress.

Contents

List of Figures

Introduction

Never Let A Serious Crisis Go To Waste

The global financial crisis which began in 2007 laid bare many vulnerabilities of the financial system. Many banks had too little good quality capital, too much liquidity risk, and too many risky assets. Banks, broker/dealers and hedge funds failed during the crisis, and matters would have been even worse had central banks not taken unprecedented actions to restore stability.

From these events came reform. The United States passed the Dodd Frank Act whose 16 titles cover financial stability, the liquidation of financial institutions, derivatives regulation and much, much else. The Basel Committee agreed a third Accord and numerous ancillary regulations, and the European Union was also neither slow nor terse in its rule making. No one has let the crisis go to waste as a motivation for regulation writing.

Mandatory clearing

This book is about one of the changes mandated as a result of those legislative efforts, the clearing of over-the-counter ('OTC') derivatives. These requirements are interesting for a number of reasons:

- They will create profound changes to the financial system;

- The need for mandatory OTC derivatives clearing is debatable, and the costs it will impose are substantial;

- The process will be implemented in a far from optimal fashion; and

- The regulations will create profits for the private entities which are at the heart of the process, the clearing houses.

Various matters must be considered as part of this story. The pre-crisis market and its infrastructure is relevant, as are some of the events of the crisis itself. We will explain what central clearing is and why some commentators thought that it was a good idea. Clearing houses are presented, and we discuss how they mitigate, create and transform

1

various risks. This leads to the question of whether central clearing as implemented unequivocally improves the financial system.

It will hardly spoil the surprise to say now that we believe that the answer to this question is no, although this conclusion can be contested, and the motivations of most rule-makers were undoubtedly good.

Design and consequences

It is difficult to write good regulations. Finance is complicated, so the rules that financial institutions must follow are concomitantly intricate. The financial system changes in response to regulation, too, so a successful rule writer has not only to draft something that works today, but they must also try to anticipate how the system might react to the new constraints that are being introduced.

Public policy requires that choices are made. Often there is no optimal approach, but rather the selection of one incomparable set of costs and benefits above others. This quandary occurs often in the construction of OTC derivatives regulation. We will examine some of the key design decisions, highlighting the trade-offs involved.

An example from elsewhere illustrates the dilemma: consider the problem of travelling into space. During the 1990s it became clear that US government-sponsored programmes were an expensive and possibly sub-optimal way of getting people beyond the atmosphere (and back). Perhaps the private sector could produce a cheap launch vehicle and bring it to market faster than NASA? Some regulations were needed to stop enterprising individuals from strapping weather balloons to a lawn chair and calling the result a spacecraft. On the other hand, if private space vehicles were too highly regulated then they would probably be uneconomic to develop. This would not achieve the desired objective of fostering new, cheaper but still reasonably safe forms of space travel.

There is no obviously correct approach here; rather there are many detailed issues. At the time of writing, for instance, the United States' Office of Commercial Space Transportation had just revised part 420 of Title 14 of the Code of Federal Regulations (14 CFR) Chapter III, updating the FAA's requirements for how to site explosives under a license to operate a launch site. This new rule is one of hundreds the OCST has to write as part of its implementation of the 2011 Commercial Space Launch Act. Writing most of these regulations involves delicate decisions about the severity of various risks, and the cost and efficacy of different risk mitigation mechanisms.

We can see that complex regulations with many choices which can affect the viability of a whole industry are not confined to finance. The post-crisis financial reforms were unusual, though, in their complexity, the speed of their enactment, and the lack of objective evidence used in their construction. In some cases it seemed to be the equivalent of deciding that all rockets had to have three fins whatever the proven benefits of four (or for that matter the possibility of dispensing with them entirely through the use of steerable exhaust nozzles). These 'three fin' regulations will influence the financial system profoundly.

The arrangement of the book

This book is organised into two parts. The first looks at the bilateral OTC derivatives market and its risks, and explains the role that OTC derivatives played in the financial crisis. The second looks at regulatory responses. In particular, we discuss OTC derivatives clearing and the changes it will bring to the post-crisis derivatives markets. The regulations which mandate clearing are analysed, as are some alternative choices of rule with different systemic consequences. We end with an examination of the likely nature and risks of the OTC derivatives markets after the current reforms have been implemented.

Each chapter consists of a discussion followed by end notes which give references and discuss some issues in greater detail (and sometimes at a greater level of sophistication). General readers will not miss the main arguments if these end notes are skipped entirely, while those interested in a detailed point will find caveats, expansions of the argument and pointers to other work.

An overview

OTC derivatives can be complicated. Financial regulations are recondite, too. Add in a soupçon of case law, a pinch of quantitative analysis and a dash of high-end information technology, and you have a situation where myriad details may be relevant. Therefore, while this book attempts to give a good introduction to many of the key issues in bilateral and cleared OTC derivatives, there will necessarily be many simplifications and glosses over potentially important detail.

There are many good books, articles and notes on the quantitative aspects of derivatives pricing, so we largely skirt those issues. This allows the book to dispense with mathematics, making the text more accessible at the cost of precision.

The book was written in the autumn and winter of 2012. Some of the regulatory initiatives we describe are not yet final, and others are likely to evolve as experience is gained and the political climate changes. In particular, many OTC derivatives regulations have not yet been finalised in either the US or the EU. Therefore while the general shape and many of the details of the post-crisis regulatory environment are known, some things can (and inevitably will) change. You are therefore strongly encouraged to check that the ground has not moved when reading any of the descriptions of the regulatory framework given in this book, or indeed anywhere else.

Market infrastructure is evolving fast, too, as are the means of trading. All of this means that no one can predict what the OTC derivatives market will look like in several years' time. We will try to make predictions, but they are necessarily extrapolations rather than certainties. (The speed of change and the level of detail we give also mean that you cannot and should not rely on any of our descriptions to be sufficiently correct that a cent should be staked on them.)

Perspective

The approach to finance we will use is to try to understand how behaviours are created by interactions between parts of the system given the rules under which they have to operate. If a behaviour is undesirable, and especially if it represents a serious systemic risk; then we want to understand what features created the problem. Was it shaky infrastructure, unhelpful incentives, asymmetric information – or even bad regulation? I think this is a more useful question than 'was that trader to blame?' or 'does this firm resemble a vampire squid?' not because the answer to those questions is likely to be 'no' but rather because no answer gives much insight. It tells us who to blame today, but not how to stop the same problem happening again tomorrow. It is only by looking at what features of the system caused the bad behaviour that we can hope to stop the mistakes of the past being repeated.

Acknowledgements

This book has benefited greatly from the insights of others. Conversations with Julian Day, David Geen and Richard Metcalfe were particularly valuable. Edwin Budding deserves a special mention for his wide and detailed knowledge of the topic and his generosity in sharing it both in conversation and as co-author of Chapter 9. Bill Hodgson brings special expertise to Chapter 7: my thanks to him, too, for that.

I learned a great deal from OTC derivatives market participants; Peter Axilrod, Nathalie Bouez, Eduardo Canabarro, Curtis Doty, Darryll Hendricks, Chris Holliman, Greg Hopper, Ulrich Karl, Gregg Rapaport, Sven Sandow, Jonathan Taylor and Henry Wayne all shared their understanding, and I am grateful to them all, and to Mark White for his diligent and fair-minded chairmanship of the Basel Committee's RMG.

I am very grateful to Sue Sharkey for her diligent proof reading and punctuation criticism. My editor Pete Baker has been supportive of this project and of my typographical predilections, for which I thank him profusely. All errors, omissions and mis-judgements remain, of course, the author's (unless otherwise indicated).

David Murphy
Spitalfields, January 2013

Part I

Understanding Bilateral OTC Derivatives

1

Over-The-Counter Derivatives

Concepts, like people, have their histories.
They are just as vulnerable to the ravages
of time as individuals.
But in and through all this they keep
a certain homesickness for
the scenes of their youth.
Søren Kierkegaard

Introduction

A derivative is a contractual relationship between two parties. Each entity makes a financial commitment. For instance, one may pay the other a sum of money in exchange for the right to buy something at a fixed price in the future; or both parties may promise to make a series of payments to the other.

One categorisation of derivatives is based on how they are transacted:

- Over-The-Counter (or 'OTC') derivatives are transacted bilaterally between the two parties; whereas

- Exchange-traded derivatives are traded on an organised platform or at an established venue. Typically the exchange (or a related party) acts as counterparty to these transactions.

OTC derivatives, then, involve a promise to make some payment or to deliver some financial asset in the future. One of the sources of risk in such transactions is the fact that the party making the promise might not keep their word. This is counterparty credit risk.

A related danger is that one party might make demands on the other as a result of the transaction that they cannot meet because they cannot

9

raise sufficient funds, or that they can only meet at excessive cost. This is liquidity risk (which can, of course, give rise to counterparty credit risk).

These two risks – counterparty credit risk and liquidity risk – will be discussed further in subsequent sections. First, though, we need to examine OTC trading and the diverse promises made once an OTC derivative has been agreed more closely. We then turn to the risks inherent in OTC derivatives trading and the size of the pre-crisis OTC derivatives market. This defines the magnitude of the problem that the regulations we will discuss in subsequent chapters have to address.

1.1 OTC Derivatives: Trading and its Consequences

We will assume a basic familiarity with swaps and options[1], concentrating here on how derivatives are transacted and the risks that result from this trading.

1.1.1 Engaging in an OTC derivatives transaction

Historically, OTC derivatives markets were simply a collection of dealers and brokers who would advertise the prices at which they might engage in benchmark transactions. A deal was typically conducted by telephone, with two parties privately negotiating the nature of the deal and the price at which it would be done. If the deal was a benchmark transaction – a five year fixed for floating interest rate swap in US dollars, say – then it could be directly compared to advertised prices. If it was less standard, then both parties would need to acquire comfort that the agreed price was acceptable. Often they would do this using a derivatives pricing model[2]. Thus for instance a six year swap might be valued using the prices of the benchmark five and seven year swaps.

More recently, electronic platforms have become commonplace. These allow platform members to view dealer advertisements and, should they wish, engage in a range of transactions. It is worth noting that regardless of the method of dealing:

- Historically in the OTC market advertised prices were often not firm commitments to trade. This is a marked contrast with some exchange markets.

- OTC markets did not include trade reporting, so advertised prices often represented the only information available to non-dealers.

- The negotiation of a trade is a purely bilateral process. If two parties can agree a transaction and they are legally able to enter into it, then they can trade without involving or reporting to a third party.

* The bilateral nature of trading inevitably meant that the responsibility for documenting and recording trades lay with the two parties involved. Standard documentation has been developed by a trade body, the International Swap Dealers Association[3] ('ISDA'). This reduced the burden of this process and assisted in the standardisation of trading terms[4].

Recent years have seen an elaboration of this process as market infrastructure and trade reporting developed, but the OTC market still remains fairly close to these roots in bilateral trading[5].

1.1.2 Market participants

The parties trading derivatives are often divided into dealers and end users. Dealers (who are often large financial institutions) make markets in OTC derivatives. They advertise standard products, create new forms of transaction, and respond to client requests for solutions to risk management problems. A substantial fraction of OTC derivatives trading is concentrated in a group of 14 large dealers known as the G14 (the 'G' for 'Global').

The class of end users includes corporates, investment managers (such as pension funds and hedge funds) and governments. Typically this group uses OTC derivatives either to hedge risk or to take it outright. For instance, a corporate might enter into an interest rate swap to hedge risk on a bond issue, or a pension fund might invest in an equity index by purchasing a call option.

1.1.3 OTC derivatives and counterparty credit risk

Counterparty credit arises whenever we are owed money[6] in the future by a party who might not pay us. The causes of that failure to pay may be simple unwillingness[7] or more likely it will be inability, for instance due to bankruptcy. All that matters is that there is a risk that we might not get paid.

Figure 1.1: Depicting a promise made via a derivative

OTC derivatives involve an agreement between two parties, and hence it is highly likely that they will involve counterparty credit risk. If A and B are counterparties to each other in an OTC derivatives transaction, then typically either A will pose counterparty credit risk to B; or B to A; or both. We will depict a promise made by A to B via an OTC derivative as in figure 1.1.

Various derivatives create different degrees of counterparty credit risk, alone and in combination. In the rest of this section we examine some common simple situations.

1.1.4 The promises made in plain vanilla options

If I sell a plain vanilla call option, I receive the premium from my counterparty at the beginning of the transaction[8]. I have further obligations to them if the option is exercised when it is in-the-money; but they have none to me. Therefore from my perspective there is no credit risk in selling a plain vanilla option.

The reverse pattern is seen with purchased options. Here we have paid for a promise: the promise that the option writer will give us the required sum if the option is in-the-money when we exercise it. For a European option, then, we are relying on the option writer to fulfil a promise at the option's maturity, a time that may be some years in the future. Absent any mitigating factors, that may represent a substantial credit risk, as the option may be worth millions of dollars at maturity.

Notice that while we may only be able to exercise a European style option at maturity, and so extinguish the credit risk we have to the option writer, the option itself has a value before that point. Standard valuation techniques such as the Black-Scholes formula can provide estimates of that value, but those approaches often assume that our counterparty will definitely honour its promise. If that is in doubt, then we may need to adjust the value of the option to reflect the fact that the counterparty may not perform. This adjustment is known as the 'credit valuation adjustment' ('CVA'), and we will have more to say about it in section 3.1.4.

1.1.5 Replacing a promise

Suppose that A makes B a promise, as in figure 1.1, and then defaults. In order to be in the same position as it was before this unfortunate event, B has to replace A's promise with one made by someone else. For instance, if the promise is in the form of an option that B has purchased, it will need to go to another market participant and buy an option on the same terms.

The cost to B of doing this is the price of the option *when it is purchased*. If this purchase is made very soon after A's default, and the market has not moved much, then this price will be very near to the mark to market of the option B had at the point of default. If however it takes B some days to purchase the replacement option, then the price may have changed somewhat[9]. Some delay between bankruptcy and close out is likely, not least due to the need to verify that the default has indeed occurred, gather information on the trade(s) which have to be replaced, get prices for these trades from the market, select the best counterparty to execute with, and actually effect the replacement.

Figure 1.2 illustrates the effect by plotting the price of a fixed strike and maturity S&P 500 call option through the Lehman Brothers default.

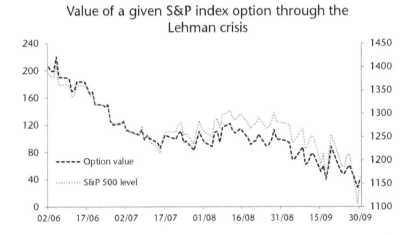

Figure 1.2: The value of a certain promise through the Lehman Crisis

On September 15th – the day that Lehman filed for bankruptcy – the option we have chosen was worth $52. Buying that same option 1, 2, 3 and 4 business days later would have cost $60, $41, $60 and $88 respectively[10].

This example illustrates two key points:

1. The 'current credit exposure' at the point of default of a counter-party is the value[11] of the promise(s) made if positive, and zero if negative, as figure 1.3 illustrates. It therefore represents the present value of the promise our counterparty has made to us at a point in time.

2. On the other hand, the ultimate cost of a failure is the cost of replacing the non-performing party. This can be substantially different from the value at the point of failure if replacement is not immediate.

Value of derivative to us	Counterparty position	Current credit exposure
Positive	They owe us money	Value of derivative
Negative	We owe them money	None

Figure 1.3: Current credit exposure

1.1.6   The promises made in interest rate swaps

Interest rate swaps represent one of the most common forms of promise in OTC derivatives. Here both parties undertake to do something: one might promise to pay a fixed amount every six months, for instance; while the other promises to pay an amount that depends on a floating rate such as Libor.

In order to analyse the value of these promises, we need to know how interest rate swaps are valued. Unfortunately that is a lot more complicated that it used to be, thanks in part to market participants becoming more sophisticated in how they value credit risk. Still, we can at least give an overview of the valuation of a fixed vs. floating interest rate swap[12]:

 * Value the fixed leg by discounting the known fixed payments back to today;

 * Determine the best estimate of the future floating payments using the prices of suitable contracts based on those floating rates (such, for instance, as interest rate futures and/or FRAs);

 * Value the floating leg by discounting the estimated floating payments back to today.

Suppose that we have a par interest rate swap. The swap being at par means that the value of the fixed leg is equal to the value of the floating leg. If the Libor curve points up, then Libors in the future will typically be above today's Libor. Early in the life of this swap then, the floating rate payer will pay less that the fixed rate payer, and later they will pay more. Thus the fixed rate payer makes net payments to the floating rate payer at first, and the situation reverses later on.

A structure where we get money now and pay it back later is often called a loan. Thus we can see that in the situation outlined, the fixed rate payer is in effect loaning money to the floating rate payer. Table 1.4 illustrates the phenomenon. Here we have taken an upward pointing Libor curve, and found the coupon which prices a five year swap to par. We then assumed that the notional was $10M, and calculated the value we expect the swap to have in 6, 18, 30, 42 and 54 months[13].

Month	0	6	18	30	42	54
Swap Value	–	$53K	$140K	$191K	$175K	$78K

Figure 1.4: Expected value of a particular five year fixed for floating swap at various points in its life

These figures can be understood as follows:

- Early in the life of the swap, the floating payments are less than the fixed ones, so we pay the counterparty more and more money. That loan has to be repaid, and the increasing value of the swap as time goes on reflects the increasing repayments due;

- Those payments are made incrementally during the life of the swap, reducing what is owed. With the yield curve we used, the peak value occurs about 3 years into the swap: this is the point at which we would lose the most were the counterparty to default[14].

- Late in the life of the swap, the payments fall fast as each coupon represents a substantial payment back to us.

This analysis was for a fixed yield curve; we simply looked at how the swap's value changed as time passed and coupons were paid, assuming that the current curve gives accurate predictions of future floating rates. Clearly this assumption is unreasonable, so we need to examine the effect of market movements.

1.1.7 When future floating rates cannot be predicted

No one knows precisely what interest rates will be in the future, but we do have information about how much they are likely to move. For instance, we could examine the historical volatility of interest rates, or we could examine the prices of interest rate derivatives and hence obtain a market-based estimate of future volatility. Either of these approaches would give us a distribution of future interest rates[15]. This allows us to construct a range of scenarios for what interest rates will be in the future. In order to be consistent with the distributions, many scenarios will explore interest rates close to the average value, while a few will explore less probable alternatives.

Figure 1.5 illustrates the idea: it shows six one year scenarios for the five year swap rate (based on pre-crisis data). We would need far more data than this in a real simulation: thousands of simulations rather than six; simulations of each tenor rather than just one; and simulations thirty rather than one year into the future. Still, the idea should be clear from this miniature example.

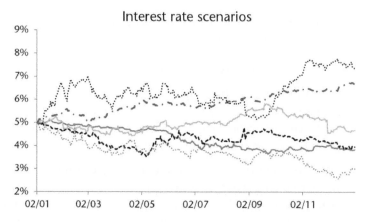

Figure 1.5: Six scenarios for the five year swap rate every business day for the next year

Each scenario gives us a path of rates through time. Each of these rates can be used to value the swap of interest. Thus each scenario gives a path of swap values. We can cut through these paths at any given time in the simulation to give a distribution of swap values at that point. Figure 1.6 illustrates the process.

In each case, the credit exposure is the positive part of the swap value. Risk managers use two key terms relating to these distributions:

- The 'expected exposure' (or 'EE') at a point in time is the average credit exposure across all scenarios; while;

- The 'potential future exposure' (or 'PFE') is a statistical measure of the credit exposure at some degree of confidence. Thus the 95% potential future exposure is the credit exposure which will not be exceeded in more than 5% of scenarios.

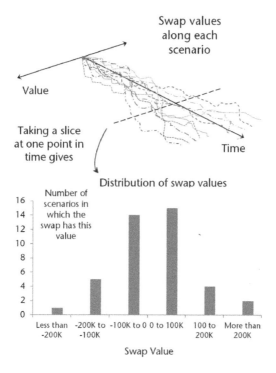

Figure 1.6: The swap value distribution in the future

Figure 1.7 shows the idea: expected exposure is, roughly speaking, the best estimate of the credit exposure, while potential future exposure is an estimate of how bad it could be at the chosen degree of confidence. Both vary through time.

1.1.8 Credit default swaps

Credit default swaps ('CDS') can be dealt with in an analogous way to interest rate swaps. The credit exposure at a given point in time is again the present value of the remaining payments, but with the twist that both the credit event payment and the value of the premium leg depends on the hazard rate for the reference credit[16]. Thus we start by inferring the hazard rate curve, and this allows us to value the CDS at any point in the future. Calculating EE and PFE requires us to calculate the joint distributions of interest rates and hazard rates at various points in the future.

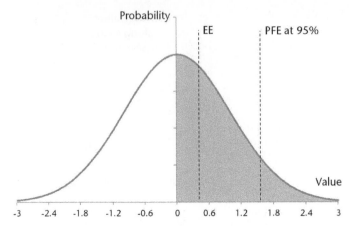

Figure 1.7: An illustration of expected exposure and potential future exposure for a distribution of swap values

1.2 The Risks of OTC Derivatives

In the last section, we saw that derivatives counterparties can fail to perform, and that it can cost us money to replace the promise that our counterparty has failed to keep. Here we examine these risks, and others that accompany OTC derivatives trading, a little more carefully.

1.2.1 Market risk

The most obvious risk of engaging in derivatives transactions is market risk. Derivatives are traded to transform risk[17], and thus it is no surprise that they change both counterparties' market risk position.

Often large derivatives dealers will be more or less hedged, meaning that their overall position does not suffer major P/L swings as the market moves. That hedged position will however be the result of trades with many counterparties. Thus if one of them defaults, the resulting post default position will be unhedged. The dealer will have to engage in new trades in order to hedge themselves.

1.2.2 Counterparty credit risk

The last section illustrated how counterparty non-performance in OTC derivatives can give rise to a loss. The extent of this counterparty credit risk is unknown, as we do not know how long it will take to replace the lost transactions, nor what the market prices will be when (or indeed if) we succeed in the replacement. There are therefore two components of counterparty credit risk: the current value of the portfolio with each counterparty, and its possible change in value between default and re-placement. The latter can be thought of as credit-contingent market risk.

1.2.3 Settlement risk

Settlement risk is the risk that a counterparty does not deliver cash or a financial instrument when they have undertaken to do so. Thus for instance the risk that we pay the strike of a physically settled call option but the counterparty does not deliver the underlying is a settlement risk.

Often there is a grace period for settlements, so that counterparties have a period of time in which to 'cure' their failure and belatedly keep their promise.

Some authors refer to counterparty credit risk as 'pre-settlement risk' in that counterparty credit risk represents a risk to the expected value today of future settlements. We do not find the distinction particularly useful – when does a future payment move from having pre-settlement risk to having settlement risk? – so we prefer to define counterparty credit risk as any risk of counterparty non-performance, i.e. including settlement risk.

1.2.4 Funding liquidity risk

Funding liquidity risk arises when demands for cash can be made which a firm might either not be able to meet, or only be able to meet at excessive cost. Clearly if a demand for cash is expected, for instance because a firm knows that it has to repay the principal of a bond which is coming due, then it can plan for it. Unexpected large demands are riskier though, and these can occur as a result of entering into OTC derivatives. Options can be exercised, credit events can occur, and collateral calls can be made; all of these can place a strain on a firm's liquidity[18].

1.2.5 Legal and documentation risk

OTC derivatives may be agreed by telephone, but then what has been agreed has to be documented. This is typically done by the exchange of documents known as confirmations. Once both parties have signed, the trade is fixed. This process gives rise to several risks all of which fall under the heading of documentation risk:

- ◆ It may take an extended period of time for the confirmation to be signed, perhaps because the bank's infrastructure is not capable of handling the current deal flow. This was for instance the case for many credit derivatives confirmations during 2003-2006, with the industry wide backlog exceeding 150,000 unconfirmed trades at its peak[19]. (We discuss this issue further in section 1.3.5 below.)

*   Two parties may have reached what appeared to be agreement by telephone, but their understanding of what was agreed differs, and as a result the trade to be confirmed is disputed. Worse, an imprecise or inaccurate confirmation may be signed, leading to the possibility of future litigation[20].

*   The terms of the trade may have an effect which differs from that envisaged by one or both parties. Comparatively rare events such as corporate restructurings or government action can reveal unexpected (and typically for at least one party unwelcome) possibilities[21].

In addition to these OTC-derivatives-specific issues, there are also legal risks which are common across a range of trading activity such as the risk that a counterparty will be deemed not to have the capacity to enter into a seemingly agreed trade, the risk of misrepresentation, and so on[22].

1.2.6 Other operational risks

OTC derivatives trading necessitates significant operational complexity. Trades have to be recorded and confirmed, payments have to be made and options sometimes have to be exercised. Trades terminate, are restructured, or novated to third parties. Moreover the business has to be accounted for and regulatory capital is required for many risks. The processes for fulfilling these requirements are often fallible, and the resulting operational risks can be substantial[23].

1.3 The Pre-Crisis OTC Derivatives Market

'Systemic risk' is the risk of the collapse of, or severe stress to, an entire financial system. It typically arises when many financial institutions are troubled at the same time, so it is natural to ask how problems at one firm can spread to others; the issue of contagion.

Later in the book, we will have much to say about the credit crisis and the reforms that grew out of it. Many of these reforms aim to reduce systemic risk. A key element of this is reducing the risk of contagion from one financial institution to others. Exposures between financial institutions created by OTC derivatives trading are potentially a cause of contagion; if a firm fails while owing a lot of money to others, a domino effect of multiple failures is possible. Therefore it is logical to examine how big the exposures created by OTC derivatives were, and hence how big a source of contagion they were. In particular we will review the OTC derivatives market at the end of 2007; this will give us an idea of the state of the market and the risks it embodied just before the most severe phase of the financial crisis.

Before we begin, it is worth mentioning why we avoid the common approach of using notionals as a measure of OTC derivatives wherever we can, despite this being the most readily available data. The notional of a derivatives transaction bears no relationship to its risks. Thus while the credit exposure of an interest rate swap is often a single digit percentage of notional, that of a CDS might be 50% (or indeed 0.01% of notional). Therefore while information on the gross notionals of various types of derivatives is available, it is of little use in assessing risk. We prefer to use more pertinent information where we can.

1.3.1 Pre-crisis OTC derivatives exposures

An OTC derivative is a private agreement between two parties, so discovering how many OTC derivatives had been traded at a given point in time, or how big the exposures they created were, is not straightforward. Two important sources of information are the BIS surveys on positions in global over-the-counter derivatives markets[24] and the ISDA margin surveys[25]. The data from these two sources is not wholly comparable[26], but we can draw some general conclusions about pre-crisis OTC derivatives exposures.

* For the 55 dealers who reported to the BIS in mid-2007, net credit exposure before collateral taken via derivatives totalled $2.7T[27].

* ISDA meanwhile estimates total collateral exchanged between OTC derivatives market participants at end-2007 as $2.1T. It also quotes the average level of collateralisation as 65%, implying that the total credit extended via OTC derivatives at end-2007 was approximately $3.2T.

This data suggests that it is not unreasonable to conclude that before the 2008 crisis, OTC derivatives created total credit exposure between financial institutions amounting to low single digit trillions of US dollars[28].

The BIS reports consolidated statistics on banks' on-balance sheet financial claims. The total claims of banks on each other represent a reasonable measure of credit exposures taken by traditional means such as interbank lending[29]. The total for end-2007 is $10.6T, demonstrating that conventional interbank lending created at least three times as much exposure as OTC derivatives.

1.3.2 How many promises were made?

There is very little data available on how many trades there were in banks' OTC derivatives portfolios pre-crisis (or indeed how many there are today)[30]. However there is some related evidence, notably:

*   LCH Clearnet at the time of writing claim to have cleared over 2.2 million trades. Combining their c. 65% share of the IRS market with the IRS market's c. 78% share of gross notionals as reported by the BIS suggests an end-2011 market of at least 4.3 million trades[31].

*   The OTC trade infrastructure service Trioptima claims to reconcile 'over 6 million trades' daily, as at June 2012[32].

*   Anecdotal evidence from G14 dealers suggest that portfolios of hundreds of thousands of OTC derivatives are not uncommon.

All of this suggests that the OTC derivatives market probably consists of high single digit or low teens of millions of trades.

1.3.3 How concentrated was the market?

Data about the concentration of the OTC derivatives market is patchy, but there are indications that the few biggest market participants together share much of the business. For instance, BIS data suggests that several markets[33] met the Department of Justice's criteria for a concentrated market at end-2007[34]. ISDA's 2010 market survey supports this view, indicating that the G14 was 82% of the total market[35].

Size of firm	Number of Master Agreements	Number of Reporting Dealers in that Class
Large	>1000	18
Medium	51-1000	40
Small[36]	0-50	39

Figure 1.8: The numbers of OTC derivatives master agreements

Most financial markets display some form of power law whereby the largest few firms account for most of the activity, so it is no surprise to see this pattern repeated in OTC derivatives. Moreover, not only do the G14 account for the majority of trading, they also have far more counterparties than smaller firms. As we discuss in the next chapter, nearly all OTC derivatives counterparties sign master agreements with banks, so the number of master agreements a bank has is a good proxy for how many counterparties they deal with. ISDA gives the data in table 1.8 for end-2007: this shows the G14 have many more counterparties than the next tier of dealers. Most OTC trades, in other words, have a member of the G14 as at least one counterparty.

1.3.4   How complex were exposures?

The vast majority of OTC derivatives are simple, standardised structures: interest rate and cross currency swaps, plain vanilla puts and calls on single underlyings, forwards and total return/equity swap structures dominate, for the following reasons:

  * Liquidity is concentrated in simple products. Dealers are naturally reluctant to trade too many highly illiquid products unless they can be easily hedged with liquid ones. Therefore a product's status tends to remain constant over time; liquid ones stay liquid, but it is quite difficult for a new product to become very well traded. For every new type of derivative which becomes a major business line – such as single name CDS – there are many which fail or remain niche products[37].

  * There is typically more valuation risk with complex products as these usually have to be valued using a model whose veracity is debatable[38].

  * Complex products are often expensive because they have to be hand-crafted. Just as many people find that an off-the-peg suit is 'good enough' for their purposes given the price of bespoke tailoring and the wide variety of ready-made products, so many end users find that combinations of standard OTC derivatives are often good enough risk management tools given the cost, opacity and potential illiquidity of hand-made instruments. That said, unusual needs are often best met by a bespoke product.

That said, highly exotic instruments continue to be traded. Some of these are tailored to meet the specific risk management requirements of clients, but one may be suspicious that others simply represent complexity for its own sake[39].

1.3.5 How efficient was the infrastructure?

The state of the OTC derivatives industry's infrastructure was sufficiently worrying to supervisors in 2005 that the FED 'hosted a meeting
with representatives of major market participants and their domestic
and international supervisors to discuss a range of issues regarding the
processing of OTC derivatives, particularly credit derivatives, and the
risk management and control issues around these instruments'[40]. This
meeting lead to a number of commitments by market participants. The
progress on meeting these, and further pledges were set out in a series of
'FED letters' over the next five years. For instance, a 2008 document[41]
sets out the achievements since the 2005 meeting and the targets that the
industry had committed to meeting:

- Major dealers reduced OTC credit derivatives (CDS) confirmation
  backlogs by roughly 93% and increased the percentage of trades
  that were confirmed electronically from 53% to more than 90%.

- Dealers had also reduced OTC equity derivatives backlogs by 70%
  from the levels of mid-2006. 95% of inter-dealer OTC equity
  derivatives trades were processed on electronic platforms at that
  point.

- 'Escalating targets' for reducing the backlog of confirmations and
  greater use of electronic trade matching were set out.

- The industry also committed to automating OTC derivatives
  trade matching.

In other words, while the infrastructure supporting OTC derivatives
had lagged behind trade volumes and best practice in the early 2000s, the
industry had already made substantial improvements by late 2007, and it
had a plan (nearly all of which was subsequently executed) to move to
a largely electronic market featuring automated trade processing. These
issues are discussed further in chapter 7.

Summary

OTC derivatives trading creates a variety of risks for market participants.
Prominent amongst these is counterparty credit risk: the failure of one
counterparty to an OTC derivative can create losses for the other if the
cost of closing-out the derivative is significant.

Two measures of risk are important here: the current value of the portfolio, which determines the current credit exposure; and the potential future values, which estimates how large the exposure might be at some future default point.

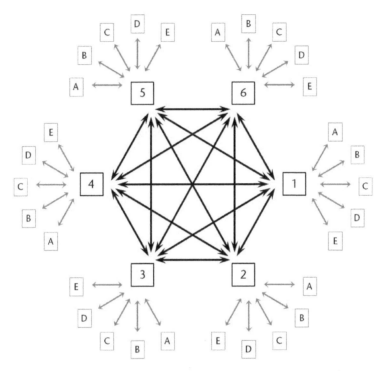

Figure 1.9: Conceptual schematic of the OTC derivatives market. The dealers are represented by the large boxes, with the thick arrows representing the large inter-dealer portfolios. End-users are symbolised by smaller boxes, with fewer trades connecting them to their dealers.

The pre-crisis OTC derivatives market was characterised by a small number of dealers serving a much larger number of end-users. Dealers had significant numbers of trades with each other, and fewer trades with end-users, as figure 1.9 illustrates.

The whole network was comprised of perhaps ten million trades, creating a few trillion dollars of gross current credit exposure. This is a substantial number, but it is about a third of the risk of the interbank lending market, and moreover is substantially mitigated by collateral – an issue we turn to in the next chapter.

Notes

[1]For a comprehensive introduction to these products, see J. Hull, *Options, Futures and Other Derivatives*, Prentice Hall 2005 or D. Murphy, *Understanding Risk: The Theory and Practice of Financial Risk Management*, Chapman Hall 2008.

[2]In other words, pricing models are used as interpolators between the known prices of benchmark instruments.

[3]ISDA subsequently kept its initials but renamed itself the International Swaps and Derivatives Association.

[4]Before ISDA produced standardised documentation, OTC derivatives were documented using dealer-specific language. That made negotiations long and complex, and furthermore meant that two swaps with nominally the same terms did not necessarily have exactly the same economics due to minor differences in wording from one dealer to the next. By creating market conventions for everything from stub periods to market disruptions, ISDA enhanced the liquidity of the market.

ISDA and related market participant initiatives can be seen as a type of 'club good' (in the sense, for instance, of J. Buchanan, *An Economic Theory of Clubs*, Economica Volume 32, No. 125, February 1965). These excludable but non-rivalous goods are created thanks to coordination. It is worthy of note that this clubbing together to solve common market problems occurred without the need for regulatory intervention.

[5]For a much more comprehensive description of OTC derivatives markets, see European Central Bank, *OTC Derivatives and Post-trading Infrastructures*, 2009 available at www.ecb.int/pub/pdf/other/overthecounterderivatives200909en.pdf.

[6]Or, which amounts to the same thing, we are owed something that is worth money.

[7]Sovereign counterparties amongst others have in the past repudiated obligations, and so there is the risk that they may do so again. Given that many sovereigns are derivatives counterparties, any such repudiation could represent a credit risk for their trading partners. See *This Time Is Different: Eight Centuries of Financial Folly*, C. Reinhart, S. Rogoff, Princeton University Press 2009 for a comprehensive history of sovereign defaults.

[8]This may not be precisely true, as the premium may only be received a few days after the start of the transaction. The risk of non-payment here is usually thought of as settlement risk.

[9]This is of course especially the case if the market is in turmoil due to A's default, as it may well be if A is a large financial institution.

[10]This substantial variation is due to the large movements not just in the S&P 500 index level but also implied volatility and interest rates that happened immediately after the Lehman default. In particular implied volatility rose substantially after the default; the effect of this offset the impact of the fall of the S&P 500 on the value of the call.

[11]There is a degree of coyness in not saying 'mark to market value' here; while most derivatives are fair valued, and hence will have a credit exposure based on that measure, there is an argument that if a swap is accrue accounted (as some banking book transactions, IFRS notwithstanding, are) then the exposure is the accounting value of the derivative, not its mark to market value. However, the replacement cost of that derivative will clearly be driven by its market value, so the position is debateable.

[12]For a much more comprehensive account, including the role of funding and CVA, see for instance M. Johannes, S. Sundaresan, *Pricing Collateralized Swaps*, Journal of Finance, Volume 62 (2007).

[13]That is, the value it would have if the predicted forward Libors actually came to pass.

[14]Fixed for floating interest rate swaps in USD are very liquid, so we could replace this trade very soon after counterparty default, and thus the likely cost of the default would be rather close to the value of the contract on the day default happened.

[15]For more details, see D. Brigo, F. Mercurio, *Interest Rate Models - Theory and Practice: With Smile, Inflation and Credit*, Springer 2006 for more details of the construction process. If the intention is to examine real world exposures, perhaps for the purpose of calculating a loan-loss type reserve, then historical data should be used; if the intent is to calculate a CVA and its sensitivities for hedging purposes, then risk neutral calculations should be made: we discuss this further in section 3.1.4.

[16]For an account of CDS pricing in the hazard rate framework, see P. Schönbucher, *Credit Derivatives Pricing Models*, John Wiley & Sons 2003.

[17]Or sometimes for other reasons, such as tax, regulation or accounting.

[18]Collateral calls represent another major source of liquidity risk; we deal with these in the next chapter.

[19]See United States Government Accountability Office, *Confirmation Backlogs Increased Dealers' Operational Risks, but Were Successfully Addressed after Joint Regulatory Action*, June 2007 available at www.gao.gov/new.items/d07716.pdf.

[20]The default of an American flooring company known colloquially as Armstrong is a good example here. Armstrong World Industries, Inc., a subsidiary of Armstrong Holdings, Inc., declared bankruptcy in 2000 but its parent did not file. Two major disputes arose from these events, both relating to the question of whether the parties to the transaction intended the trade to refer to Armstrong World Industries, Inc. or Armstrong Holdings, Inc. For more details, see P. Harding, *A Practical Guide to the 2003 Isda Credit Derivatives Definitions*, Euromoney (2004).

[21]When Railtrack Plc, a UK company which owned and managed British rail infrastructure, was put into administration in 2001 as a result of an application to the High Court by the then Transport Secretary, Stephen Byers, it became clear that at least one major market participant did not construe the relevant credit default swap documentation as permitting the delivery of convertible bonds, while its counterparty did. See Harding, *op cit.* for a fuller account.

[22]C. Jackson gives a more comprehensive account in *Legal risk optimisation*, Risk Magazine, September 2002 available at www.risk.net/risk-magazine/feature/1506604/legal-risk-optimisation.

[23]S. Bruel subdivides OTC derivatives operational risk into that arising from valuations, collateral management, reconciliations, settlements, pre-trade decision support, trade capture, counterparty communications, clearing and novations: see *Addressing End-to-End Risks and Inefficiencies in OTC Derivatives*, February 2010 available via www.capitalize-on-change.com/resources.aspx for more details. M. Power, *The Invention of Operational Risk*, ESRC Centre for Risk and Regulation, June 2003 available at eprints.lse.ac.uk/21368/1/DP16.pdf has a broader discussion of operational risk in trading and banking activities.

[24]At the time of writing, the most recent BIS survey was available via www.bis.org/publ/otc_hy1205.htm.

[25]Available via www.isda.org/statistics/marginsurveys.html.

[26]Amongst other things, the BIS and ISDA data reflect slightly different time periods and reporting entities.

[27]This is after enforceable netting arrangements are taken into account, but before collateral.

[28]The OCC's data on Bank Trading and Derivatives Activities provides a useful check on the magnitude here. Their Q1 2008 report cites net current credit exposure of $465 billion for US banks. Given that these figures do not include non-US banks nor non-bank US derivatives activity, a global total of several trillion seems reasonable. The OCC report is available at www.occ.gov/topics/capital-markets/financial-markets/trading/derivatives/dq108.pdf.

[29]This data is available via www.bis.org/statistics/consstats.htm.

[30]The ISDA operations benchmarking surveys (available via www.isda.org) provide some direct data on new 'events' (which include new trades between firms, novations, and terminations but excluding inter-company trades). One can combine that information with the maturities profiles given in the BIS data to get a sense of the total number of trades in the OTC derivatives market, but the results seem anomalously low. Reasonable assumptions give a firm-to-firm network of only a million trades at end-2007, a number that seems roughly an order of magnitude too small.

[31]The LCH Clearnet data was taken from www.lch.com/swaps/swapclear_for_clearing_members, BIS data from www.bis.org/publ/otc_hy1205.pdf. Since IRS notionals are on average larger than those of equity, credit or commodity derivatives, this calculation likely somewhat understates trade numbers.

[32]See www.trioptima.com/services/triResolve.html.

[33]Notably some JPY and GBP interest rate derivatives and most Asian equity derivatives.

[34]The BIS publish Herfindahl-Hirschman indices ('HHI') based on notionals in various markets. The DOJ's criteria for a moderately concentrated market is an HHI of

between 1,500 and 2,500; above that the market is deemed to be highly concentrated. (See www.justice.gov/atr/public/guidelines/hhi.html for more details.)

[35]See www.isda.org/media/press/2010/press102510.html for more details.

[36]Small dealers may not be ISDA survey responders, so this line almost certainly underestimates the number of small OTC derivatives dealers.

[37]The Federal Reserve Bank of New York Staff Report *An Analysis of OTC Interest Rate Derivatives Transactions: Implications for Public Reporting*, No. 557 (March 2012) available at www.newyorkfed.org/research/staff_reports/sr557.pdf contains a helpful analysis of the split between the trading of standard, benchmark instruments and less liquid products. M. Fleming et al. find that trading in the standard 2-, 3-, 5-, 10- and 30-year tenors represents around 57% of the G4 IRS activity.

[38]There may for instance be several models which could be used for the product, each of which gives different valuations, or there may be a choice of calibration of the model. See M. Morini, *Understanding and Managing Model Risk: A Practical Guide for Quants, Traders and Validators*, Wiley 2011 for a further discussion of model risk.

[39]One of the 'advantages' of trading a complex derivative is that it may be difficult for competitors to price or risk manage.

[40]Federal Reserve Bank of New York, *Statement Regarding Meeting on Credit Derivatives*, September 15, 2005, available via www.ny.frb.org. This represents a 'club good' approach in the sense of note 4.

[41]*Summary of OTC Derivatives Commitments*, July 31 2008, available via www.ny.frb. org. At the time of writing all of the FED letters are available on this website, but some of the links on the OTC Derivatives Supervisors Group page data.newyorkfed.org/ markets/otc_derivatives_supervisors_group.html are broken. Any reader who is interested in following the details of the industry's commitments and subsequent improvements in OTC derivatives market infrastructure is advised to follow links from the relevant press release relating to each FED/Industry meeting.

2

The Nature of the Counterparty Relationship in Bilateral OTC Derivatives

Look at the two of us in sympathy
with everything we see
I never want anything, it's easy
you buy whatever I need
But look at my hopes, look at my dreams
the currency we've spent
I love you, you pay my rent
Pet Shop Boys*

Introduction

Many parties in the derivatives markets have more than one trade with a given counterparty. The existence of these portfolios gives rise to issues of netting: when can we look at risk on a net basis, and when is it gross? This chapter is concerned with those problems and with the legal machinery that addresses them. In particular we look in some detail at the usual forms of documentation used for bilateral OTC derivatives trades.

Market infrastructure also becomes a significant concern once we look at the scale of inter-dealer exposures. How do market participants agree on the trades they have with each other and what they are worth; how do they agree on what payments have to be made; how do they reduce their exposure to each other? The answers to these questions go hand-in-hand with the legal analysis since market participants need to ensure that they

---

adhere to the undertakings they have made in the documents they have signed. Efficient and effective market infrastructure is essential to ensure that these promises are kept.

2.1 Portfolios and Payment Netting

Two large OTC derivatives dealers might well have tens or hundreds of thousands of trades between them. If most of those trades were interest rate swaps (as they might well be), then there would likely be hundreds of payments due on each business day. Clearly there is significant operational risk if each of those payments is made separately. Moreover, separate payments create substantial settlement risk: if I have to pay you $100,000 today and you have to pay me $75,000, my credit exposure to you is $75,000 despite the fact that I have no net exposure. The OTC derivatives market has evolved a number of conventions to reduce these risks.

2.1.1 What is payment netting?

Payment netting is the process of replacing two or more gross payments due on the same day by a single net payment. Thus in the example given, I would pay you $25,000. Some degree of payment netting[42] is usually practiced in the OTC derivatives markets. However:

- Payment netting is usually only done *within* a single currency. This is because banks typically manage their cash separately in each currency. Netting only within a currency also removes the potential for dispute over FX rates.

- Netting typically only takes place with respect to payments between two legal entities. Given that large financial institutions often have more than one legal entity which trades derivatives, this means that there are often multiple USD payments from, for instance, the group of companies headed by JPMorgan Chase & Co. to the group headed by Deutsche Bank AG.

Payment netting as practiced dramatically reduces the number of payments between OTC derivatives market participants and thus substantially decreases settlement risk.

2.1.2 When does payment netting work?

Payment netting can be simply a convenience. We agree to net payments, but as a legal matter the gross amounts are still owed. Thus for instance if you went bankrupt, it might still be the case that I owed you

$100,000 despite our agreement to net payments. The ability to reduce a debt from a gross to a net amount is known as the right of set-off. If I have the legal right of set-off against you, then I do indeed only owe you $25,000 and payment netting would reflect the legal reality of the situation.

The law of set-off has a long history[43]. Whether a party has it against another depends on a number of factors including the governing law(s) of the transactions between them, the bankruptcy law governing the failed party, and comparability of the claims[44]. OTC derivatives market participants strive to achieve the right of set-off because it dramatically reduces exposure. The right of set-off is relatively easy to achieve in many jurisdictions, and indeed some have altered their legislation to facilitate it[45]. Thus bilateral payment netting can be enforced between most if not quite all OTC derivatives market participants.

The multiplicity of legal entities involved in large financial institutions does however generate an issue: while *bilateral* set-off might work, *trilateral* set-off where one group company tries to set-off a credit against a debit to an affiliate is much more problematic[46]. Therefore market participants are often only completely confident of the effectiveness of netting between pairs of legal entities.

2.1.3 Market infrastructure supporting payment netting

With hundreds of thousands of trades between large counterparties, the business of figuring out who owes what to whom on any given day can be onerous. Various pieces of market infrastructure have developed to assist with the determination of the amount and to assist in the actual settlement. For instance, Deriv/SERV (a subsidiary of the large US clearing and settlement body DTCC[47]) offers an automated cashflow matching and netting service for equity derivatives. Users tell Deriv/SERV what trades they have with each other and what payments are expected: the company reconciles these and facilitates orderly settlement.

The importance of global market infrastructure like this is easy to understate: without it, there is a much greater risk that market participants will not agree what net payment needs to be made on a given day, or will not actually make it. In ordinary times such a failure would probably be resolved without major stress on market participants, but in a crisis any failure to receive expected cash can cause panic and exacerbate liquidity risk[48].

Another major infrastructure achievement is the development of fast gross settlement systems. CLS (for 'continuous linked settlements') is an example of this which supports the FX spot and derivatives markets. It is both a system linking members, and a supporting bank[49]. CLS receives payment instructions from both parties to a trade. These instructions are authenticated and matched, and instructions generated for a future movement of cash. If the instructions do not match, then both parties are notified. When an amount in one currency is due to be exchanged for an amount in another, CLS simultaneously settles each pair of matched instructions by making the corresponding debit and credit entries to the parties' accounts at CLS Bank. Thus for instance some spot FX trades are settled on the day of trading. Each party's net funding requirement is determined and communicated so that parties have certainty of any payments they need to make into the system at the start of the next business day. CLS thus reduces settlement risk in the FX market and provides certainty of liquidity requirements for those trades that it settles.

2.2 Default and Close Out Netting

We would be rather fortunate if every counterparty default happened as we were settling the last transaction with them. It is much more likely that our counterparty will stop performing during the life of one or more derivatives. In this section we look at what can happen in this case.

If our counterparty is not performing then we will usually want to replace them. Therefore we will typically want to close out all our transactions with them, and make a claim on our counterparty's estate for what is owed. There are two contrasting situations here:

- If we can make a single net claim for the value of the whole portfolio of trades we have with them, then counterparty exposure is as low as possible, given the circumstances. We set off transactions with a positive value to the counterparty against those with a negative value, coming to a final net value. This can of course result in us making a positive payment to the counterparty (or their bankruptcy trustees) if we owe them money.

- If we cannot make a net claim – if net close out is not permitted – then we have to pay them the value of each transaction where we owe them money, and we have to make a claim against them for each transaction with credit exposure. This 'gross close out' evidently increases counterparty credit risk.

Clearly net close out is desirable[50]: the key to achieving it is a legal document known as a 'master agreement'.

2.2.1 Master agreements

A derivatives master agreement is legal glue. It seeks to bind together all of the transactions executed between two parties and (together with various auxiliary documents) to govern the terms of them. By signing a master agreement, the parties signal the intention of treating all the trades between them as aspects of a single whole. Thus conceptually if two parties have a valid signed master agreement, when they trade a swap they are not entering into a new, separate transaction, but rather varying the terms of their existing agreement to include the cashflows of this new swap: figure 2.1 illustrates the idea of close out netting. The documentation agreed sets out (among other things) when a counterparty is in default and hence can be closed out, and on what basis close out is to be achieved.

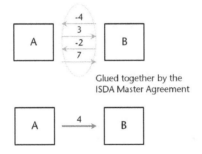

Figure 2.1: The ISDA master agreement facilitating netting by glueing together four transactions so that a single net payment is due.

ISDA has published two major editions of its master agreement in 1992 and 2002, and these are by far the most commonly used master agreements in OTC derivatives trading[51]. Both seek to reduce disputes by providing extensive definitions of the terms of the agreement; both bind transactions done under the master agreement together.

2.2.2 When does the glue hold?

You can write more or less whatever you want in a legal agreement, but clearly stated intent is no guarantee of enforceability. The key issue for close out netting is whether a bankruptcy judge would respect the agreement[52], or whether they would instead seek to impose gross close out.

ISDA at the time of writing has opinions for 55 jurisdictions that close out netting would be respected[53]. These include all the major OTC derivatives market venues. Moreover, close out netting has been very effective in practice[54]. Thus if two potential trading partners have signed a master netting agreement, and positive opinions on the effectiveness of close out netting in the relevant jurisdiction(s) exist, then both parties can be reasonably sure that a single net claim can be enforced after counterparty non-performance[55]. The set of all transactions between two counterparties under a single Master Agreement which jointly enjoy close out netting is known as a netting set.

2.2.3 Closing out

The efficacy of close out netting means that parties can often be sure that their claim should a counterparty default is that of a net amount. The next question that arises is when they can claim. Many bankruptcy codes, including that of the US, have the concept of an 'automatic stay', under which creditors of a bankrupt entity are automatically stayed from enforcing contractual rights against the failed party without the Bankruptcy Court's authorisation or a specific statutory exception. The US bankruptcy code (and many other countries' codes) contain safe harbours which protect the rights of OTC derivatives counterparties to close out transactions. This means that parties typically can close out on a timely basis after their counterparty has suffered a credit event.

A more delicate question arises when we consider if close out *must* occur. Often a party will want to close out as quickly as possible after default. However there are at least two situations where they may wish to delay:

1. It may take some period of time to establish the size of the claim. Typically this is due to operational difficulties and/or the presence of upcoming cashflows (so that the party might for instance find it convenient for Libor to fix so that the next coupon of a swap is known). It is hard for this author, at least, to see how such delays could last more than a few days.

2. Less reasonably, a party may take the view that the market is moving in their favour, and thus may wish to delay close out in order to increase the size of their claim (or reduce the size of their payment).

It is in my view unfortunate that the 1992 and 2002 ISDA Master Agreements have facilitated the second type of delay. This issue (known as 'the 2(a)(iii) problem' after the relevant clause in the Master Agreement) is currently under discussion following a case in the United States where it was ruled that the non-defaulting party could not indefinitely delay close out[56]. This case does not cast doubt on the efficacy of prompt close outs, but it does suggest that parties should not delay for economic (as opposed to operational) reasons.

2.2.4 The benefit of netting

Close out netting helps any portfolio with more than one trade. However, it typically helps bigger portfolios much more than smaller ones. This is because as a portfolio gets bigger, it is much more likely that the risk of a new trade will be diversified by some positions that are already in the portfolio. Thus as portfolios increase from ten to a hundred to a thousand trades, the net risk tends not to go up in orders of magnitude too, but rather at a much slower rate. This is especially the case for dealer portfolios. These portfolios are mostly comprised of client trades, and different clients tend to diversify each other[57].

Netting promotes efficiency, in that it allows active market participants to trade frequently and only consider their net rather than their gross risk position. The gross portfolio is still important for two reasons, though.

1. Operational risk sometimes depends on the number of trades or gross payments; and

2. In close out, there is no guarantee that bids will be available on a whole portfolio. In order to close out a large portfolio, then, a participant might have to split it into pieces[58]. Thus there is no guarantee that the value of a portfolio in close out depends only on its net risk.

2.3 Credit Support: Margin and Collateral

Suppose a counterparty wants to enter into an OTC derivatives transaction, but the credit exposure it would generate is troublingly large. One of the things that could be done to reduce this risk is for the counterparty to agree to post something – ideally cash, but perhaps bonds or some other asset – to reduce the net exposure. The idea is that this collateral can be sold and the proceeds used to offset losses on the portfolio in the event of the counterparty's default. Collateral is therefore a form of 'credit support'. There are others, too, such as the provision of a guarantee from a third party or the purchase of credit derivative protection.

We denote the situation where A posts collateral to its counterparty B against an exposure created by a portfolio of OTC derivatives as in figure 2.2.

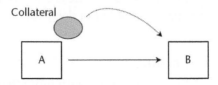

Figure 2.2: Depicting collateral against the credit exposure created by a portfolio of OTC derivatives

2.3.1 The mechanics of collateral

A number of issues are pertinent to OTC derivative collateralisation including the following:

+ How is the amount to be posted determined? In particular, does the full exposure have to be collateralised, or less than that? Sometimes a 'threshold' is agreed below which no collateral is required[59]. On other occasions a counterparty may be willing to over-collateralise, posting a higher value in collateral than the exposure.

+ Who determines what the exposure is, and how often is that determined?

+ Is collateral unilateral (only one party has to post) or bilateral (both must post)?

+ If collateral is bilateral, is it gross (each party posts the amount required) or net (only the difference between the two amounts must be posted)?

+ After the amount is determined and a call to post collateral is made, how long does the counterparty have to meet the call?

+ How often is collateral posted? This may be daily, weekly, monthly, or even just once during the life of the trade.

+ What can be posted? It is just cash, cash and securities, or something more esoteric?

+ How is collateral transferred and held?

+ What interest or other return is paid on collateral, and when must collateral be returned?

These questions are typically settled between two counterparties in the credit support annex ('CSA') to the ISDA master agreement. This might set out for instance that one party is the calculation agent, that they calculate the value of the exposure once a week, and that they then call for collateral if the difference between the exposure and the current value of collateral held is greater than $1M. The counterparty then has a period of three days to transfer extra collateral which may be in the form of USD, GBP or JPY cash or government bonds in those currencies. Cash posted earns interest at the overnight rate, and collateral must be returned the next business day after a calculation showing that there is an excess.

Typically failure to post collateral subject to the terms of the CSA is an event of default. This is known as 'credit support default': it means that after a failure to post which is not cured during any applicable grace period, the counterparty's portfolio can be closed out.

Figure 2.3 illustrates the effect of collateral where calls are made monthly on the first of the month and collateral settles four days later. There is a $6M threshold, so collateral has to be posted if the portfolio value is in excess of this amount[60].

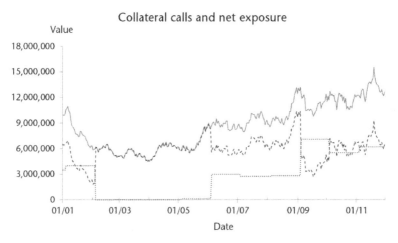

Figure 2.3: An illustration of the effect of collateral. The value of the portfolio is shown as the solid line; collateral value as the dotted line; and the net exposure as a dashed line.

Note that just as it is a specific legal entity that is counterparty to a trade, so it is a specific legal entity that is party to a master agreement and its associated CSA. The terms of CSAs vary significantly, notably in terms of what is acceptable collateral and what thresholds are present. Moreover, a large dealer may have hundreds of different types of agreement with different counterparties. It might even have different CSAs in place for deals between different subsidiaries of the same group.

2.3.2 Credit risk measures with collateral

We introduced the notions of expected exposure and potential future exposure to quantify the credit risk of a single transaction in section 1.1.7. These can easily be extended to portfolios under a master netting agreement and subject to a CSA. We simply construct sufficiently detailed scenarios so that all of the significant risk factors in the portfolio change; at any point in time on any scenario, the net portfolio value is simply the sum of the values of all of the transactions within it, given the risk factor moves. Figure 2.4 illustrates the process.

We then apply collateral subject to the terms of the CSA as described above to obtain the net exposure after collateral in each scenario. Then:

* The 'expected exposure' (or 'EE') at a point in time is the average net credit exposure after collateral across all scenarios; while;

* The 'potential future exposure' (or 'PFE') is a statistical measure of the net credit exposure after collateral at some degree of confidence.

These measures are often used by dealers to determine whether a new trade introduces too much credit risk. Thus a credit risk department might perhaps require that before any new trade is conducted, the PFE of the counterparty's portfolio including the proposed trade is calculated. If the PFE at any point exceeds some limit – $50M for a BBB corporate perhaps – then the trade cannot be executed. The sales person must find some way to restructure the transaction so that the credit risk is lower, or they must persuade the counterparty to sign a new CSA which lowers risk.

2.3.3 The lowest credit risk...

The lowest credit exposure arises when a counterparty agrees to post exactly the amount they owe us as quickly as possible, and where what is posted is highly liquid and has an unambiguous value. An agreement to post exactly the value of the exposure bilaterally every day in cash[61] would therefore be highly desirable.

Recently, a number of G14 dealers have developed a 'standard' CSA which is similar to this[62]. Such a CSA would reduce the counterparty credit risk created by OTC derivatives to the gap between the value posted at the last successful collateral call (presumably soon before the default,

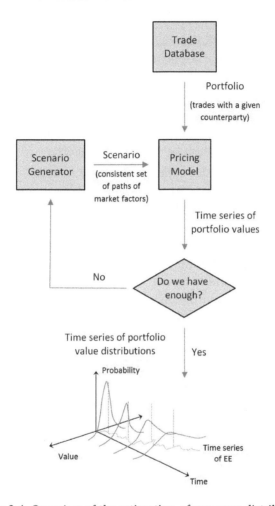

Figure 2.4: Overview of the estimation of exposure distributions

given that calls are made each business day) and the final replacement cost of the portfolio.

We will use the term 'tight CSA' for a cash-only, bilateral, zero threshold, daily margin, daily mark-to-market CSA. This term includes the standard CSA; it implies credit support arrangements that ensure that counterparty credit risk is low[63].

2.3.4 ... does not go hand-in-hand with the lowest liquidity risk

Tight CSAs reduce counterparty credit risk, but they do so at a considerable cost:

- Counterparties have to agree on what trades they have with each other. For inter-dealer portfolios of 100,000 or more trades (and where the trade population changes daily), that 'reconciliation' may not be entirely straightforward[64].

- They then have to agree what each of those trades is worth. Given that both parties might have their own proprietary models, that might not be straightforward either: in fact, 'valuation disputes' are not uncommon between large dealers.

- Next, the transfer actually has to be made. That requires the transferring party to find the cash. Given that this amount can be large, there is significant liquidity risk from tight CSAs.

This discussion should make it clear that a tight CSA is probably not appropriate for the average end-user. They neither have the operational infrastructure required to meet daily calls nor do they necessarily have spare cash lying around to meet them. Clearly a dealer who is willing to agree a looser CSA – monthly calls, say, and a high threshold – might well be a more attractive counterparty to a corporate than a dealer who insists on arrangements that create less credit risk.

It is also clear that there is a trade-off between counterparty credit risk and liquidity risk. Daily bilateral cash collateral calls reduce exposure at default, but they mean that both parties must always have cash available to meet the next call. If they cannot raise that cash in the short time available, then they are in credit support default. This is more than a theoretical possibility, as the next section illustrates.

2.3.5 AIG's credit support default

Pre-crisis, the American Insurance Group, known as AIG, was one of the largest insurance companies in the world[65]. In addition to its traditional insurance activities, AIG was active in the OTC derivatives market. Specifically a subsidiary of AIG, AIG FP, entered into over $500B of credit default swap contracts, mostly writing protection[66].

AIG was AAA-rated when AIG FP began to build up its OTC derivative portfolio, and many counterparties at the time were willing to deal with it on that basis without requiring collateral. However, some of them wanted to protect themselves against declines in AIG's credit quality, so they built 'triggers' into the CSA they agreed with AIG FP. These required the firm to post collateral if it was downgraded too far. A downgrade trigger introduces substantial liquidity risk in that it requires a firm to find more cash just when its credit quality has declined.

AIG was downgraded several times during the crisis. As a result, it had to post collateral. The amounts of collateral AIG were required to post were substantial, as figure 2.5 demonstrates[67]. AIG was not equal to the burden, and the firm was forced to seek government assistance[68]. The liquidity risk created by trigger CSAs was an essential element in its failure.

Counterparty	Amount Posted ($B)
Société Générale	4.1
Deutsche Bank	2.6
Goldman Sachs	2.5
Merrill Lynch	1.8
Calyon	1.1
Barclays	0.9
UBS	0.8
DZ Bank	0.7
Wachovia	0.7
Rabobank	0.5
KFW	0.5

Figure 2.5: The collateral amounts over $500M provided by AIG to various counterparties after the firm began receiving government assistance

2.3.6 AIG's valuation disputes

AIG also offers a vivid insight into valuation disputes and their impact on collateral calls during the crisis. A well-publicised example are Goldman Sachs' calls against AIG[69]. In short form[70], the reported story through to the autumn of 2007 was:

Pre-history Goldman entered into a number of trades with AIG FP whereby Goldman bought protection on various securities, mostly asset-backed securities ('ABS').

The two firms' CSA allowed Goldman to call collateral if AIG lost its AAA rating and if the value of the securities protected fell sufficiently.

July 2007 AIG having been downgraded and the ABS market having fallen, Goldman sent a $1.8B collateral call to AIG FP. AIG FP executives disputed the size of the call, claiming that the underlying securities had not fallen in value as much as Goldman claimed. Both sides admitted that the securities concerned were illiquid in current market conditions and that an accurate mark to market was challenging[71].

August 2007   After weeks of dispute and without having received their cash, Goldman reduced their call to $1.2B[72]. AIG FP suggested paying Goldman a 'good faith' deposit of $300M. Goldman counter-bid $450M, and this amount was paid. The payment did not resolve the dispute between the firms.

September 2007   Goldman made a further call of $1.5B based on its valuations. AIG did not pay.

November 2007   At this point other counterparties had made or were making substantial collateral calls, and AIG's liquidity position was becoming increasingly stressed. This eventually led to a government bail-out in September 2008.

For this author, the interesting points about this affair are the extended period over which valuations were disputed and the significant amounts involved. Goldman's willingness to reduce the size of its call in August might perhaps represent uncertainty over the true valuation; an element of unwillingness to irritate a frequent trading partner might also be a factor. But in any event it shows that substantial extended disputes over the value of a portfolio of OTC derivatives transactions were possible.

2.3.7   Forms of margin

Two pieces of terminology from the exchange-traded derivatives market are now increasingly used with regard to OTCs. These are 'initial margin' (or 'IM') and 'variation margin' (or 'VM'). Initial margin provides some protection against the change in value of a portfolio of derivatives between the last successful margin call and close out, while variation margin protects against changes in value from trade inception to today. In a perfect margining situation, then, the VM posted by a counterparty would equal the change in the value of their portfolio with us, while IM would cover any plausible increase in value between the last successful VM call and close out[73]. Figure 2.6 illustrates the idea.

Prior to the crisis it was unusual for one dealer to agree to post IM to another: efforts were concentrated on ensuring that VM reflected the mark-to-market of the joint portfolio as accurately as possible. More recently, regulations which will require joint posting of IM have been proposed: we discuss these in chapter 5.

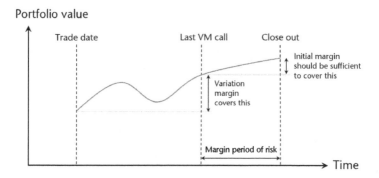

Figure 2.6: The uses of initial and variation margin

2.3.8 *Margin and due diligence*

It is important to note that the ability to call for margin does not discharge the responsibility to do due diligence on your counterparty. Collateral can mitigate the loss given default of a counterparty, but it does not change the fact of that default, and can even, as the example of AIG indicates, cause it. Therefore, despite the temptations to the contrary, it is important to properly review a proposed counterparty, and to understand the impact of their proposed transactions and credit support arrangements.

2.4 Where Does Your Margin Go? Rehypothecation & Funding

We have used the term 'post' to refer to the transfer of collateral from one party to another following a call – but what does this mean? This question is particularly important as the party who has posted the collateral needs to know what kind of claim they have for its return should the person they have posted it to suffer a credit event. Giving other people money, after all, creates credit risk.

There are two important forms of collateral transfer:

- In a 'title transfer', the secured party takes legal possession of collateral. There then may or may not be restrictions on how that collateral can be used.

- In the granting of a 'security interest', the posting party retains ownership of collateral, but the secured party acquires an interest in it. The intent is that this interest can be 'perfected', allowing the secured party to seize and sell the asset if necessary, but without them enjoying ownership prior to any perfection[74].

Different jurisdictions support one or both of these forms, and we examine them in more detail below.

2.4.1 Third party custodians

Collateral is not necessarily just a bilateral matter. Often a third party custodian is used, so that the securing party transfers collateral to the custodian who then grants rights to the party who wishes to be secured, as figure 2.7 depicts. This arrangement potentially offers lower credit risk, especially if the custodian is highly-rated[75] with few or no activities other than holding collateral, but it does make the legal analysis of exactly who has what rights more complex.

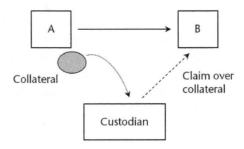

Figure 2.7: The role of a third party custodian

2.4.2 Title transfer

Title transfer represents the riskiest form of collateral movement from a credit risk perspective in that the counterparty has our asset. It is also often the only form of transfer which can be used for cash[76], a form of margin that is often mandatory. Inevitably, then, financial collateral is often posted by title transfer.

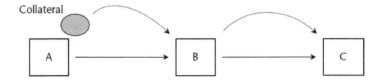

Figure 2.8: An illustration of the rehypothecation of collateral

There are a number of restrictions which can be applied to posted collateral. For instance, unrestricted collateral is often 'rehypothecated', meaning that the party it is posted to then reuses it as its collateral against an unrelated third party exposure. Figure 2.8 depicts a rehypothecation: A posts an asset as collateral to B who then on-posts the same asset to C.

If rehypothecation and other forms of reuse (such as outright sale) are restricted, then a party at least knows that the collateral remains with the counterparty they have posted it to.

Unrestricted title transfer is particularly risky if there is over-collateral-isation. If I give you €1M of collateral against an OTC derivatives portfolio which is only worth €800,000, then effectively I have unsecured credit risk to you of €200,000. The situation often exists either because it has been agreed in the CSA or because exposure has declined but the excess collateral has not yet been returned to the counterparty[77].

Rehypothecation has substantial benefits from a liquidity perspective. It means that a dealer does not have to find (and fund) fresh collateral against its own exposures, but rather can use collateral that has been posted to it. These benefits were persuasive before the crisis, with many dealers encouraging their clients to sign CSAs which permitted collateral reuse. The practice is now declining somewhat[78], not least due to the difficulties Lehman's clients had in regaining possession of rehypothecated collateral (and indeed some collateral that the client claimed should not have been reused[79]).

The discussion above makes it clear that there is another credit risk vs. liquidity risk trade-off regarding rehypothecation. Banning it would decrease credit risk: there would be no more 'chase the collateral' games as administrators attempt to follow rehypothecation chains after a bankruptcy[80]. On the other hand, the liquidity needs of dealers would be both higher and more volatile without reuse.

2.4.3 Segregation

Another technique for enhancing the safety of collateral is the require-ment for 'segregation'. Essentially this requires the party receiving the collateral to keep it separate from (that is, not 'co-mingled' with) its own assets. The CFTC's explanation of how segregation works for the clients of a class of US derivatives market participants known as futures commission merchants ('FCMs') illustrates the idea:[81]

- All customer funds used on 'designated contract markets' (i.e. ex-changes) must be kept apart ('segregated') from the FCM's own funds. This includes cash, securities or other property deposited by the FCM's customers to collateralise or guarantee futures trading.

+ Segregated accounts must be titled for the benefit of the FCM's customers.

+ Acknowledgements must be provided that would preclude a bank or clearing house from recognising a right of offset against the account for the FCM's debts.

+ Customer funds in segregation have a bankruptcy preference in the event of FCM insolvency.

+ To the extent that customer funds are not sufficient to pay customer claims, the remainder of what customers are owed will participate pro rata in the distributions to unsecured creditors of the bankrupt FCM.

In other words, these rules, together with a bankruptcy framework which ensures that segregated assets are not drawn into the estate of a failed FCM[82], keep collateral separate and make it likely that it can quickly and easily be returned to an FCM's clients should the FCM fail.

That is the theory, and it has worked in practice. Before moving on, though, we should acknowledge that segregation is only as safe as the process used for it. When collateral is not segregated as the rules require that it should be, clients face substantial credit risk. The next section discusses a prominent example of this unfortunate phenomenon.

2.4.4   When segregation fails: the case of MF Global

MF Global was a major global derivatives broker. Its business included both exchange traded and, to a lesser extent, OTC derivatives trading. The firm survived through the credit crisis but it suffered various difficulties (including fines from regulators and a rogue trader), and by 2009 it was not viewed as very well capitalised by the market. Due in part to these concerns, MF Global suffered increasingly serious liquidity stress. The firm was unable to find either a buyer or a lender, and it was forced to file for bankruptcy in October 2011.

After the failure it became clear that the firm had met some demands for cash by illegally transferring segregated customer funds to group companies and then on to third parties. At the time of writing, the deficiency between the amount that should have been in segregated accounts and the amount MF Global's bankruptcy trustee has been able to find is $1.6B[83]. Much of this sum represents amounts that are owed to retail or small business customers.

There are a number of factors which may have had a role in the MF Global losses. MF Global's loose policies and compliance failures themselves; the lack of direct supervision by the CFTC[84]; and the interaction between US and looser UK segregation rules all played a part[85]. But the fact remains that segregation was not fully effective and MF Global's clients lost money as a result[86].

2.4.5   OTC derivatives collateral segregation after the crisis

Post crisis legislation has transformed the treatment of collateral. For instance, both the United States' Dodd Frank Act and the European Union's Regulation on OTC derivatives, central counterparties and trade repositories ('EMIR') has rules on the segregation of OTC derivatives collateral. Dodd Frank requires that customers must be offered the opportunity to segregate with an independent third-party custodian any collateral that does not constitute variation margin[87], while EMIR requires 'appropriate' segregation, with the details yet to be agreed[88].

2.4.6   Collateral levels and types

The annual ISDA margin surveys give useful information on the nature and degree of collateralisation in the OTC derivatives markets. The highlights from the most recent survey at the time of writing[89] are:

- Surveyed parties reported that a total of 137,869 collateral agreements were in use at the end of 2011.

- 84% of all collateral agreements were bilateral.

- 71% of all covered transactions were subject to collateral agreements, although this includes spot FX (as these are often covered by the same master agreement as OTC derivatives). The G14 reported a higher degree of collateralisation: 84%.

- Cash was c. 79% of collateral received and 76% of collateral delivered in 2011. Government securities represented much of the rest.

- An average of 91% of collateral was eligible for reuse, and 83% was actually reused.

- The 2012 survey does not contain details of collateralisation by counterparty type, but the 2011 survey does. This indicates that average levels of collateralisation vary from 160% (i.e. significant over-collateralisation) for hedge funds, through 79% for banks and broker/dealers, to 37% for non-financial companies and below 25% for governments, supranationals and local/regional entities. In other words, the major classes of counterparty not posting collateral are state, regional and municipal governments, supranational and government agencies, and corporate end-users.

2.4.7   Collateral haircuts

The ISDA margin survey makes it clear that cash is the predominant form of collateral in OTC derivatives market. There are many good reasons for this: cash has an unambiguous value; that value does not display the kind of volatility that the value of a bond might; and cash is immediately available. Other assets are not so attractive for the collateral taker. Receiving parties typically impose a discount of the value they ascribe to non-cash collateral reflecting its possible decline between a default and liquidation of the collateral. This 'haircut' might be as little as 0.5% for a short term US government bond posted against a USD exposure, or more than 15% for a long term European government bond. Haircuts for lower-rated bonds, corporate bonds or equities can be much higher reflecting the greater risk of large changes in their value.

Cash collateral typically earns interest at some overnight rate such as EONIA or FED funds (or at a spread to it). This interest usually belongs to the collateral poster, so posted cash accumulates at the agreed rate. Similarly, returns on bonds posted as collateral typically accrue to the poster, so when a bond posted as collateral pays a coupon, that coupon forms part of the collateral posted.

2.5 Novation, Standardisation and Simplification

If one party to an OTC transaction wishes to terminate it before the trade's contractual maturity then they can approach the other party and negotiate an early termination. The terms that they can agree may however not be attractive. In this case, it may be possible to agree a 'novation' (or 'assignment'). Here a third party agrees to take over the responsibilities of the exiting party, perhaps in exchange for a fee paid or received.

Novation typically cannot take place without the consent of the re-maining counterparty, not least because the entering party might be of significantly lower credit quality than the exiting one and/or have a materially less favourable CSA. Often the contracts concerned specify that consent for a novation cannot be unreasonably withheld, though.

In practice novations are reasonably common among OTC derivatives market participants.

Figure 2.9 depicts the process. B wishes to exit its transaction with A, assigning its rights and obligations under the derivative to C. (Note that in general B will have other trades with A which it may well not wish to assign.)

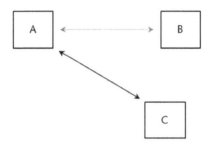

Figure 2.9: Depicting an OTC derivatives novation

The desire to facilitate novations provides another motivation for the standard CSA. If both the entering and the exiting party have a tight CSA with the remaining counterparty, then agreement on the value of the transaction at the point of novation is more likely to be achieved, and market liquidity will be enhanced. This consideration brings up an issue we will discuss further in the next chapter: how the CSA between two parties influences the value that they attribute to OTC derivatives transactions between them. First, though, we want to examine another development in the OTC markets: that of the novation protocol and the subsequent standardisation of credit derivatives. The chapter then ends with a discussion of how bilateral OTC derivatives relationships can be simplified.

2.5.1 Uncertain novations

In the early days of the credit derivative markets, novations were rare. However as hedge funds became increasingly important market players in the early 2000s, novations became more commonplace. Around 2005 it became clear that some market participants were assigning trades without obtaining the prior consent of the counterparty. This created uncertainty over the validity of the assignment, and consequently with the identity of the party from which subsequent payments were due. Supervisors raised concerns, and the industry subsequently agree to a novation protocol whereby market participants agreed to obtain written consent by close of business on the date the trade was assigned[90].

2.5.2 Liquidity and contract standardisation

The novation protocol assisted the CDS market, but it did not solve all of its issues. One problem was that CDS used to trade based on a spread, so that for instance a five year single name CDS on a corporate might be quoted by a dealer at 510/490 bps, meaning that one could buy protection for 510 bps per year or sell it and receive 490 bps. CDS spreads changed over time. This meant that if I come back to terminate or assign a trade after a year, not only would I have a non-standard maturity – four years – but the swap is also likely to be trading at the 'wrong' coupon. This creates a difference between on- and off-the-run CDS trading on the same name. Any assignment would involve a potentially contentious calculation of the fee payable to compensate for this 'basis'.

These issues were resolved in 2009 with the CDS 'big bang' and 'little bang'. Essentially these processes involved the standardisation of contracts[91]. In particular standard coupons were introduced, so that all single name corporate CDS would now trade on a fixed spread, with the difference between that and the market spread being made up in an upfront payment. The standardisations imposed in the two bangs increased the liquidity of the CDS market substantially[92].

A related initiative was the establishment of a network of Determinations Committees. These, among other things[93], decide whether a credit event has occurred for the market as a whole. The Committee may then organise an auction which sets the cash settlement price for CDS. This process means that settlement prices are less likely to be disconnected from the underlying bond market even when the CDS market is large compared to that in reference instruments[94].

2.5.3 Novation and collateral

Novation is a mechanism whereby one party can transfer its rights and obligations under a contract to a third party. The third party replaces the original party as a counterparty to the contract. However, those rights and obligations include credit support, so the new arrangements will include whatever has been agreed in the relevant CSAs.

Once the trade has moved, then, collateral requirements will be recalculated both between the original party and its old counterparty (given that they may jointly have other trades which have not been novated), and between the third party and its new counterparty, and whatever calls for

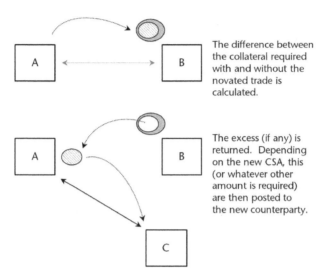

The difference between the collateral required with and without the novated trade is calculated.

The excess (if any) is returned. Depending on the new CSA, this (or whatever other amount is required) are then posted to the new counterparty.

Figure 2.10: The collateral movements accompanying an OTC derivatives novation

(or returns of) collateral are required by the respective CSAs will be made. Each calculation will use the relevant CSA, so for instance if there was no collateral requirement between the original party and its counterparty, but there was one for the novated trade, then collateral will have to be posted after novation. Figure 2.10 illustrates the process.

2.5.4 Simplification through trade compression

Bilateral OTC derivatives trading can lead to many trades between counterparties, often with little net risk. This is because unlike the securities or futures market, where buying eight of something then selling five of the same thing gives a net position of three, in OTC derivatives, trading only reduces the number of trades if the old trade is cancelled or novated away when the new one is entered into.

CDS standardisation helped here, in that it at least reduced the number of different products, but there has been no comparable initiative for interest rate swaps, and anyway some process was needed for removing redundant trades.

The answer to this issue is an operation known as 'trade compression'. This is a multilateral process whereby a number of counterparties sign up to a service provider. All participants make the portfolios that they have with each other available to the service provider (usually subject to product limits, so that for instance they might all agree to IRS compression one currency at a time).

The service provider constructs a list of trade cancellations (some partial) for each participant. This list has the property that if all participants agree and effect the proposed cancellations, then each participant is left with the same risk position and portfolio value as before[95], but with fewer trades. The compression process is designed to remove redundant trades, for instance where there is a bilateral offset (e.g. A has a trade with B and B has the same trade with A, perhaps on a different notional) or a loop of trades (e.g. A has a trade with B, B has the same trade with C, and C has that trade with A)[96]. For inter-dealer portfolios, trade compression can reduce the number of trades by 90% or more, so it is a powerful tool for reducing trade numbers.

Summary: the structure of OTC derivatives arrangements and infrastructure

The bilateral OTC derivatives market is built on five key pieces of documentation which together define the precise promises made by each pair of counterparties:

1. The master agreement; and

2. Its 'schedule' provides a framework for all the OTC derivatives transaction between the two parties.

   These documents include various representations (for instance that the party is legally able to enter into derivatives); a definition of the events of default after which a party can close out; and the netting provisions. The schedule also allows some degree of customisation of the master agreement itself so that for instance the termination provisions can be tailored to some degree. Finally, it contains various administrative and tax details.

3. The CSA details the nature of the credit support provided by each party to the other.

4. The definitions provide the framework for the documentation of OTC derivative transactions, defining key terms.

5. Each trade then has a confirmation which sets out the terms of the derivative using terms defined in the definitions.

One of the key reasons for the success of this documentation and credit support framework has been its effectiveness in ensuring that counterparties have a right of set-off. As a result of this success, credit risk in the inter-dealer market is based on net exposure, and the majority of this exposure is mitigated by cash collateral.

OTC derivatives market infrastructure has developed substantially since its early telephone- and fax-based days. In particular it now facilitates efficient trade reconciliation and collateral movement for many transactions[97]. Reconciliation failures and valuation disputes are nevertheless still possible, especially for illiquid transactions.

Collateral agreements are widespread in the OTC derivatives market but tight CSAs are not universal. There remain substantial uncollateralised exposures, particularly between dealers and both corporate and sovereign counterparties.

Notes

[42]Dealers often net within an asset class, making for instance a single net USD payment with respect to credit derivatives. However, due to systems issues, netting payments originating from different asset classes is less common: separate USD payments might well be made for the credit derivatives and equity derivatives portfolios.

[43]For (many) more details, see R. Derham, *The Law of Set-Off*, Oxford University Press 2010.

[44]Set-off between two claims is difficult to achieve if both claims do not have the same seniority.

[45]See for instance the Herbert Smith briefing *The Federal Law "On Clearing and Clearing Activities" and related amendments to Russian legislation* available via www.herbertsmith. com for information on recent changes to Russian law which enhance set-off rights.

[46]The recent case of UBS vs. Lehman, discussed for instance in White Case's Futures and Derivatives Law Report *Lehman Bankruptcy Court Denies Contractual Right to Triangular Setoff*, February 2012, available via www.whitecase.com is typical. Here Judge James Peck of the Bankruptcy Court for the Southern District of New York denied UBS's assertion of a trilateral set-off right between two different UBS affiliates and Lehman.

[47]For more on the DTCC and its functions, see V. Morris, *Guide to Clearance & Settlement*, Lightbulb Press 2009.

[48]A more comprehensive account of settlement risk and intraday liquidity can be found in A. Ball et al., *Intraday liquidity: risk and regulation*, Bank of England Financial Stability Paper No. 11 (June 2011) available at www.bankofengland.co.uk/ publications/Documents/fsr/fs_paper11.pdf. The final days of Lehman Brothers provide

a good example of the funding stress created by a loss of confidence: see for instance J. Stempel, *Lehman sues JPMorgan for billions in damages*, Reuters 2010, available at www.reuters.com/article/2010 /05/26/us-lehman-jpmorgan-lawsuit-idUSTRE64P6J720100526.

[49]For more details, see *About CLS* (2012) available via www.cls-group.com.

[50]Some commentators have argued that close out netting is undesirable for instance because it reduces counterparty due diligence: see for instance see M. Roe, *The Derivatives Market's Payment Priorities as Financial Crisis Accelerator*, ECGI Law Working Paper No. 153 (2010). We find this argument unconvincing as the amounts at stake are still substantial.

[51]For more details, see P. Harding, *Mastering the ISDA Master Agreement: A Practical Guide for Negotiation*, Financial Times Prentice Hall (2002).

[52]The unenforceability of certain 'flip clauses' in US bankruptcy is a good example of a seemingly effective agreement that was not respected. See for instance Herrick's note *Bankruptcy Court Invalidates Flip Clauses* (2010) available at www.herrick.com/sitecontent.cfm?pageID=29&itemID=12964. Further complexity is added by the fact that the other major law used to document OTC derivatives transactions – English law – ruled differently on a substantially similar case: see Mayer Brown's *Like London buses: some recent English derivatives decisions*, Derivatives Week 22 August 2011, available at www.mayerbrown.com/news/detail.aspx?news=1382.

[53]See www2.isda.org/functional-areas/legal-and-documentation/opinions/.

[54]As ISDA says, 'We have performed a survey of industry participants who are very active in the derivatives markets. This reveals no instances where firms have found that courts do not respect the netting provisions of a master netting agreement where ISDA has a relevant opinion': see www.isda.org/c_and_a/pdf/The-effectiveness-of-netting.pdf. There are however other issues which pertain, such as the 2(a)(iii) problem discussed below.

[55]It should be noted that credit events under both the 1992 and 2002 Master Agreements are broader than just bankruptcy: they include failure to pay, misrepresentation and (something that will occupy us later) credit support default. The legal analysis of close out therefore also needs to include the effectiveness of close out in these situations.

[56]The case concerned is that of Metavante Corporation versus Lehman. Metavante relied on 2(a)(iii) to suspend payments to Lehman without closing out: Judge Peck held that the safe harbour provisions in the US Bankruptcy Code did not allow the firm to withhold performance under a swap for an unlimited period if it did not terminate. See Cadwalader's note *Litigation Challenges Counterparty Right to Withhold Payments under Section 2(a)(iii) of ISDA Master Agreement as Violation of Automatic Stay Provisions of U.S. Bankruptcy Code* (2009) available at www.cadwalader.com/assets/client_friend/081109Litigation_Challenges_Counter party_Right.pdf for more details.

[57]A detailed demonstration of this effect can be found in the ISDA research note *A Note on the Impossibility of Correctly Calibrating the Current Exposure Method for Large OTC Derivatives Portfolios* (June 2011), which also demonstrates that a consequence

of the non-linear growth of netting benefit is that any approach to the capitalisation of risk in OTC derivatives portfolios that adds the risk contributions trade-by-trade is either imprudent for small portfolios or vastly over-conservative for large ones (or both).

[58]This leads to the concept of 'too big to close out', whereby a dealer's portfolio is so large that, whatever its net risk, closing it out would be a colossal task.

[59]Some collateral agreements specify a minimum transfer amount ('MTA') as well as a threshold. If the difference between the exposure and the collateral held is lower than the MTA, no collateral call is made. This reduces the operational burden of collateral calls.

[60]We also assume that neither party posts initial margin to the other, and that the collateral does not change in value.

[61]Strictly, cash in the same currency as the exposure.

[62]The standard CSA is rather more complex than we have outlined, having in particular features to transfer cash in one currency but keep notional balances (which earn interest at the appropriate rate) in others. See ISDA's *Overview of ISDA Standard Credit Support Annex* (2011) available via www.isda.org for more details.

[63]In particular we do not assume that a tight CSA permits payments in one currency while notional balances are kept in others, nor do we imply currency restrictions.

[64]Various companies such as Trioptima provide trade reconciliation services to achieve this aim.

[65]The Special Inspector General for the Troubled Asset Relief Program's July 2012 quarterly report, *AIG Remains in TARP as TARP's Largest Investment* available via www.sigtarp.gov has a fuller account of AIG's situation and mis-steps.

[66]The 2007 AIG annual report suggests that AIG had traded a notional of $561B at that point.

[67]Note that these amounts, taken from www.aig.com/aigweb/internet/en/files/CounterpartyAttachments031809_tcm385-155645.pdf represent only collateral posted after AIG received government support. There were substantial postings prior to this date too.

[68]Chapter 8 of my book *Unravelling the credit crunch*, Chapman and Hall (2009) has a longer description of credit support default and the fall of AIG.

[69]For more detail and supporting documentation see the Financial Crisis Inquiry Commission's website at www.fcic.gov/report (mirrored at fcic-static.law.stanford.edu). Subsequent notes in this section refer to documents available at that website, using their date format.

[70]See *Goldman AIG Collateral Call timeline* (2010-07-01).

[71]CBS has made available an insightful internal AIG memo from the crisis period at www.cbsnews.com/htdocs/pdf/collateral_b.pdf. It says in part: 'Due to the extreme illiquidity of the reference bonds and the current environment, all of the CSA calls we have had for the CDO negative basis trades we currently have are friendly discussions rather than disputed calls. All of the dealers have been willing to enter into a dialogue

to try and best sort out the CSA calls as they appreciate that there is no clear market to use'.

[72] For more on Goldman's pricing methodology, see the *Goldman Sachs - Valuation and Pricing Related to Initial Collateral Call on Transactions with AIG* (2010-08-31).

[73] Note that the term variation margin is used in two slightly different senses in the literature. The convention we use is that it means the *total* amount of VM called over the life of the portfolio; we use 'variation margin call' for the amount called from one day to the next. Note however some authors use 'variation margin' for the latter amount.

[74] Achieving this intent can be difficult, as Pinsent Mason discuss in their Banking & Restructuring note *New rules on financial collateral fail to remove old uncertainties*, April 2011, available www.pinsentmasons.com/PDF/NewRulesFinancialCollateral.pdf.

[75] Another advantage of third party custodians is that they can usually be replaced if their credit quality starts to deteriorate without the need to terminate or novate the trades they hold collateral for.

[76] Some legal frameworks do not permit the granting of a security interest over cash.

[77] Large payments on OTC derivatives typically give rise to over-collateralisation for at least a day; the collateral is there precisely because a big payment is due, and hence the exposure does not fall until after it has been made. There are substantial legal and operational difficulties to netting the payment and the collateral movement, so substantial over-collateralisation for a day or two is commonplace in this situation.

[78] M. Singh and colleagues have studied this phenomenon. In work with J. Aitken, *The (sizable) Role of Rehypothecation in the Shadow Banking System*, IMF working paper WP/10/172 (July 2010), the authors suggest that rehypothecation represented more than half of the activity of the shadow banking system, while in *Velocity of Pledged Collateral: Analysis and Implications*, IMF working paper WP/11/256 (November 2011), Singh discusses the role of rehypothecation as a money multiplier, and shows rehypothecation chains have shortened since the failure of Lehman creating a deleveraging effect. Both papers are available via www.imf.org.

[79] See the Orrick Client Alert *Rehypothecation by Lehman leads to Fund Litigation*, 3rd October 2008 available at www.orrick.com/fileupload/1494.pdf for more details.

[80] For an interesting discussion of this, see C. Johnson, *Derivatives and rehypothecation failure – it's 3:00 p.m, do you know where your collateral is*, 30 Arizona Law Review 949 (Fall 1997).

[81] See www.cftc.gov/IndustryOversight/Intermediaries/FCMs/fcmsegregatio nfunds.

[82] FCMs, the theory goes, cannot file for bankruptcy under Chapter 11, but rather must be liquidated under CFTC Regulation 190 and subchapter IV of Chapter 7.

[83] The amount is taken from the *Testimony of James W. Giddens, Trustee for the Securities Investor Protection Act Liquidation of MF Global Inc.* in front of the U.S. Senate Committee on Agriculture, Nutrition and Forestry, 1st August 2012 available via dm.epiq11.com/MFG/Project.

[84]The job was instead sub-contracted to that potentially oxymoronic class of entities, the 'self-regulatory organization'.

[85]The MF Global bankruptcy trustee's *Report of the Trustee's Investigation and Recommendations* (4th June 2012) available via dm.epiq11.com/MFG/Project contains a longer discussion.

[86]The US House Staff Report on MF Global (November 2012) makes the following insightful recommendation: 'The futures market cannot function unless customers are confident that FCMs will safeguard their funds. To restore investor confidence in the futures markets and help ensure that an FCM does not misuse customer funds in the future, the Subcommittee recommends that Congress consider enacting legislation that imposes civil liability on the officers and directors that sign a FCM's financial statements or authorize specific transfers from customer segregated accounts for regulatory shortfalls of segregated customer funds'.

[87]Strictly, this is something that swap dealers and major swap participants must offer customers in connection with uncleared OTC derivatives.

[88]JPMorgan's *Regulatory Reform and Collateral Management: The Impact on Major Participants in the OTC Derivatives Markets* (Winter 2012) available via www.jpmorgan.com contains a summary of the state of play at the time of writing. The situation will inevitably evolve not least because ESMA has to finalise rules implementing the EMIR provisions.

[89]This is the 2012 survey available via www.isda.org.

[90]For more on this and the other topics of this chapter, see *New developments in clearing and settlement arrangements for OTC derivatives*, Committee on Payment and Settlement Systems (March 2007) available at www.bis.org/publ/cpss77.pdf.

[91]The Bank of America Merrill Lynch Credit Derivative Strategist Research Note *The Big Bang: A Guide to the Standardized CDS Contract*, 24 February 2009 and the Markit magazine article *Small Bang for the Buckets* (Autumn 2009) contain fuller descriptions of, respectively, the big and little bangs.

[92]This is not to say that liquidity is excellent. Recently the FED found that 'A majority of the single-name reference entities traded less than once a day, whereas the most active traded over 20 times per day. Few specific reference entities were consistently active [over time].' Moreover 'more than half of all transactions were between G14 dealers' so the market was quite concentrated. For details, see K. Chen et al. *An Analysis of CDS Transactions: Implications for Public Reporting*, Federal Reserve Bank of New York Staff Report No. 517 (September 2011) available at www.newyorkfed.org/research/staff_reports/sr517.pdf.

[93]Other responsibilities of the Determinations Committee include the determination of succession events and the identification of substitute reference obligations when the originals are no longer available.

[94]J. Helwege et al.'s Federal Reserve Bank of New York Staff Report *Credit Default Swap Auctions* No. 372 (May 2009) has a further discussion of the CDS auction process.

[95]In practice there is a tolerance for how perfectly the replacement portfolio needs to replicate the original. The higher the tolerance, the fewer trades are needed in the compressed portfolio.

[96]See Box 2.4 in the IMF's *Global Financial Stability Report* April 2009, available at www.imf.org/External/Pubs/FT/GFSR/2009/01/index.htm for a further discussion of the removal of redundant trades in compression. The leading provider of OTC derivatives trade compression services at the time of writing is Trioptima: more details can also be found on their website www.trioptima.com.

[97]E. Ledrut and C. Upper's *Changing post-trading arrangements for OTC derivatives*, BIS quarterly (December 2007) available at www.bis.org/publ/qtrpdf/r_qt0712i.pdf contains a further discussion of the state of and issues with market infrastructure in the key pre-crisis period.

3

The Valuation and Risk of OTC Derivatives

DUCHESS: *And thou comest to make my tomb?*
BOSOLA: *Yes.*
DUCHESS: *Let me know fully therefore the effect*
  Of this thy dismal preparation
John Webster

Introduction

It is time to look in more detail at how OTC derivatives are valued, and how some of the risks that they create are measured and capitalised. In this chapter, the modern approach to derivatives valuation is surveyed, credit valuation adjustments are discussed, and a widely-used approach to modelling portfolio counterparty credit risk is presented. We also review some of the risks inherent in the taking of collateral, so-called 'credit support risks'. The situation where there is a strong (and unhelpful) association between the exposure we have and the credit quality of the counterparty is considered, and the chapter ends with an outline of how counterparty credit risk models are used by some banks to calculate regulatory capital requirements.

3.1 Derivatives Valuation under a CSA

In chapter 1, we indicated that the way to price a derivative was to figure out what cashflows we expect – or, better, to deduce the distribution of those cashflows – then discount them back to today. This approach is broadly correct, but there are several issues:

- ✦ In general, there may be cashflows from collateral as well as ones from the derivative. We need to take these into account.

- ✦ We need to include credit effects in valuation, via the calculation of a CVA.

- ✦ The rate that we discount back at is not obvious; should it be the risk free rate, the rate we fund at, the rate we have to pay interest on collateral at, or something else?

- ✦ How, if at all, do we account for CSA optionality, whereby our counterparty might be able to post margin in Euros, say, or US dollars?

We do not have space to answer these questions in their full (highly mathematical) detail, but we will indicate the general argument and their impact on market practice.

3.1.1 Replicating portfolios and collateral

The theory of no arbitrage is central to derivatives pricing. At its simplest, it says that there are no free lunches. This means that if we can come up with a strategy which replicates the payoff of a derivative, the cost of carrying out that strategy must be equal to the value of the derivative (for if it wasn't, we could come up with a free lunch by buying the cheap thing and selling the expensive thing).

The standard derivation[98] of the Black-Scholes partial differential equation, of which the famous Black-Scholes pricing formula for plain vanilla options is a solution, is based on this approach. A portfolio consisting of a cash position and a position in the underlying of the derivative is created, and this is rebalanced to ensure that it has the same payoff as the derivative.

The key issue here, though, is that this strategy replicates the payoff of the derivative at maturity; it does not replicate the on-going cashflows of a collateralised position. To do that, we need a different strategy that not only produces the right final result, but also reflects the movements of cash that could occur under the particular CSA in place between the counterparties. This alters the final result, introducing in particular a term that depends on the return on collateral[99]. The key point is that the value of an OTC derivative depends on the CSA in place with the counterparty. Changing the CSA between two parties changes the value of the whole portfolio of derivatives they are jointly counterparties to[100].

3.1.2 OIS discounting

The observation that pricing changes based on the nature of credit support arrangements between counterparties, together with market movements during the credit crisis which made the differences between naïve and CSA-sensitive pricing more significant[101], led market participants to adopt a new approach to OTC derivatives pricing which we will call 'CSA-specific valuation'. This takes a (relatively) simple form if we assume a tight CSA, and this particular form of CSA-specific valuation is known as 'OIS discounting'. It therefore represents a reasonable basis for quoting prices, as tight CSAs are commonplace.

3.1.3 CSA optionality

A CSA that only permits the posting of Euro cash collateral gives a different value for a Euro/Dollar cross currency swap to one that only permits the posting of Dollars. What about one that lets a counterparty post Euros or Dollars? Clearly here the counterparty has the option to do whatever is cheapest, and this option has value[102]. Should we account for this 'CSA optionality' in pricing derivatives with the counterparty? The answer is clearly yes, but how to do this exactly is the subject of some debate[103]. The desire to avoid this problem provides another motivation for using a type of CSA where it does not arise.

3.1.4 CVA

A credit valuation adjustment is the difference between the portfolio value if contracted with a risk free counterparty and the true portfolio value that takes into account the possibility of the counterparty's default, with values being taken in both cases under the same CSA. In other words, CVA is the market value of counterparty credit risk, given the credit support arrangements we have[104].

Tight CSAs typically generate very low CVAs as they mean that there is only exposure to the movement in the value of the portfolio over, at most, a few days. Other arrangements – especially CSAs with high thresholds or long periods between margin calls – can generate significant CVAs.

Consider again the scenarios that were introduced in sections 1.1.7 and 2.3.2. At any given point in time, were the counterparty to default at that moment, then we would lose the expected exposure. This is a loss in the future, so it has to be discounted back to today. Moreover, we do not lose the whole amount, since our claim is (typically) *pari passu* with senior debt, so the loss given default is one minus whatever recovery we expect on the counterparty times the discount factor, times the expected exposure.

The probability of suffering this loss is simply the probability that the counterparty will default at this time. Therefore the contribution to the CVA from the potential loss at this point in time is just the loss given default times the probability of default. The total CVA is simply the sum of all of these potential losses from now until maturity of the portfolio[105].

The CVA is a real cost: customers will typically see swaps quoted without CVA, but an appropriate CVA will be charged based on the CSA they have, so the price that they can deal at might be rather different from the quote[106]. This CVA adjustment can be opaque to clients, not least because it depends on the portfolio that they have with the dealer.

The problem that arises immediately is the size of the unilateral CVA. If we assume that all of our counterparty's credit spread is compensation for default – a standard if overly-conservative assumption – then the probability of non-performance for most counterparties is so high that few swaps would trade if the dealer tried to charge this CVA. Moreover two parties who each calculate unilateral CVAs on the other can never agree a trade, as they both try to charge a premium. One pragmatic solution is to move to bilateral CVA.

3.1.5 Bilateral CVA

Bilateral CVA takes into account the possibility of both parties defaulting. It is therefore a symmetric measure that can perhaps be agreed between two parties to a trade. Moreover, taking account of both parties' credit quality means that the bilateral CVA is smaller than the unilateral CVA, and so clients are more likely to find prices that include it acceptable.

The 'own credit' component of CVA (sometimes known as 'DVA' for 'debt valuation adjustment') is typically defined as the difference between the value of the portfolio assuming the calculating party is default-risk free and the value reflecting default risk. Changes in our own credit quality therefore impact this component of the CVA[107].

3.1.6 Why CVA?

It may seem arbitrary to separate the price of an OTC derivative into a credit risk free component and a CVA. The reason for this is to allow the market risk of the derivative to be hedged separately from the credit sensitive element. The relevant product area – equity derivatives, interest rate derivatives, or whatever – hedges all of its derivatives as if they were credit risk free. This allows them to treat a long and a short position in the same derivative as a perfect hedge, regardless of the credit quality and the CSAs in place. CVA is managed separately, typically on a whole firm basis; the CVA desk is therefore responsible for the firm's entire counterparty credit risk portfolio.

3.1.7 Summary: Factors In OTC Derivatives Valuation

In the preceding sections we have seen that the valuation of a portfolio of derivatives depends on the following factors[108]:

- The market factors needed to value each derivative in the portfolio separately;
- The CSA between the two parties;
- The return on any collateral posted (e.g. the overnight rate on cash);
- The credit quality of the counterparty if collateralisation is not perfect; and similarly
- Own credit quality, again assuming imperfect collateralisation.

3.2 Estimates of Default Risk and CVA Management

Default is inherently uncertain: if we knew that a counterparty was going to default, then we would deal with them on very different terms to the usual ones. This uncertainty means that we will have to work with necessarily imperfect estimates of the likelihood that a counterparty will not perform[109]. There are two major approaches here, each leading to a different approach to CVA management.

3.2.1 Historical default estimates

The frequency of default of similar counterparties to the one at issue can be estimated from historical data. For instance, one might use a credit rating of the counterparty to infer its likely future probability of default. As always, the future may not be like the past, so this estimate may be unreliable, but one may be able to gain some comfort that a given ratings system provides reasonable probability of default estimates[110]. Figure 3.1 illustrates the approach.

This method of calculating CVA is broadly similar to the estimation of a forwarding looking loan loss provision in the banking book[111]. CVAs which use historical estimates tend to be associated with less active

Credit Rating	Probability of Default
AAA	0.005%
AA	0.02%
A	0.06%
BBB	0.4%
BB	1.5%
B	10%
CCC	30%

Figure 3.1: An example of real world one year probabilities of default associated with a given credit rating

management: the dealer takes the view that it is in the business of extending credit, and this includes extending credit via OTC derivatives. Provided that this credit is properly priced[112] – via the CVA – then there is no inherent problem in this.

3.2.2 Market-based default estimates

The alternative to historical approaches to default probability is the 'market based' method. Here a counterparty's credit spread is used to infer an estimate of probability of default. For instance, it is straightforward to infer a probability of default by assuming that the whole of the credit spread is compensation for default risk, and then fixing a recovery at, say, 40%. The resulting probability is typically much larger than would be inferred using a historical approach. Two researchers put it this way:[113]

> Spreads on corporate bonds tend to be many times wider than what would be implied by expected default losses alone. . . In 1997–2003, for example, the average spread on BBB-rated corporate bonds ... was more than eight times the expected loss from default.

This is because the credit spread includes compensation for non-default risks such as credit spread volatility and liquidity[114]. A probability backed out from credit spreads is sometimes called a 'risk neutral probability'. These risk neutral probabilities are useful in so far as, being market-based, they facilitate hedging, but they should not be confused with real-world default probabilities.

Consider a counterparty with a CSA that generates significant CVA. We charge the counterparty this amount at trade inception. If the counterparty's credit quality subsequently declines (and exposure does not change) then the CVA will increase, and we will take a loss. The risk of this can be hedged in the market-based approach. Specifically, in this view, the total CVA is something whose value depends on a variety of market factors (the parameters which drive the value of the portfolio with each counterparty) and on each counterparty's credit spread. These sensitivities can be hedged by trading in suitable instruments, for instance buying sufficient CDS to remove the exposure to widening credit spreads[115]. If this hedging is performed successfully then we lock in the value of the unilateral CVA charged at trade inception, and thus are not at risk of unilateral CVA losses.

The qualification 'unilateral' in the previous paragraph highlights an important issue: hedging the 'own credit' component in bilateral CVA is problematic. Bilateral CVA goes up and we take losses[116] if our credit quality increases[117], so we want to sell credit protection on ourself to hedge this. There is currently no completely effective way to do this[118].

3.2.3 Sovereign CVA

The CVA generated by OTC derivatives exposures with sovereigns is a particular issue for many dealers. Most sovereigns are reluctant to agree to post collateral[119], and some of them have substantial portfolios, so they generate a significant CVA. To hedge this CVA, dealers would need to buy CDS. The CDS market in many sovereigns is not liquid enough to permit this hedging without the market being moved[120], so CVA hedging pushes out sovereign bond spreads, increasing governments' borrowing costs. Perhaps it might be in sovereigns' interests to post collateral after all.

3.2.4 Default risk vs. credit spread risk

The fact that credit spreads typically provide more compensation than is fair for default risk (mentioned in section 3.2.2 above) makes it clear that credit spread risk and default risk are different things. Credit spreads can move for reasons other than changing perceptions of default, and these other factors introduce extra volatility – and thus risk – into credit exposures that are marked to market. To make this more precise, consider two situations:

1. A bank has a loan portfolio which is accrue accounted and funded to term. The bank is sufficiently well capitalised that it can hold this portfolio to term.

2. A bank has a bond in its trading portfolio (so that it has to be marked to market).

In the first case the bank is only exposed to default risk, while in the second it has the additional risk of the non-default components of the credit spread. The first position will require less capital than the second; historical default estimates would be appropriate to measure risk in the first case, while market-based ones would be more suitable in the second[121].

3.3 Counterparty Credit Risk

We have already seen (at least in outline[122]) how to calculate EE and PFE for a portfolio of exposures to a single counterparty. We can then apply any credit risk mitigation given by the CSA, such as collateral, and deduce our net EE and PFE. This section begins with an examination of that netting process in a little more detail. Then we go on to look at how the measures of risk for each counterparty are aggregated to produce an estimate of total counterparty credit risk.

3.3.1 Effective measures

EE is the average positive exposure of our distribution of portfolio values at any point in time, as figure 1.7 illustrated. It is natural to take the average of these EE(t)s: the result is called 'expected positive exposure' or 'EPE'. A related term is 'effective EE': like EE, this is a function of time, and for any point it is the maximum of the current EE and the past effective EE. Thus effective EE is non-decreasing, as figure 3.2 illustrates. 'Effective EPE' is the average of the effective EE(t)s.

The EPE is an estimate of the average amount the counterparty owes us during the life of the current portfolio, and thus it represents a kind of loan equivalent amount.

3.3.2 The margin period of risk

It is natural to ask how collateral reduces EE and hence EPE. This clearly depends on how long it takes to

- Value the current portfolio and the collateral posted;
- Call for extra collateral if permitted by the CSA;
- Note that we have not received the called-for amount;
- Give a grace period required in the CSA to the counterparty;

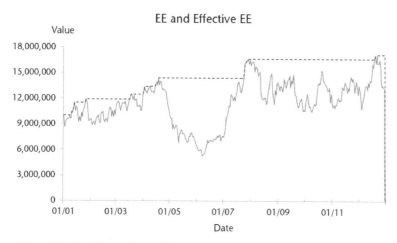

Figure 3.2: An illustration of the difference between EE (shown in the solid line) and effective EE (shown in the dashed line)

- Put them into default;
- Perfect and liquidate the collateral; and
- Replace all the transactions in the portfolio.

This period, known as the 'margin period of risk' (or 'MPOR') , will be several days even with a tight CSA. Counterparty credit managers often assume a ten day MPOR for large OTC derivatives portfolios. If the collateral is entirely cash, the portfolio is composed of highly liquid risks, infrastructure is good[123], and grace periods are short, then a five day margin period of risk may instead be reasonable.

The margin period of risk means that collateral does not reduce the current exposure, but rather the exposure in the past. A 5 day MPOR means that there is a business week of lag between the exposure and the collateral value. Thus we have to use a lagged amount of collateral[124] in calculating net exposure.

Once the mitigatory effect of collateral has been properly accounted for, we have good EE and PFE profiles for each counterparty, and EPE is a good 'loan equivalent' measure of risk. Or is it?

3.3.3 Loan equivalent exposure

Banks want to be able to combine the default risk of their derivatives portfolio with that taken in other areas in order to estimate their total default risk. One way to do that is to use a loan equivalent amount, so that a varying derivatives exposure is represented by a fixed number. The portfolio's EPE is an obvious candidate for that fixed number, but we may be concerned that simply using the average EE is not prudent due to the variability of exposure. It turns out[125] that that concern is justified, especially if the portfolio is concentrated, and we should increase the exposure somewhat. The factor we need to multiply EPE by to get a prudent exposure amount is known as alpha. It depends somewhat on the portfolio, but taking alpha equal to 1.4 is reasonably safe.

Now that we have alpha times EPE as the loan equivalent amount for each counterparty, the question arises as to how to combine these into an aggregate risk measure.

3.3.4 Default comovement models

In order to aggregate exposures to different counterparties, we need to know how often they will default together. If counterparties' defaults are uncorrelated, then multiple defaults will happen rarely, and even portfolios composed of numerous different creditors will seldom suffer many defaults. On the other hand, if there is a strong relationship between defaults, then a large number of defaults are much more likely.

The minefield analogy helps to explain this. Imagine a minefield with randomly scattered mines. If we wander around this field, then we are quite likely to encounter one or two mines blowing up, but rather unlikely to set off ten or fifteen in quick succession. On the other hand, if the same number of mines are planted in clumps, we might miss all of them and thus suffer no losses at all; or we might come across a densely mined area and so experience many explosions in a short period of time. Default comovement is analogous to mine clumping: many bad things happening in a short period of time is much more likely if it is high than if it is low.

There are a number of mathematical models of default comovement[126]. The simplest of these is the Gaussian copula model[127] and there are many others[128]. Most of these models, including all the best known and widest used ones, share the following features:

* The model postulates some relationship between default-related quantities[129];

* This model has some free parameters[130] which must be calibrated;

* Some data – either the prices of traded securities or historical credit information – is used to calibrate the model;

- The model then makes predictions about the likelihood of multiple defaults.

A good example of this is the model used to determine the regulatory capital for default risk within the Basel II internal ratings based ('IRB') framework. This assumes that the default risk in a financial institution can be modelled in a certain mathematical form[131], and then fixes the calibration of the model via supervisor-set default correlations[132].

3.3.5 Problems with these models

The problem of how to think about the relationship between the defaults of different companies is a difficult one. For instance, if we knew how to do this then pricing CDO tranches would be straightforward. The reason it isn't is that in times of stress, lots of defaults occurring together becomes quite likely, whereas it is much more improbable ordinarily. The difficulty of modelling this and related phenomena[133] means that there is no widely-agreed model of default comovement. Even worse, market measures of default comovement are only observable for a very limited number of portfolios, essentially only those underlying the liquid credit indices. Therefore we are in the undesirable situation of not knowing what the right model for the relationship between defaults is, and not having the data to calibrate what models we do have for most portfolios of interest[134].

In the face of these (substantial[135]) problems, firms typically adopt a pragmatic approach. They pick some relatively simple default comovement model, and use this to aggregate the exposures to single counterparties into an estimate of the complete counterparty credit risk distribution.

3.3.6 Portfolio counterparty credit risk

A risk measure should quantify how much we might lose were a situation to unfold badly. Risk estimation often proceeds by first estimating the distribution of total returns at some time horizon, then taking some high percentile of it as the risk measure. This is what we do for counterparty credit risk, but with one slight modification. This relates to the average of the distribution. For market risk, this is often zero, or close enough to zero that we can ignore it. For credit risk, it isn't; there are often significant expected losses. Risk managers therefore typically distinguish:

- 'Expected loss' or 'EL', which is the average of the portfolio loss distribution; from

* 'Unexpected loss' or 'UL', which is some high percentile (99.9% perhaps) of this distribution.

Figure 3.3 illustrates the ideas. It is generally viewed as good practice to provision for expected loss, and to support unexpected loss with capital.

The Credit Risk Loss Distribution

Figure 3.3: Expected and unexpected loss for the credit risk loss distribution

3.3.7 CVA and portfolio counterparty credit risk

A CVA which has been calculated using historical estimates of counterparty default is akin to a traditional loan loss reserve: it acts as an EL provision[136]. The position of a market-based CVA is rather less clear: it is at least as big as an EL provision, but being hedged, it behaves differently. Perhaps the right way to look at it is to consider the analogous example of an option sold to an end-user. The end user pays for the option at the start of the contract, and does not hedge. The dealer receives the premium and locks in that value by hedging, ensuring that whatever the market does, they do not materially gain or lose[137]. Similarly the end user without a tight CSA pays CVA up front and has no further payments; the dealer hedges that CVA to ensure that whatever happens, they do not suffer losses from counterparty non-performance[138].

The alternative to paying CVA up front is to agree to a tight CSA: but then you pay collateral as you go. In effect, CVA is a one-off fee to be exempt from further demands on liquidity, while a tight CVA is a promise to fund your counterparty however much your portfolio with them might be worth[139].

3.3.8   MPOR, IM, and ignoring CCR

Even the most tolerant of readers must have thought that the process of deriving a measure of a firm's total OTC derivatives counterparty credit risk is a complicated one. Can we do without it? That is, can we arrange matters so that there is no risk, and so there is nothing to estimate?

It is clear that we can reduce CCR to very low levels with every counterparty, but at a very substantial cost. If, for instance, we had a very tight CSA and in addition charged IM based on some high percentile of a very conservative model with a holding period given by the MPOR[140], then we could be reasonably sure[141] that the CCR was low enough that the costs of estimating it are not worth the benefits. On the other hand, this approach would demand such a high level of IM that either no one would deal with us; or, if they were forced to, we would have created a great deal of liquidity risk for them.

Another issue with this approach is that it assumes that collateral *always* works. We are dealing with very high confidence intervals, after all, so if we use the single tool of collateral to remove all counterparty credit risk from OTC derivatives trading, then we need to be sure that collateral will be ineffective less often than our desired safety standard. Basel II uses a 99.9% standard, so to be sufficiently prudent, we would need to be sure that collateral worked nine hundred and ninety nine times in a thousand. Lawyers who are experienced in the legal risks of collateralisation (let alone collateral managers who understand the operational risks) might be hard pressed to give assurances that this is so.

The author's view is that without the kind of counterparty credit risk system we have described, it is very difficult to know how much aggregate risk remains after margining. This in turn means that it is hard to know if there are sufficient financial resources to bear that risk. Calculating net unexpected loss for CCR and capitalising that risk seems more prudent than hoping that margining makes up for not having a sophisticated model for measuring residual CCR.

3.4   The Risks in Credit Support and Procyclicality

What both parties to a collateralised transaction want is that the collateral posted does not fall in value. The poster does not want to have to post more collateral to top up the balance, as that creates liquidity risk; it also increases counterparty credit risk for the party it has been posted to. Cash in the same currency as the exposure is therefore ideal collateral: it is also ideal from the perspective of portfolio valuation, as we saw earlier. However, the poster may not have sufficient cash in the right currency available. In that case, there are two potential issues[142]:

1. The risk that the collateral may change in value, leaving the portfolio less well collateralised than it should be; and

2. The risk that haircuts on one or more items of collateral may increase, forcing extra collateral to be posted.

3.4.1 Collateral value risk

The simplest situation where collateral value can change is cash collateral in a different currency to the exposure. Here we have FX risk, and thus (as discussed in section 2.4.7), some haircut will typically be imposed to protect the collateralised party. This should depend on the volatility of the FX rate, with more volatile currencies attracting higher haircuts.

Government bonds are also frequently used as collateral. Here there is interest rate risk, and hence longer term bonds – which typically have longer durations and thus are more sensitive to movements in interest rates – attract higher haircuts[143]. Haircuts are usually calibrated for interest rate risk only; there is an assumption that there is no credit risk in a government bond. However, as the recent Euro crisis has demonstrated, government bonds can change in value for reasons other than interest rate risk. Thus one of the things that can happen in a sovereign crisis is that all the parties who use that sovereign's bonds as collateral become less well collateralised.

3.4.2 Haircut risk

In a bilateral OTC derivatives transaction, collateral haircuts are typically agreed in the CSA. This means that they can only change if the CSA is renegotiated. CSA negotiations often take weeks, and a new CSA is only signed when both parties agree to it. Therefore one of the (unforeseen) advantages of the bilateral market is that it is rather difficult for haircuts to be changed, and thus for one party to suffer from the liquidity risk created by a haircut increase[144].

The situation is less happy for exchange traded (and indeed cleared OTC) derivatives. Here collateral haircuts are not subject to negotiation: they are set by the exchange and can change with very little notice. Thus for instance a haircut increase might be announced on Wednesday, used for calculating margin at close of business on Thursday and thus affect Friday's margin delivery. This creates a considerable liquidity risk.

A good example of this can be found by examining the haircuts applied to Irish government bonds. Figure 3.4 illustrates the very substantial margin calls that posters of these bonds faced during 2011[145].

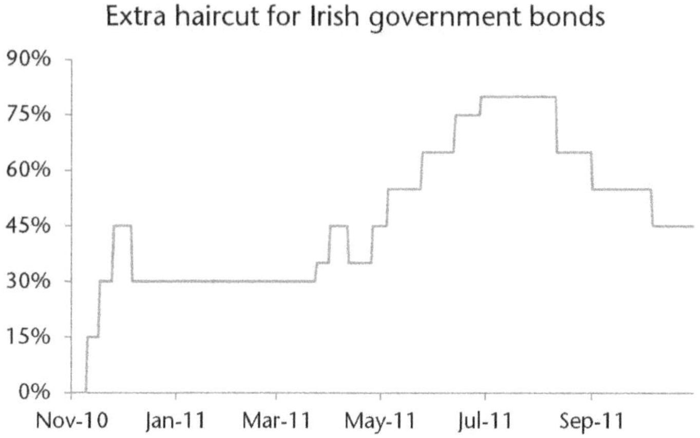

Extra haircut for Irish government bonds

Figure 3.4: The variation of the haircut required on Irish government bonds in the early Euro crisis

3.4.3 Procyclicality of haircuts

Procyclicality refers to a phenomenon whereby something changes with the cycle. It is often used with regard to risk measures: value at risk is procyclical because in good times, volatilities and correlations are low, leading to a low measure of risk; but when a crisis occurs, volatilities and correlations rise, increasing the risk estimate for the same portfolio. Thus value at risk estimates based on ordinary conditions can understate what losses may occur in a crisis.

Haircuts which depend on the current volatility of an asset display a similar procyclicality. In good times, haircuts are set at low levels, encouraging market participants to use that asset as collateral. When a crisis hits, a series of undesirable events can occur:

- Holders of the asset take losses;

- Haircuts increase where they can. This increases the financing cost of the asset, notably in the overnight repo market;

- Some leveraged holders of the asset may have to sell, causing further price falls;

- Haircut increases cause a liquidity drain, increasing stress on market participants.

Clearly the procyclicality of haircuts can increase systemic risk. It can also affect the market in the collateral asset itself, since if haircuts increase substantially, market participants may try to protect themselves against further increases by selling the bond and substituting a different, less volatile form of collateral. This causes the prices of seemingly safe bonds to rise as they become preferred forms of collateral. Meanwhile there are further falls in the prices of already stressed and out-of-favour assets.

It is perhaps counterintuitive that this phenomenon is less significant for lower quality assets. The reason is that assets everyone knows are volatile attract high haircuts at all times, and thus they remain good collateral even after a price fall. A 200% over-collateralised position is still 150% over collateralised after a 25% fall in collateral value. Thus it is AAA or AA-rated bonds which are at the greatest risk from the procyclicality of margin, not CCC-rated ones.

3.4.4   When cash is not available

The risks of posting non-cash collateral lead to the question: 'why not just post cash?' For banks, there is no good answer to this question, but for other classes of counterparty, there are. For instance, an investment fund may wish to be fully or nearly fully invested: forcing the fund to keep a substantial proportion of its assets in cash simply to post as collateral on derivatives is inefficient[146]. Non-financial corporates, too, may be cash constrained and thus unwilling to post cash margin. This is especially so for lower credit quality companies: their cost of funds is substantially in excess of OIS, so requiring cash collateral is a real cost to them.

3.4.5   The procyclicality of margin requirements

Haircut procyclicality can arise when the assets posted as margin have market risk. The underlying portfolio being collateralised in an OTC derivatives relationship usually has market risk too. This means that its margin requirements can rise in a crisis[147]. This is another form of procyclicality.

The effect can be considerable. For instance, some common approaches exhibit a two or three fold variation in IM requirements for typical portfolios between good and bad times[148].

Note that if complete collateralisation is required[149], then increases in required margin act as a brake on the amount of risk that can be absorbed.

Procyclical margin requirements do not just imply that institutions will suffer liquidity stress on existing trades in a crisis; they also mean that new trades create a need for cash that cannot reasonably be met. For a fixed level of liquidity, then, increasing IM requirements reduce the markets' ability to transfer risk.

3.4.6 Portfolio valuation risk

We saw in the last chapter that AIG had a substantial extended margin dispute over its portfolio of CDS with Goldman. This is an example of valuation risk, whereby counterparties may occasionally disagree[150] over the value of a portfolio of derivatives, and hence may differ over the amount of margin which should be posted. The risk here is not just the counterparty credit risk on the difference between the 'true' portfolio value (under the relevant CSA) and the value of margin held[151]. There is also the issue that margin calls cannot be based on an arbitrary valuation: they must be commercially reasonable. Ultimately, this is something that can and has been litigated[152].

3.4.7 Initial margin disputes

If the valuation of portfolios is difficult to agree, how much more difficult might it be for two dealers to agree on their risk? Neither is likely to want to trust the other's model: hence neither will be eager to lose responsibility for calculating initial margin. This gives rise to the potential for serious disputes if two way initial margin is required for inter-dealer trades. Moreover the enormous range of transactions in the inter-dealer market means that it is unlikely that any single third party could credibly mediate all disputes. This issue is therefore a substantial barrier to the use of initial margin on inter-dealer bilateral OTC derivatives.

3.4.8 When enough is too much

One of the concerns that has been raised about the post-crisis financial system centres on the rise of collateralised vs. uncollateralised transactions[153]. This is not just an issue relating to derivatives: the inter-bank lending market has declined precipitously, especially in Europe[154]; instead, banks are borrowing on a collateralised basis from central banks. Five issues immediately arise:

1. Is there enough collateral to back a substantial fraction of the credit between financial institutions that has to be extended for the economy to function?

2. If an asset such as a government bond is widely used as collateral, and its value falls (perhaps due to concerns about the credit quality of the issuer), is the resulting margin-call-driven liquidity drain on the financial system destabilising?

3. Does the decline of unsecured lending mean that conventional monetary policy is markedly less effective[155]?

4. Does collateral work well enough, given our dependence on it? The concern here is that collateral has become so important a risk-reduction mechanism that any risk to its effectiveness (whether legal or operational) could be hugely destabilising. Should more emphasis be placed on other mechanisms to mitigate risk such as capital?

5. If only a narrow range of high quality liquid assets are permitted for use as collateral, some market participants will have to transform the ineligible assets they have into eligible ones. Will this collateral transformation introduce significant new systemic risks?

A full discussion of these issues would take us too far out of the way, but it is worth mentioning them in passing as increased attention on such matters could have a profound effect on regulation.

3.5 Wrong Way Risks

Suppose we lend money to someone to buy a house as follows:

- We lend them the entire purchase price, or very nearly all of it;

- We ask that they make no payments on the loan for the first two years, or only a low payment compared with a conventional (amortising) mortgage;

- After that, the loan interest rate is set at a high level, perhaps Libor plus six or seven percent;

- We conduct little due diligence on the affordability of these higher loan payments to the borrower, or their credit quality generally.

This type of lending was, in essence, a major cause of the sub-prime crisis[156]. It is evident that the borrower's ability to repay the loan depends on house prices. If house prices rise strongly during the two year low interest period, then they can sell the house for more than the loan balance (or refinance into another loan, as the house remains good collateral for such a mortgage). If, however, house prices fall, then they cannot afford to pay the higher payments and whoever sells the house – them or us after repossession – it will be worth less than the loan balance.

Any situation where the credit quality of a loan depends strongly on an external factor gives rise to the risk that the factor will move the wrong way and hence the loan will become much riskier.

In derivatives, there are three forms of this factor dependence:

1. As the factor moves, our exposure increases due to changes in value of the portfolio of exposures;

2. As the factor moves, our exposure increases because the collateral we have becomes less valuable (and we cannot immediately call for more of it);

3. As the factor moves, the probability of failure of our counterparty increases.

Situations occur where there are more than one of these three connections. Indeed, we have this in the mortgage example: as house prices fall, the collateral on our loan gets less valuable and the probability of default of the borrower increases. The situation where exposure rises (situation 1. or 2. above) as counterparty credit quality falls (situation 3.) is known as 'wrong way risk'[157].

3.5.1 Specific and general wrong way risk

Regulators[158] have articulated a more elaborate idea; they identify 'specific' and 'general' wrong way risk, saying that:

> A bank is exposed to 'specific wrong-way risk' if future exposure to a specific counterparty is highly correlated with the counterparty's probability of default. For example, a company writing put options on its own stock creates wrong-way exposures for the buyer that is specific to the counterparty[159].

In contrast, general wrong way risk arises when the credit quality of the counterparty may be 'correlated with a macroeconomic factor which also affects the value of derivatives transactions'[160].

The distinction supervisors propose is hard to apply, since it is not clear where specific wrong way risk shades into general wrong way risk. To see this, consider one of the paradigmatic examples, that of CDS. This is important partly because the value of a CDS can change rather quickly, and partly because certain types of CDS exhibited pernicious forms of wrong way risk during the crisis[161]. To make the discussion concrete, let us consider entities in the Santander group as protection sellers. The group is Spanish, and includes large Spanish and Portuguese retail banks, Banco Santander Totta being one of the latter.

It is clear that if the parent Banco Santander sells protection on its affiliate Banco Santander Totta, then there is significant specific wrong way risk. Indeed, supervisors explicitly flag situations where there is a legal connection between the entity selling protection and the reference instrument as examples of specific wrong way risk. But what about Banco Santander selling protection on the Kingdom of Spain? Santander has significant resources outside Spain, and a Spanish credit event does not necessarily imply insolvency of its banks, but there is nevertheless a close relationship between sovereign credit quality and that of the banks incorporated in that sovereign. Clearly protection sold on Spain by, say, Bank of America would not entail the same wrong way risks as that sold by Santander.

This discussion simply illustrates that it is sometimes difficult to distinguish between specific and general wrong way risk. Unfortunately the distinction is important because it has regulatory consequences[162], so banks are required to implement some form of split between specific and general wrong way risk.

3.5.2 Wrong way and correlated collateral risks

Wrong way risk is often obvious at trade inception. Unfortunately it is also commonplace. Companies typically want to trade derivatives that relate to their business. Indeed, the whole purpose of derivatives for a corporate is usually to transform risks that they are exposed to, so there will likely be a high correlation between their earnings and the value of their derivatives, although often this will be 'right' rather than wrong way. Furthermore, the only assets that a corporate might have to pledge as collateral could have a value which is highly correlated with the derivative. This 'correlated collateral' risk is a close relative of wrong way risk.

Another issue is that the value of the assets some corporates have available to post as collateral might instead be tied to the corporate's credit quality. A copper consumer, for instance, may wish to enter into a copper swap to hedge its costs in the future, and the only asset it might have available to pledge is physical copper. It may well be best for the economy as a whole if risks like this are taken by banks who are both able to hedge them and well enough capitalised to withstand the residual risks; if such transactions are unavailable or unaffordable to corporates, that simply leaves the risk with less well capitalised entities which are less able to manage them. Therefore there is a trade off between financial stability considerations – which would suggest that risks like this are conservatively capitalised – and broader macroeconomic ones – which do not commend unnecessary timidity in wrong way or correlated collateral risk taking.

It may well make sense for a dealer to take correlated collateral risk such as in the copper producer example, especially if it is sufficiently over-collateralised[163]. However, it should do so knowingly. Supervisors require that dealers 'must have procedures in place to identify, monitor and control cases of specific wrong way risk, beginning at the inception of a trade and continuing through the life of the trade', which is prudent.

3.5.3 General wrong way risk

Many wrong way risks are obvious, as in the copper consumer example above. The concept of general wrong way risk, however, includes some that are not, including in particular situations where there is simply a loose correlation between exposure and credit quality. When stock markets go down, credit spreads tend to go up, for instance, so any equity index put could be said to have general wrong way risk since as the put becomes more valuable, the credit quality of the writer may tend to decrease.

Regulatory requirements here are imprecise. They suggest that banks 'must identify exposures that give rise to a greater degree of general wrong-way risk'. Some firms have developed elaborate models to meet this stipulation[164]. The problem is not that general wrong way risks are not real – they are – but rather that it is difficult to know what the underlying causal relationships are. On the one hand, data may well suggest a general wrong way risk that disappears in stressed conditions; on the other, it may not display one that does appear when the going gets tough. Therefore analysis of realised correlations between exposures and credit quality must be complemented with stress and scenario analysis.

3.5.4 Right way risk

If an exposure becomes larger as credit quality *increases*, then we have right way risk. For instance, if we had had a copper producer hedging their production, then as the copper price went up, their earnings would increase as would the value of the collateral they had posted. This would offset the increase in the value of the copper swap to their counterparty.

This seems helpful and it is, with one caveat: if the swap is long-dated, then from the producer's side of the trade, the swap will fall in value faster than the increase in value of the posted collateral[165], giving rise to a margin call. The producer's business is more valuable but it may not have any extra liquidity, yet it has to meet the margin call on whatever terms the CSA sets out. Thus it may have liquidity risk despite having accurately hedged its exposure.

3.5.5 *Wrong way exposures in portfolio counterparty credit risk models*

Situations with wrong way risk pose a challenge to CCR models, in that exposure and default cannot then be simulated independently; since each depends on the other, such an approach would be imprudent. This can be addressed in a number of ways. The easiest is to exclude the problematic transactions from the model and add their risk back in to the exposure profile at the end: this is simple, but it typically overstates the risk. A better approach is to jointly simulate default and market movements so that the wrong way risk can be explicitly included. This is problematic too, though, firstly because supervisors do not allow it for regulatory purposes, and secondly because it complicates the calculation[166]. A more pragmatic solution might be to sign a separate, tight CSA for the wrong way transaction(s), and so to have distinct margin amounts for the wrong way and normal portfolios.

3.6 Regulatory Capital Requirements for Default Risk in OTC Derivatives Portfolios

The methods of the previous sections form the basis of the approach taken to calculating capital for default risk in the Basel Accords[167]. The capital requirement for OTC derivatives is fixed by the answers to two questions:

1. How will regulators let us estimate the loan equivalent amount generated by a given OTC derivatives portfolio?; and

2. What capital do regulators require for that loan equivalent risk?

In order to answer these questions, we need to say something more about the Basel approach to determining regulatory capital requirements.

3.6.1 *Alternative approaches*

In many areas of the capital accords the Basel Committee give several alternatives. Typically there is a simple alternative designed for smaller or less sophisticated banks. This usually (but not always) produces a higher capital requirement. One or more advanced methods are provided, but banks have to meet certain standards before they are permitted to use these more risk-sensitive approaches.

Multiple alternatives are provided for banks to answer each of the questions discussed above. We will set out only the most sophisticated alternative, partly because it is closest to best practice, and partly because most large dealers use them[168].

3.6.2 Determining loan equivalents for regulatory purposes: the internal models method

The sophisticated approach to determining regulatory counterparty credit exposure is known as the internal models method, or 'IMM'. As the Basel Committee put it:

> *A qualifying internal model for measuring counterparty credit exposure must specify the forecasting distribution for changes in the market value of the netting set attributable to changes in market variables, such as interest rates, foreign exchange rates, etc. The model then computes the firm's CCR exposure for the netting set at each future date given the changes in the market variables. For margined counterparties, the model may also capture future collateral movements.*

The model is required to calculate effective EPE as discussed in section 3.3.2, and the loan equivalent is given as alpha times effective EPE, where alpha is typically[169] 1.4.

Firms who wish to use the IMM approach must meet an extensive list of requirements which range from back testing[170] of the models through model validation to governance requirements and a 'use test' (whereby firms have to demonstrate that they use their model for internal risk management and management reporting purposes as well as for the calculation of regulatory capital).

Supervisors define the margin period of risk used in IMM models[171]. For transactions with daily margin and daily mark-to-market, the MPOR is ten days[172]. However, if any of the following conditions is met, the MPOR doubles to twenty days:

- There are more than 5,000 trades in the netting set during the previous quarter;

- An item of collateral is illiquid; or

- One or more transactions in the netting set cannot easily be replaced.

These criteria substantially increase capital requirements for large netting sets or sets containing exotic derivatives.

3.6.3   Capital requirements for default risk: the IRB

Capital for default risk[173] is calculated under the Basel advanced approach using a fixed formula (as we mentioned in section 3.3.4 above). This takes as inputs estimates of the probability of default of each counterparty, the exposure to them, the recovery[174] and the maturity of the exposure. The output of the formula is the capital charge for the counterparty, and these are added up to determine the total capital.

This methodology is known as the internal ratings based approach or IRB. The name comes from the fact that banks use their own internal estimates of probability in the IRB.

The IRB applies the same approach to default risk whether it arises from OTC derivatives, lending, or some other source. However a degree of conservatism is built into the framework through the estimation of exposure: for a loan this is the amount owing, but for an OTC derivatives portfolio it is effective EPE, which is almost always larger than the amount currently owed[175].

Notes

[98]See for instance Chapter 2 of my book *Understanding Risk: The Theory and Practice of Financial Risk Management*, Chapman Hall 2008.

[99]V. Pitarberg's *Funding beyond discounting: collateral agreements and derivatives pricing*, Risk magazine (February 2010) available at www.risk.net/digital_assets/735/piter barg.pdf has the details.

[100]This result is moreover independent of CVA or DVA.

[101]During the credit crisis the Libor-OIS spread increased dramatically, as did both tenor basis and cross currency basis spreads. These effects meant that Libor discounting was no longer sufficiently accurate for pricing OTC derivatives.

[102]If you can choose between placing EUR cash earning EONIA and USD cash earning Fed Funds then you have a series of options on the EONIA/Fed Funds basis swap spread.

[103]Not least because some of the hedge instruments you would want to address CSA optionality, such as options on basis swaps, do not trade.

[104]See M. Pykhtin, S. Zhu, *A Guide to Modelling Counterparty Credit Risk*, GARP Risk Review (July/August 2007) available at ssrn.com/abstract=1032522 for a further discussion of CVA.

[105]Note that we had made various assumptions in deriving the unilateral CVA as one minus the recovery times the sum of the PD-weighted LGDs notably that there is no wrong way risk. See J. Gregory's book *Counterparty Credit Risk and Credit Value Adjustment* Wiley (2012) for more details.

[106]CVA can even be negative on a new trade if it reduces the risk of the customer's portfolio with the dealer; in this case the customer would get a better price than the market quote.

A related issue here is anonymous trading: if market participants do not know the counterparty (and hence the CSA) at the time of trading – as they might not in some SEFs – then they will have to impose tight CSAs on all potential counterparties.

[107]This makes DVA a controversial component of earnings: see for instance Tracy Alloway's story in the Financial Times *Banks face profits hit as fog descends* (12th October 2012). One thing to be said in favour of DVA from a financial stability perspective is that it is countercyclical: DVA increases as a firm's credit quality goes down, partially offsetting the other negative effects of that process. On the other hand, a firm can only fully monetise DVA by defaulting, so its inclusion in earnings is questionable.

[108]It is worth noting that the definition of 'close out amount' in the ISDA master agreements leaves questions unanswered about some of these factors. Specifically is there any requirement when calculating a close out amount to take account of the CSA one has with the party being closed out, or the CSA one has with a party providing a quotation? The recent case of Lehman Brothers International (Europe) (in administration) v. Lehman Brothers Finance SA (citation [2012] EWHC 1072 (Ch)) established that under English law a party determining a close out figure under the 2002 master should proceed on the assumption that, but for the termination, the transaction would have proceeded to contractual maturity. This 'continuity' principle had already been laid down for the 1992 Master. Whether this means that either unilateral or bilateral CVA have absolutely no role in determining close out amount is, however unclear (at least to this author).

[109]The probability of an event of default under an ISDA master is not quite the same as the probability of default of a typical senior bond; ISDAs often trigger before senior debt, despite ranking *pari passu* with it. ISDA receivables tend to have higher recoveries than senior debt, partly as a result of this.

[110]More details on the validation of such estimates can be found in *Studies on the Validation of Internal Ratings Systems*, Basel Committee on Banking Supervision Working Paper No. 14 (May 2005) available at www.bis.org/publ/bcbs_wp14.pdf.

[111]There is some debate as to whether the requirement in both IAS and US GAAP to use a fair value approach for most derivatives precludes the use of historical approaches to estimate CVA. Despite this concern, the audit profession seems to have been willing to permit historical default estimates to be used for CVA calculation in a number

of financial institutions. The Ernst and Young Survey *Reflecting credit and funding adjustments in fair value* (2012) shows four banks out of nineteen survey respondents using purely historical PDs and a further two using a blend of historical and market PDs.

[112]This of course assumes that this credit risk is also properly monitored and properly capitalised.

[113]See J. Amato, E. Remolona, *The credit spread puzzle*, BIS Quarterly Review (December 2003) available at www.bis.org/press/p031208.htm. It should be noted that this implies that if credit can be funded at the risk free rate (a big assumption) then there is an excess return to be made by taking credit risk. This appears to be true, but it depends on the taker having enough capital to support losses and on being able to fund the risk taking to final term.

[114]See L. Chen et al., *Corporate Yield Spreads and Bond Liquidity*, Journal of Finance Volume LXII No. 1 (February 2007).

[115]A more accurate statement is that those sensitivities where a suitable hedge instrument exists can perhaps be hedged. The problem for some banks is that many of their counterparties do not have easily traded credit protection, since only a thousand or so names are liquid in the CDS market. If your counterparty is not one of these liquid thousand, then it may be necessary to use a proxy hedge. J. Gregory in his presentation *Managing CVA* at Riskminds 2011 (available via www.cvacentral.com) states that this proxy hedging issue arises for more than 90% of counterparties.

[116]This assumes that 'own credit' losses go through the P/L rather than the equity account. Accounting standards are by no means internationally agreed here. It is clear, though, that if own credit adjustments do not affect earnings, then the rationale for hedging them is rather less clear.

[117]On the other hand, if our credit quality decreases enough, the own credit component of bilateral CVA will be bigger than the unilateral CVA, and so we can offer better prices than the market on 'loose' CSAs. The fact that worse quality dealers can offer better prices is one of the less attractive features of bilateral CVA.

[118]We *can* sell credit protection on ourselves as ISDA receivables (such as amounts owing on CDS) ranks *pari passu* with senior debt, and hence at 40% recovery, say, a CDS claim of $100M will receive $40M. Thus we should receive roughly the market premium times our estimated recovery as premium for selling CDS on ourselves. Sadly though recoveries for financial institutions tend to be uncertain and sometimes low, so this is not economically efficient. The alternative is selling protection on a basket of similar names, but as a well-known dealer anecdotally discovered when Lehman defaulted, that method involves taking significant basis risk.

[119]The exceptions at the time of writing are Portugal and Ireland and the UK. See for instance the Bank of England news release *HM Treasury and Bank of England announce technical changes to selected foreign currency operations* (June 2012) available at www.bankofengland.co.uk/publications/Pages/news/2012/063.aspx. A separate issue is that

sovereigns often demand one way CSAs so that dealers have to post collateral to them if the portfolio moves against the dealer: this can create substantial liquidity risk.

[120]These liquidity issues have not been improved by the European Union's ban on 'naked short' sovereign positions: see *Commission Delegated Regulation No. 918/ 2012* available at ec.europa.eu/internal_market/securities/docs/short_selling/ 20120705-regulation_en.pdf.

[121]This discussion presents a dichotomy: historical or market-based. This is a reasonable high level view, but there are many more choices in practice. For instance, one need not assume that all of the credit spread is compensation for default: instead a liquidity component can be estimated, as for instance in J. Dick-Nielsen, *Corporate bond liquidity before and after the onset of the subprime crisis*, Journal of Financial Economics Volume 103 (2012). If this component could in addition be hedged, then one would have a market-consistent model that produced PDs (and hence CDS hedges) that were less over-stated than the usual approach.

[122]Gregory, among others, has the details.

[123]So that in particular there is daily portfolio reconciliation and straight through collateral processing.

[124]It is a little more complicated than that: if exposures have increased uniformly in those five days, then the statement is correct. If they had a whipsaw down then up, though, there is some danger that we returned collateral after the down, but did not receive any more during the up. ISDA's *Best Practices for the OTC Derivatives Collateral Process* (June 2010) available at www.isda.org/c_and_a/pdf/ ISDA-Best-Practices-for-the-OTC-Derivatives-Collateral-Process.pdf has a further discussion of the issues here including points we have not had space to discuss such as minimum transfer amounts and grace periods.

[125]E. Canabarro et al., *Analysing Counterparty Credit Risk*, Risk magazine, Volume 16, No. 9 (2003) give the details.

[126]'Comovement' rather than 'correlation' because 'correlation' implies a certain mathematical relationship which does not necessarily hold: 'comovement' is a broader term.

[127]See D. Li, *On Default Correlation: A Copula Function Approach*, Risk Metrics Working paper 99-07 (September 1999).

[128]L. Isla, S. Willemann, *Correlation modelling – from vanilla to exotic* Barclays Capital Structured Credit Strategist (2007) and C. Albanese et al., *A Comparative Analysis of Correlation Approaches in Finance* available via papers.ssrn.com/sol3/papers.cfm?abstract_ id=1769302 discuss the standard approach to correlation modelling and a number of variants of it.

[129]Such as the asset values of obligators.

[130]E.g. base correlations.

[131]Specifically, the asymptotic single risk factor approach. The BCBS note *An Explanatory Note on the Basel II IRB Risk Weight Functions* (July 2005) available at www.bis.org/ bcbs/irbriskweight.htm discusses the foundations of this approach in more detail.

[132]P. Kupiec's *Basel II: A Case for Recalibration* (2006) available at www.imf.org/external/np/seminars/eng/2006/macropr/pdf/Kupiec.pdf contains a highly pertinent criticism of the Basel II calibration.

[133]Such as the correlation crises which occasionally plague tranche markets; see J. Noss, *Extracting information from structured credit markets*, Bank of England Working Paper No. 407 (December 2007) available www.bankofengland.co.uk/publications/Documents/workingpapers/wp407.pdf for a model with 'becalmed' and 'catastrophe' regimes, and A. Kherraz, *The May 2005 correlation crisis: Did the models really fail?*, Portuguese Finance Network 4th Finance Conference (June 2006) available via www.fep.up.pt/conferencias/pfn2006.

[134]To say that default correlation markets are incomplete is rather like saying that a single aluminium panel and a half full tank of hydrogen peroxide form an incomplete rocket.

[135]The problem is made slightly simpler by the fact that while the largest portfolios are with (highly correlated) dealers, the largest EPEs typically are not. If there is reasonable diversification in the portfolio of exposures, then using a Gaussian copula calibrated to an upper tranche of a credit index may not be too bad.

[136]Sadly the Basel Committee does not allow it to be used as such for regulatory purposes: see question 26 of the Basel Committee's *Basel III counterparty credit risk - Frequently asked questions*, (November 2011) available at www.bis.org/publ/bcbs209.pdf.

[137]This is assuming that hedging is perfectly effective, of course.

[138]Or, more precisely, they do not suffer losses from changes in either the perception or the reality of counterparty non-performance.

[139]For more on this perspective see C. Albanese, *Optimal Funding Strategies for Counterparty Credit Risk Liabilities* (2011) available at www.riskcare.com/wordpress/wp-content/uploads/2011/05/Revolvers.pdf.

[140]The 99.9% 10 day expected shortfall from an extreme value model calibrated with data including the credit crisis, for instance.

[141]At least absent wrong way risk.

[142]There is also the subtler risk that the value of the collateral may increase, leaving the poster over-collateralised, and hence increasing their unsecured exposure to their counterparty.

[143]This means that when interest rate volatility rises, haircuts on government bonds may go up. The 2th July 2011 memo *Collateral Haircuts* from CME Clearing available via www.cmegroup.com is an example of this kind of increase.

[144]The Committee on the Global Financial System therefore suggest that bilateral OTC derivatives margining practices are not strongly procyclical for this reason: see *The role of margin requirements and haircuts in procyclicality*, CGFS papers No. 36 (March 2010) available at www.bis.org/publ/cgfs36.pdf.

[145]This data is from LCH.Clearnet, and reflects haircuts on Irish governments for Repoclear as announced in LCH.Clearnet Ltd Circulars.

[146]A good example here is a pension fund using inflation swaps to reduce its asset/liability mismatch: see Scottish Widows, *A brief history of Liability Driven Investing* (June 2011) available via www.swip.com.

[147]Haircuts and initial margin are similar in that they are both intended as protection against the risk that the value of something – collateral in one case, the underlying portfolio in the other – changes. In both cases too the size of the protection required depends on how much that value can change.

[148]D. Heller and N. Vause in *Expansion of central clearing* (BIS Quarterly Review, June 2011) give a variation of between 3 (for IRS) and 5 (for CDS) in the total amount of IM a CCP would require from clearing members.

[149]There is no reason why all OTC derivatives should be fully collateralised. After all, one of the key functions of banks is to extend credit.

[150]In the words of Mike Clarke, at the time Global Head of Collateral Management and Client Valuations at UBS, 'There were a small number of large and intractable margin disputes': see the presentation *Practical Counterparty Risk Management* at the 2009 Credit Markets Symposium, available from www.richmondfed.org/conferences_and_events/banking/2009/pdf/cms_2009_clarke.pdf.

[151]This rather assumes that, absent an attempt to sell the portfolio, there is such a thing as its true value. The author doubts this, preferring instead to think of the value of all portfolios as inherently uncertain to some degree.

[152]In its answer to a lawsuit alleging failure to meet a valid margin call, Paramax Capital state that a representative of their counterparty intimated that 'subjective valuation methodologies' would be used to keep the value of the portfolio 'at a level that would not trigger calls for additional margin payments'. The representative said that was possible, Paramax's answer states, due to the 'unique and bespoke nature' of the transaction. When the counterparty made a large margin call soon after the trade closed, Paramax refused to meet it. See UBS AG v. Paramax Capital, No. 07604233 (N.Y. Supreme Court Dec. 26, 2007). The parties subsequently settled out of court. The issue here for this author is the difficulty of justifying any models-based valuation to a judge: one might not feel sanguine about the prospects of success in any suit relating to a collateral call on a bespoke transaction whose value is, by its very nature, subject to debate.

[153]See M. King, *Saving for broke: Why zero is the place to start*, Citibank Research Presentation (August 2012).

[154]B. Cœuré, Member of the Executive Board of the ECB, gave a good summary of the issues here in his speech *The importance of money markets*, Morgan Stanley 16th Annual Global Investment seminar (16th June 2012) available at www.ecb.int/press/key/date/2012/html/sp120616.en.html.

[155]In particular, does monetary policy transmission work reasonably well without unsecured inter-bank lending?

[156]See my book *Unravelling the Credit Crunch*, Prentice Hall (2009) for more details.

[157]For a further discussion, see *Wrong-way risk in OTC derivatives and its implication for Japan's financial institutions*, Bank of Japan Review 2012-E-6 (June 2012), available at www.boj.or.jp/en/research/wps_rev/rev_2012/data/rev12e06.pdf.

[158]This is in Basel III: see *Basel III: A global regulatory framework for more resilient banks and banking systems*, Basel Committee on Banking Supervision (December 2010) available via www.bis.org/bcbs/basel3.htm.

[159]The earlier Basel II definition is 'Specific Wrong-Way Risk arises when the exposure to a particular counterpart is positively correlated with the probability of default of the counterparty due to the nature of the transactions with the counterparty.'

[160]The wording comes from an ISDA letter to the Basel Committee, *Re: Calculation of regulatory capital for counterparty risk*, September 2001, available at www.isda.org/c_and_a/pdf/RGresserLetter-Sept701.pdf.

[161]CDS (and related financial guarantees) written by the monolines on ABS are a good example: see my book *Unravelling the Credit Crunch*, Prentice Hall (2009) for more details.

[162]See the Basel III text and the accompanying *Basel III counterparty credit risk - Frequently asked questions*. CDS with specific wrong way risk are taken out of the netting set with the counterparty for regulatory purposes. They are then assumed to have an exposure at default equal to the expected loss assuming that the reference asset is in default.

[163]Over-collateralisation levels of 150% or more are not uncommon in such situations.

[164]See for instance J. Cespedes et al., *Effective modeling of wrong way risk, counterparty credit risk capital, and alpha in Basel II*, Journal of Risk Model Validation, Volume 4, No. 1 (Spring 2010).

[165]In other words, the swap is leveraged.

[166]This is not just a computational problem: one also has the issue of selecting a plausible mathematical relationship to model the wrong way risks, something that is not without hazard.

[167]See *Basel II: International Convergence of Capital Measurement and Capital Standards: A Revised Framework - Comprehensive Version* (June 2006) available at www.bis.org/publ/bcbs128.htm.

[168]Information on which approaches a given bank is permitted to use, and for what, is difficult to discover. It is probably fair to say that rather few banks can use all the advanced methods for everything, and many of them can use some advanced approaches for some parts of their business. There is a good case that this information should be required as part of bank's pillar 3 disclosures.

[169]The rules do permit firms to model alpha, but such 'own alpha' estimates are floored at 1.2, and the modelling process is complex, so there has been scant take up of this option. Note, too that the effective EPE is calculated as the average of the first year's effective EEs, and that in Basel III (but not Basel II), the calculation requires the use of stressed market data. See the Basel Committee's *Basel III: A global regulatory framework for more resilient banks and banking systems* (December 2010) available at

www.bis.org/publ/bcbs189.htm for more details of the modifications Basel III makes to the Basel II capital framework.

[170]See the Basel Committee's *Sound practices for back testing counterparty credit risk models* (December 2010) available at www.bis.org/publ/bcbs185.pdf.

[171]We have, once again, glossed over some details here. There are two methods for dealing with collateral: handling it within the model calculation of effective EPE, and a 'shortcut' method: see the Basel II document for more details

[172]This is an exception for netting sets consisting only of repo-style transactions: here the MPOR is five days.

[173]Technically, default risk and credit spread migration risk.

[174]Or, in Basel terminology, probability of default, exposure at default (which can be greater than current exposure for instance for a line of credit) and loss given default (i.e. one minus the recovery).

[175]The use of stressed EPE in Basel III, together with other measures (such as the increased asset value correlation) further increases this conservatism.

4

The Role of OTC Derivatives in the Crisis

What the vulgar call chance
is nothing but a secret and conceal'd cause.
David Hume

Introduction

Consider these three statements[176]:

> *"Derivatives were at the center of the financial crisis of 2008."*
> *"What caused the Crisis? Derivatives."*
> *"I view derivatives as time bombs, both for the parties that deal in them and the economic system."*

Given these views, and many others in a similar vein, one might think that derivatives played a central part in the recent financial crisis. This is far from the truth. In this chapter we explore the roles actually played by derivatives in the crisis, highlighting both the vulnerabilities that were revealed and the issues that received much comment but which did not make a major contribution to financial stress. In particular, the securitisation process which led to the creation of many 'toxic' assets is discussed. We show how this technology facilitated risky mortgage lending, and what part credit derivatives played in the process. A brief history of the crisis is presented, with subprime mortgages as the trigger but not the only cause of the massive losses which swept over the financial system starting in 2007. We discuss some of the vulnerabilities which, in retrospect, imperilled the system, touching in particular on the connections between financial institutions created both by OTC derivatives and by other market features.

4.1 The Dogs That Barked and the Dogs That Didn't

The vast majority of OTC derivatives markets were not important contributors to the crisis. Losses due to equity, FX, interest rate, and commodity derivatives were immaterial[177]. The crisis was primarily a crisis of credit instruments and of funding, as financial crises usually are[178]. OTC derivatives[179] had two roles:

1. Credit derivatives were instrumental in transferring exposure; and

2. OTC derivatives, along with many other features of the financial system, increased the interconnectedness between financial institutions and hence may have made the system less robust.

The following sections examine these phenomena. First, though, a (very) short summary of the growth of mortgage backed securities in the United States. This sets the scene for a description of the events of the crisis itself[180].

4.1.1 Securitisation

Suppose a financial institution has made some mortgage loans. While each individual loan is risky as the borrower might not repay the loan, a large collection of mortgages usually has fairly regular, predictable cashflows. This means that they can be used as collateral to back a security.

To take advantage of this, the financial institution sets up a company known as a *special purpose vehicle* or SPV. In a 'cash securitisation', the SPV buys the mortgages. It gets the money to pay for them by issuing bonds to outside investors. In the simplest structure, these bonds just pass on whatever cashflows there are on the underlying mortgages to the bond holders (at least after the originating institution has taken a fee). Figure 4.1 illustrates this 'securitisation' process.

Bonds backed by residential mortgages are known, reasonably enough, as residential mortgage backed securities, or 'RMBS'. More generally an asset-backed security or 'ABS' is any security backed just by a ring-fenced pool of assets[181] rather than the promise to pay made by a creditor.

4.1.2 The originate to distribute model

In the decade or two before 2007, a new model of mortgage lending became increasingly important in the United States. Instead of banks originating mortgages and holding them on their own balance sheets,

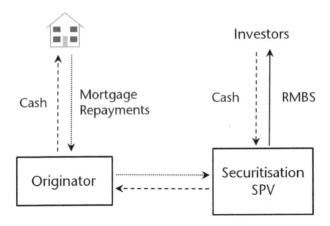

Figure 4.1: An illustration of a simple cash RMBS securitisation

institutions instead securitised the loans they had made. These 'private label' RMBS[182] became the vectors of a growing risk transfer from mortgage originators to investors. By 2000, half a trillion dollars of mortgage backed securities were being issued annually[183].

The use of securitisation to pass on the risk of loans is known as the 'originate to distribute' model as the originator extends the mortgage loan with the intent of securitising it. This model does not require that the originator is a bank: as the loans are mostly funded by the issuance of securities, there is no need for deposit funding. From 1990 to 2007 this model allowed a large number of non-bank mortgage lenders to develop, and indeed banks' share of retail mortgage originations shrank dramatically during this period[184].

The originate to distribute model changed incentives in the mortgage market. When originators had to bear the risk of the loans they made, they tended to be conservative about who they lent money to. When the risk was instead borne by RMBS holders, and originators were paid based on the number of loans that they made, there was a disincentive to be prudent. This change in incentives eventually had disastrous consequences.

4.1.3 Tranched RMBS

A key technique in the design of RMBS was tranching: instead of a single class of securities, the securitisation SPV issues multiple tranches. These are paid in order, so the top or 'super senior' tranche gets paid first, followed by the senior and mezzanine tranches, then the equity tranche last. Defaults on the collateral pool erode the tranches from the bottom up, so the equity is first to suffer losses, followed by the mezz, with the super senior suffering only if all the lower tranches have been exhausted. The super senior tranche thus has the lowest return as it bears the lowest default risk. The low risk[185] allows it to receive a high rating, often AAA.

Retail mortgages from 1998 to 2007 experienced rather low default rates. This meant that it seemed to be easy to create a lot of highly rated securities from a pool of mortgages. By 2006, the AAA-rated tranche(s) would represent over 90% of a good quality mortgage securitisation. Figure 4.2 illustrates a typical tranche structure from the period[186].

Class	Size	Rating	Notes
A	AAA	94%	Super senior
B1	Aa2/AA	2%	Senior
B2	A2/A	1.5%	
B3	Baa2/BBB	1%	Mezz
B4	Ba2/BB	0.6%	Mezz
B5	Ba2/BB	0.4%	Mezz
C	Not rated	0.5%	Equity (retained)

Figure 4.2: A typical 2006 RMBS deal

The ability to create a lot of AAA-rated securities from a collection of mortgages was important because there was a great demand for AAA-rated assets. That in itself was an interesting phenomenon which is discussed in the next section.

4.1.4 The safe asset hypothesis

One explanation for AAA-rated tranches finding such ready buyers focuses on the imbalance between the supply and demand of truly safe assets. Prior to the crisis, there was substantial demand for safe assets created by the fast growing emerging economies, pension funds, and indeed the need for collateral in financial transactions. Supply, according to this narrative[187], did not rise fast enough to meet demand, and so the financial system created 'pseudo-safe assets' via securitisation and tranching. The risk of these AAA tranches became widely held across the financial system, and their risks were not widely appreciated, partly because their performance was good for a long period, and partly because there were few affordable alternatives.

4.1.5 CDOs of ABS

Securitisation and tranching were too useful to confine to the mortgage market, especially with demand so high for AAA-rated tranches. Asset backed securities were created using collateral ranging from credit cards and student loans to car loans and the revenues from pubs. 'Collateralised debt obligations' ('CDO's) became a ubiquitous feature of the financial system during the 2000s.

The first tranched CDOs were static: assets were transferred into a securitisation SPV, tranches were issued, and that was that. Soon, though, managed deals were created. Here an asset manager was appointed with responsibility for trading the collateral pool. The manager could buy and sell collateral (subject to some constraints), and thus had some discretion about which assets backed the tranches.

CDOs of ABS became popular too. Here, rather than buying loans, the securitisation vehicle bought ABS. In many cases, it bought tranches of other securitisations. The 'demand' from CDOs of ABS allowed securitisation issuers to dispose of unsold tranches: this was particularly an issue with RMBS mezz tranches, which had few natural buyers, so these tranches were often bought into CDOs of ABS[188].

4.1.6 Subprime mortgages

The US experienced an enormous growth in access to mortgage credit in the run up to the crisis. The number of households with a mortgage increased by 20% from 1997–2005, and mortgage debt grew five times faster than GDP[189]. There were a number of factors at play here, notably:

- ✦ Low interest rates, thanks to the Greenspan FED's 'great moderation', which made the interest payments on loans more affordable;

- ✦ Lax mortgage underwriting, especially from some of the new non-bank entrants to the mortgage market;

- ✦ The Tax Reform Act of 1986 increased the attractiveness of mortgage debt compared with other loans due to the preferential tax status of mortgage payments;

- ✦ The evolution of new types of mortgage, such as adjustable ARMs, which reduced initial payments. These new loans types were predominantly funded by securitisation: in other words, the originators did not bear much of the risk of these mortgages[190].

- Mortgages where the amount lent was a higher percentage of the value of the house became commonplace. These high loan-to-value ratio (high 'LTV') loans reduced the down payments required from house buyers.

Another important trend in the run up to the crisis was that mortgages increasingly relied only on the perceived collateral quality (i.e. the value of the house), with the borrower's credit becoming less important[191]. Mortgage lending to the high credit quality individuals (those with a FICO score above 700) only grew slowly; most of the growth came from lower quality mortgage borrowers. Thus for instance FICO 600-700 loans were less than 20% of all mortgages in 1995, but more than 40% in 2003[192].

All of these trends led to house prices becoming an increasingly important and initially hidden risk factor in US mortgages and the securities that depended upon them. Good quality borrowers with low LTV mortgages have 'skin in the game'. Houses prices have to fall 25%, for instance, before a borrower with a 75% LTV loan has no incentive to keep paying their mortgage. Loans with a 90 or 95% LTV (perhaps where the residual is also borrowed) are robust only under much smaller falls in house prices, especially if the lender has no recourse to the borrower other than the mortgaged property[193]. This is particularly the case for mortgages with low initial rates which are unaffordable once the rate resets: such loans can only be refinanced into a new low-rate loan if house prices have risen. Thus many of the new types of mortgage loan originated from 1995–2007 were vulnerable to falls in house prices.

Broad US house prices levelled off in late spring 2006 after years of rises. By 2007, the average price had fallen by 10% from the peak, with larger falls in newer areas with a larger number of subprime loans[194].

As we might expect, US mortgages suffered very substantial default and loss rates once house prices started to decline. More than a third of 2007-vintage subprime mortgages were delinquent eighteen months after the loan was made, for instance. These problems, and expectations of future losses, caused the prices of RMBS generally and subprime RMBS in particular to fall dramatically[195]. These falls then fed through into the prices of securities based on RMBS, such as CDOs of ABS. Mortgages both directly and in the form of ABS had been an increasingly large component of banks' (and broker/dealers') balance sheets[196], so these losses were visited upon a wide range of financial institutions. This was the beginning of the financial crisis, which we turn to next.

4.2 A Very Short History of the Financial Crisis

In this section a brief account of the events of the financial crisis which began in 2007 is presented. These provide the backdrop and motivation for many of the regulatory reform efforts discussed later in the book.

4.2.1 The early crisis

The first signs of impending problems came in the prices of sub-prime mortgages. By the spring of 2007, the prices of subprime-backed RMBS had begun to fall, with even AAA-rated tranches beginning to show signs of stress during the summer, as figure 4.3 illustrates[197]..

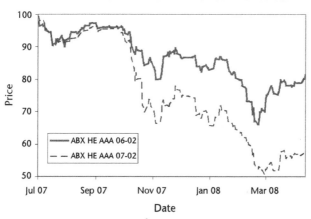

Historical Prices of two Markit ABX HE Indices

Figure 4.3: Price history of two of the Markit ABX AAA Indices representing pseudo-safe assets

The market had begun to fear that such mortgages were not going to perform well. If that happened, then many of the securities which depended on them would not repay their principals[198]. A key sign that the subprime problems were severe was the suspension of redemptions on three investment funds by BNP Paribas in August 2007. The French bank acted because illiquidity in the ABS market was preventing it from calculating the value of the funds[199]. This suggested that uncertainty over the value of RMBS had become so severe as to disrupt the market. The problems rapidly spread to credit assets as diverse as leveraged loans, commercial mortgage backed securities, and asset-backed commercial paper[200]. Soon after this, some institutions started to have problems raising money.

4.2.2   The funding crisis

The contagion from RMBS to broader credit then into funding instruments indicated fundamental vulnerabilities of the financial system:

* They were too leveraged, with too little good quality capital. This meant that when doubts started to arise about the value of their assets, investors became nervous about the viability of the institution as a whole because there was insufficient capital to absorb plausible losses. This, in turn, discouraged them from lending to institutions that they had doubts about;

* They had too much volatile funding, which meant that a loss of confidence quickly led to a funding crisis.

This issue was first evident in the most vulnerable areas such as ABCP conduits and SIVs, but it rapidly spread to regulated institutions. First Bear Stearns then Lehman Brothers gave stark demonstrations of how over-reliance on short term funding such as repo left a firm vulnerable to a loss in confidence[201].

Bear Stearns was ultimately rescued, thanks to a purchase by JPMorgan (encouraged by the New York FED). It was solvent at the time of purchase: JPMorgan paid $10 per share. This emphasises the importance of being unable to fund as a failure mechanism.

Lehman, of course, was allowed to go bankrupt. Here too liquidity was a key element in the firm's distress. As Lehman's bankruptcy examiner put it[202]:

> *Confidence was critical. The moment that repo counterparties were to lose confidence in Lehman and decline to roll over its daily funding, Lehman would be unable to fund itself and continue to operate.*

Most large financial institutions survive because they can borrow. The confidence of the funding market is a vital component of financial stability. For a fragile institution, trying to borrow too much can push it over the edge: not only might that attempt fail, but the act of trying to raise unexpectedly large amounts of funds can raise further doubts which mean that even routine funding roll overs cannot be executed.

4.2.3   Bailouts and borrowings

After Lehman, problems in financial institution funding were so severe that there was a real danger – and certainly a perceived danger – of widespread financial system collapse. Many authorities intervened in unprecedented size and sometimes in unconventional ways. In September and October 2008 alone[203]:

- The two US agencies Fannie Mae (the Federal National Mortgage Association) and Freddie Mac (Federal Home Loan Mortgage Corporation) were rescued by the US government in one of the largest bailouts in US history.

- Wells Fargo bought Wachovia, Merrill Lynch hastily agreed to be taken over by Bank of America, and the two remaining broker/dealers, Goldman Sachs and Morgan Stanley, converted themselves into banks in order to be able to access central bank funding at the FED window.

- AIG was saved from the brink of collapse by the US Federal Reserve who lent the firm $85B at a high rate[204] and in exchange for warrants granting them the right to buy 79.9% of the firm's equity for a nominal amount.

- Various central banks including the FED, the Bank of England, the ECB and the Swiss National Bank announced measures to stabilise the liquidity markets via the injection of funds and the widening of collateral requirements[205].

- The US introduced the Troubled Asset Relief Program, initially making $250B available to directly recapitalise US financial institutions. It quickly purchased $125B in preferred stock from a range of banks including Citigroup, JPMorgan, Bank of America and Wells Fargo. Various other nations also injected capital into troubled institutions, with the UK in particular spending more than £35B on a range of firms including RBS.

- Washington Mutual was seized by supervisors and most of its assets sold to JPMorgan in the US; Bradford & Bingley was nationalised in the UK, as was Glitnir in Iceland and Fortis in the Benelux countries. Hypo Real Estate was rescued by a consortium of the Bundesbank, the ECB, and German private sector banks.

Steps like this, combined with coordinated central bank rate drops and liquidity injections, stabilised the financial system. Many institutions recovered, although a few (including AIG and RBS) remained in government control.

4.3 Credit Derivatives in the Crisis

Credit instruments played a key role in the crisis, so it is not surprising that derivatives based on them were also involved. We look at credit derivatives as assemblers of ABS, and at unfunded risk taken via credit derivatives.

4.3.1 Credit derivatives as assemblers

Section 4.1.1 discussed the mechanics of the simplest kind of securitisation, a 'cash' deal. Cash securitisations are constructed by the securitisation vehicle buying the collateral[206] that backs the CDO. There is another, more sophisticated class of securitisation known as a 'synthetic' deal. Here some or all risk is swapped into the securitisation vehicle using CDS. Figure 4.4 illustrates the difference.

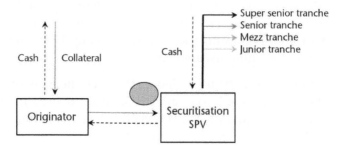

Figure 4.4: An illustration of cash (above) and synthetic (below) securitisations

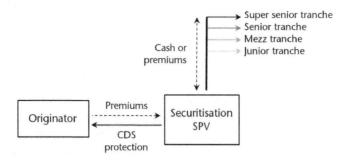

Synthetic securitisations do not require that the securitisation SPV owns the underlying collateral[207]. This was convenient for the marketers of ABS, as it meant that they were not constrained by the supply of securities in making CDOs. If you only have cash CDOs available, then in order to sell, say, a AAA-rated tranche of an RMBS-backed CDO, you had to actually buy all of the backing RMBS, put them in a securitisation vehicle, and issue tranched securities. (You then had the problem of what to do with the other tranches.) For synthetics, sourcing CDO collateral was not an issue: you did not have to own something in order to issue securities 'backed' by it[208].

It is undeniable that CDS were used to assemble securities that suffered very substantial losses. Moreover, synthetic securitisations were about a third of all structured finance CDOs[209], so their role was not nugatory.

4.3.2 Shorting into synthetic CDOs

Managed synthetic securitisations were also central to allowing some investors to profit from the crisis. For instance, in the (well known) Abacus transaction[210], a large hedge fund, Paulson & Co. wished to buy protection on a collection of RMBS in order to profit if their value fell. A synthetic CDO was structured referencing the desired securities so that Paulson could get the exposure they wanted. The investors in the CDO were thus, in effect, writing protection to Paulson, although they may not have known this. When the crisis intensified and value of the securities backing Abacus fell, Paulson made money and the investors lost. The amounts involved in this single trade are substantial: Paulson is said to have made a billion dollars on Abacus[211].

The SEC alleged that the firm that structured this trade, Goldman Sachs, should have disclosed Paulson's economic interest to securitisation investors. Goldman settled and 'acknowledged that its marketing materials for the subprime product contained incomplete information'. The firm paid a record $550M fine[212].

There are differing opinions on the lessons to be drawn from this. Certainly there should have been more disclosure of the economic motivations for the transaction. But beyond this, should entities be allowed to buy protection on securities that they do not own, as Paulson did? The ability to go short improves efficiency and price discovery in the market. But, unlike a well-regulated equity market where going short involves borrowing the security, credit derivatives allowed shorts to take their position without borrowing the underlying security and without their position being visible. Shorting has to be done this way as there is almost no borrow market for ABS (or indeed most corporate bonds). It does, though, raise the issue of trade reporting: investors should at least be able to compare the size of the cash market with the synthetic one so that they can better understand what is driving prices.

4.3.3 Risk taking using credit derivatives

In addition to their use in synthetic CDOs, CDS were used in a variety of risk-taking strategies before 2008. For instance, 'negative basis trades' involved dealers buying bonds, then buying credit protection on them using CDS (or analogous contracts such as financial guarantees). The idea was essentially that the dealer could fund the bond cheaply and, if the CDS spread was sufficiently lower than the credit spread on the bond (i.e. the basis was negative) then an 'arbitrage' gain could be made[213]. Similarly, CDS – particularly CDS on credit indices – were used to 'hedge' positions ranging from AMPs (a position which ultimately lost UBS billions of dollars[214]) to bespoke CDOs. Finally, a range of market participants ranging from hedge funds through to insurance companies used CDS to take risk: AIG (discussed in section 2.3.5) was an example of this.

4.3.4 Did using credit derivatives intensify the crisis?

Without CDS, there would have been no synthetic CDOs, no negative basis trades, and much less structured finance activity generally. That would clearly have lessened the intensity of the financial crisis[215].

CDS acted in another unhelpful way in the crisis thanks to their private nature. No one – supervisors included – knew the totality of risks which had been transferred via CDS and to whom[216]. This opacity contributed to the loss of confidence in financial institutions as the crisis moved into the funding phase. A related issue was counterparty credit risk: significant amounts of credit risk taking had been done without collateral agreements, and when it became clear that this risk taking had created losses which were large enough to imperil the institutions concerned, the focus shifted to their counterparties. Put simply, if an investment bank had bought so much protection from an insurer that the insurer could not afford to pay, then the problem became the bank's. Disputes followed between the banks and their counterparties. By this point much of the damage had been done as investors began to doubt the true value of the banks' derivatives receivables. In this sense counterparty credit risk was a significant factor, even though ultimately the losses from this risk type were relatively minor.

4.4 OTC Derivatives and Interconnectedness

The UK Financial Services Authority ('FSA') undertook a loss attribution exercise after the crisis to ascertain which investment banking activities generated losses for the firms that they regulated[217].

Product type	Total losses ($B)
Pseudo-safe assets[218]	87
ABS assets	51
CVA losses	45
Leveraged loans	18
Corporate CDS	11
Other derivatives losses	14
Counterparty defaults	8
Other securities and FX losses	6

Figure 4.5: FSA's analysis of losses suffered by regulated firms during the financial crisis

Figure 4.5 summarises the results of this analysis. It substantiates the discussion above concerning the primacy of credit instruments in creating direct losses. However, it does bring up some other issues, such as CVA risk. Losses on this, and other instabilities resulting from OTC derivatives, are the topic of this section.

4.4.1 CVA losses

In the previous section we saw that a feature of the use of CDS to take credit risk before the crisis was the absence of tight CSAs with certain counterparties. In particular, banks often bought credit protection from insurance companies without demanding daily margin. As the crisis deepened, these CDS became more valuable to the banks, and hence CVAs rose. The insurance companies' credit quality fell, also increasing the required CVA. The combination of these two factors created the $45B CVA loss in figure 4.5. Clearly CVA risk was capable of creating substantial losses.

It is worth noting here that this loss could not, by its nature, be permanent. Each counterparty either performed or defaulted. If a counterparty performed, then its CVA went to zero. If it failed, then the loss became a default loss. CVA losses therefore represented the price of increasing *concerns over* eventual counterparty non-performance, not the cost of that non-performance itself[219]. The difference between these two was particularly pronounced for firms using market-based CVA. Credit spreads for some insurers went out to thousands of basis points. This generated very large CVAs. Some of these insurers subsequently defaulted, but others did not (although they did in many cases enter into litigation over their CDS transactions[220]). There is no reason to believe that a market-based

CVA represents the market's best guess of the eventual realised losses, and so it proved in this case[221]: CVA losses were much bigger than the eventual cost of non-performance.

4.4.2 Interconnectedness

The interconnectedness of financial institutions is a double-edged sword. On one side, it improves opportunities for risk distribution and hedging, facilitates the availability of a wide range of transactions which can be tailored to institutions' needs, and enhances financial system efficiency. On the other, it can make the financial system more fragile. Small or idiosyncratic shocks are spread, harmlessly; but large ones can lead to failure, especially if many institutions suffer the same vulnerabilities[222].

There are a number of forms of interconnectedness[223]. The first, direct form occurs when one firm has a direct exposure to another[224]. The failure of its counterparty may cause it losses which imperil it. Counterparty credit risk in OTC derivatives causes direct interconnectedness; interbank lending and repo are other, more important and more systemically risky forms. Still, OTC derivatives contributed to both the reality and perception of interconnectedness among dealers during the crisis.

Indirect interconnectedness is more delicate. Here the failure of a firm causes market prices of assets to fall, either because the firm (or its administrators) liquidates its holding of those assets, or simply because there is a general flight to quality. Firms holding those assets suffer mark to market losses. Thus there can be contagion from one firm to another even without direct exposure. Indirect interconnectedness was very important in the ABS markets during the crisis.

Infrastructural interconnectedness occurs because many financial institutions use the same pieces of financial markets infrastructure. These range from payment systems though securities custodians[225] to the subject of the second half of this book, central counterparties.

Finally, sovereign interconnectedness is the phenomenon whereby all the financial institutions in a country, and perhaps some outside it, rely on sovereign credit quality, central bank operations, and other governmental features. If a country becomes distressed, its banks will not prosper.

4.4.3 Unwinding OTC derivatives

Whatever the reality of total OTC derivatives inter-dealer exposure, there is no doubt that unwinding the OTC derivatives portfolio of a G14 dealer is a large task. Lehman was not a first rank swaps dealer, and yet its book of cleared trades (which were all standard transactions) took more than two weeks to unwind[226]. Prior to Lehman, there was a widespread view that authorities would not let a bank that was 'too complex to unwind' fail; this may have contributed to market participants willingness to sign loose CSAs. After all, why worry about your credit exposure to a party if they will be bailed out in any case?

It can reasonably be argued that this view was wrong. Still, one of its premises – that unwinding a major dealer in stressed markets is systemically risky – was sound, and the nature of bilateral close out in the OTC derivatives market was to blame. Clearly there are advantages to policies which make it much less likely that a big OTC book has to be closed out during a crisis.

The risk of a destabilising unwind of a large OTC derivatives portfolio has been somewhat mitigated as part of other post-crisis regulatory changes. As we mentioned in section 2.2.3, supervisors in many countries are introducing (or modifying) 'resolution' procedures by which financial institutions can be taken over by authorities. This process often includes provisions preventing immediate close out and allowing for the assignment of derivatives to an entity which could run them to maturity or work them out on an orderly basis.

4.4.4 OTCs in stress

It is worth noting here that many of the improvements in market infrastructure resulting in part from the FED letter process (discussed in section 1.3.5) meant that the OTC market did not display prophesised instability during the crisis. The market survived the Lehman default[227]. The crisis did not display widespread disagreements over who had traded what with whom. Major credit events were not disputed, and the auctions held to settle these credit events operated smoothly.

The failure of Lehman and the stress on Bear Stearns and AIG might have passed off in an orderly fashion, but this is not to say that OTC derivatives had no impact. Not only was AIG in particular brought down by its derivatives trading, but OTC derivatives novations also increased stress on many institutions[228]. Counterparties who were worried about their credit exposure to, say, Bear Stearns novated profitable trades to other counterparties. The receiving counterparty was typically not anxious themselves to take extra exposure to a troubled broker/dealer, so they would only accept the novation if they had a tight CSA with Bear Stearns. That in turn meant that Bear Stearns had to collateralise most or all of the exposure post novation. The effect of counterparty risk reducing novations was therefore to produce a liquidity drain on an already stressed institution[229].

4.5 Broader Vulnerabilities

The total notional of subprime mortgages originated before the crisis amounted to less than $2T. Even if all of these mortgages were worth nothing – something that was far from true – subprime lending by itself could not have caused the crisis. There were simply not enough subprime loans to create the losses experienced across the financial system[230]. Subprime mortgages were the trigger for the crisis, but other factors were important contributors to the size of losses which eventually occurred.

Here we examine some of the principal vulnerabilities revealed by the crisis. These include the amount of capital institutions held; liquidity risk; and the lack of institutional transparency. We summarise these failings not so much to add to the already-substantial literature on the crisis, but rather to motivate some of the changes in regulation discussed in the next chapters. First, though, we need to set some context.

4.5.1 Frameworks

Financial institutions operate in a unique, and perhaps uniquely limiting framework. This is formed from a number of elements: accounting standards, regulatory capital, market regulation and financial markets infrastructure ('FMI') all play a part. This framework operates as a series of constraints which together determine the nature of financial institutions. Different constraints would produce different behaviours. For instance, automated trade processing infrastructure reduces operational risk, but it is expensive to connect to. Thus it acts to enhance both robustness and market concentration as only larger firms can afford the infrastructure needed to trade.

4.5.2 Banks, broker/dealers, insurers and others

The regulatory environment for various types of entity is the most important constraint on the financial system. For our purposes, four different types of entity are relevant[231]:

 • Banks are entities with a banking license. Typically this means that they can (and often do) take deposits. Banks can have multiple branches in different jurisdictions sharing assets and liabilities. Thus they can be centrally funded. They are typically regulated by the bank supervisor of their home country; this regulator will have rules which (broadly[232]) implement the Basel Accords. In the United States, bank holding companies are lead-regulated by the FED. Other countries either use this model – the central bank as bank supervisor – or have a separate banking supervisor such as Germany's BAFIN.

* Broker/dealers are mainly trading rather than banking entities. In the United States, broker/dealers used to form a major class of entities, with five large institutions competing with banks in the capital markets[233], although none of these remain as broker/dealers. US-domiciled broker/dealers are lead-regulated by the SEC. The EU applies (broadly) the same supervisory framework to broker/dealers as to banks, so the distinction is less relevant in Europe.

* Insurance companies typically have an entirely different regulatory framework to other entities. In the United States this is based on state insurance commissioners, while in the EU various arrangements pertain ranging from integrated supervision with banks and broker/dealers (for instance in the UK) to a separate supervisor (e.g. Italy).

* Hedge funds used to have rather light regulation provided that their investors were sufficiently qualified. This is now changing, with (slowly) increasing hedge fund regulation being matched by a broadening in the permitted investor base.

4.5.3 Capital regulation

One key aspect of regulation concerns capital. Supervisors set rules which define both how much capital an institution has and how much it needs, given the risks it runs. Institutions must keep enough capital to comply with these rules, so if capital falls (for instance because the institution loses money), or risks rise, then the institution must either raise new capital or cut its risk.

Capital rules differ markedly between entities. Thus for instance the same risk in a bank, a broker/dealer, and an insurance company attract very different capital requirements, while none at all is required in a hedge fund. This sets up a crucial incentive structure for cross sectoral risk transfer.

4.5.4   Capital, leverage and loss absorption

There is general accord that banks had too little capital before the crisis, and too little good quality capital in particular[234]. The issue was even more severe for the five large SEC-regulated broker/dealers[235].

This widespread agreement on the desirability of more capital can mask a more fundamental question, that of what this extra capital would be for. It is worth bearing in mind that raising capital *requirements* does not necessarily mean that regulated institutions can absorb more losses, since they have to remain well capitalised at all times. Extra required capital is in effect trapped, and not available to meet losses without triggering supervisory intervention.

In general, capital can have a variety of roles including:

+ Absorbing going concern losses;

+ Absorbing losses during resolution or bankruptcy (so-called 'gone concern' loss absorption);

+ Giving confidence to liability holders that their debt or deposit will be repaid when due; and

+ Ensuring that the firm's owners have some 'skin in the game' which may[236] deter imprudence.

4.5.5   Funding liquidity risk

The immediate failure mechanism for large institutions during the crisis was liquidity risk: for Bear Stearns and Lehman, over-reliance on repo played a large factor; while for banks, the stress in unsecured funding was important too. This demonstrated the well-known fact that lending long and funding short leaves institutions vulnerable to a run on funding[237]. Any other transaction which can expose the bank to an unexpected large demand for funds can be functionally equivalent to funding short, too.

Liquidity and capital are often spoken of as comparable issues, and indeed reforms of regulations in each area receive separate volumes in Basel III. They differ substantially in character however. There has been at least thirty years work in quantifying market and credit risks, and much of this work has fed through into the definition of capital requirements. In contrast, funding liquidity risk has not been so extensively researched, and measures of it remain fairly crude. Quantification is difficult not least because deposits (among other liabilities) have behavioural maturities which are often much longer than their contractual maturity: people tend just to leave their money with a bank despite being able to withdraw it. We know from many examples – most recently Northern Rock – that we cannot rely on this always being the case: but equally if we take the most conservative interpretation of the maturity of insured deposits and use that as the basis of liquidity risk regulation then we will likely make it rather difficult for banks to intermediate credit. There is a strong argument that the economy requires banks to perform some degree of maturity transformation, but measuring how much they are doing and limiting excesses is more difficult.

4.5.6 *Institutional transparency*

Loss of confidence in an institution is a key ingredient in causing a funding crisis. Investors start to doubt whether a firm is 'really' solvent, and so withdraw credit. Typically as an accounting matter the firm is solvent: its financial statements show positive net worth. So this doubt amounts to concern that the firm's financial statements over-state the value of its assets and/or under-state its liabilities. In the case of Lehman, for instance, retrospective analysis indicates that many of its holdings were over-stated by material amounts compared with best valuation practice[238]. Thus another key vulnerability is institutional opacity: the fact that large firms were not sufficiently transparent meant that legitimate doubts could arise over their solvency. This is partly an issue of disclosure and partly one of supervision. Investors did not have enough information, and they doubted that supervisors (or auditors) were sufficiently rigorous in their review of valuations.

4.5.7 *The regulatory & accounting frameworks for unfunded risk takers*

While CDS were in many cases the mechanism by which risks were transferred from originators to ultimate holders, they were not of themselves purposeful. We need to ask why a range of parties – notably insurance companies – took large amounts of ABS risk, and why, when this turned out badly, they did not have sufficient capital to support their losses. There are two main threads to this narrative:

1. The regulation of insurance companies in general, and the monoline insurers in particular, was plainly inadequate. These companies were permitted to use very high levels of leverage, to have high levels of concentration in certain risk classes, and to estimate the capital they required in ways that flattered their risk profile. Absent a regulatory constraint, and (mistakenly) seeing a

higher return from higher leverage, the insurers took more and more ABS risk.

2. The accounting framework for insurance companies permitted risk to be taken on a non-market to market basis[239]. This in turn meant that investors had little visibility of potential earnings volatility, and thus did not penalise the insurers for their rising risk until it was far too late.

These observations serve to remind us that it is not just the tools by which risk is taken that are important: the institutional framework matters too. Arguably the insurers would have found other ways to take the same housing-based risk without CDS; had they been subject to prudent leverage requirements, however, this behaviour would have been much less dangerous to financial stability.

Plausible concerns regarding OTC derivatives and financial stability after the crisis

We have discussed the main vectors by which OTC derivatives contributed to the vulnerabilities of the financial system. Reasonable people have differed over what policy lessons to draw from this; indeed, some of these disagreements and the consequences of different policy choices will be key issues in the rest of the book. Here we summarise the discussion above by listing some of the main concerns that official observers of the crisis have raised. This will then motivate the post-crisis regulatory policy changes examined in the next chapter. These concerns are[240]:

- Many financial institutions, including some banks, insurance companies and broker/dealers, were too highly leveraged with too little good quality capital.

- Many financial institutions also had too much funding liquidity risk due to over-reliance on short term funding or vulnerability to calls on their funding (such as margin calls).

- Risk transfer in some markets was opaque[241], and both supervisors and investors had insufficient knowledge about which institutions had which risks. This made many large firms vulnerable to a loss of confidence.

- Many financial institutions were too interconnected, giving rise to concerns that their failure would cause widespread financial instability.

- As a related matter, large financial institutions were typically so complex that their bankruptcy would have been destabilising. There were no credible plans for the resolution of a systemically important financial institution.

- While counterparty defaults did not cause major losses during the crisis, rising CVA did, and the risk of this was not considered in the regulatory capital framework.

OTC derivatives did not cause the crisis, but they did facilitate some aspects of risk transfer that led to it, and they did exacerbate some pre-existing vulnerabilities.

Notes

[176]From, respectively, the Economic Collapse blog (theeconomiccollapseblog.com), the Seeking Alpha blog (seekingalpha.com), and Warren Buffett.

[177]It is notable that none of the participants in the Financial Crisis Enquiry Commission's hearings in the role of derivatives in the financial crisis point to anything other than credit derivatives as direct causes: see the testimony available at fcic.law.stanford. edu/hearings/testimony/the-role-of-derivatives-in-the-financial-crisis.

[178]C. Kindleberger, R. Aliber in *Manias, Panics and Crashes: A History of Financial Crises*, Palgrave Macmillan (6th Edition, 2012) give an account of the common features of financial crises. To summarise a long argument in a short phrase, excessive credit extension causes crises.

[179]We do not count asset backed securities as derivatives but rather as securities, because that is what they are. Some ABS such as the tranches of synthetic CDOs may have been assembled using derivatives, and those of course count, but the tranches don't. We discuss synthetic CDOs in section 4.3.1 below.

[180]A longer account can be found in my book *Unravelling the Credit Crunch*, Chapman Hall (2009).

[181]Strictly, the promise is made by the SPV that issues the ABS, but since the only sources of cash that SPV has are the ones in the collateral pool, the assets (absent any support from the originator, anyway) are the only things backing the security.

[182]'Private label' in distinction to 'agency' RMBS: the first RMBS had been issued by Federal Agencies. These transferred prepayment risk to investors but were guaranteed against default risk by the Agency. Private label RMBS transfer both prepayment and default risk.

[183]See *The 2009 Mortgage Market Statistical Annual, Vol. 2, The Secondary Market*, Inside Mortgage Finance Publications (2009).

[184]R. Green, S. Wachter, *The Housing Finance Revolution*, 31st Jackson Hole Economic Policy Symposium (August 2007) available at www.kansascityfed.org/publicat/sympos/2007/PDF/2007.08.21.WachterandGreen.pdf contains a longer account of the changes in the US mortgage market.

[185]This is a simplification, ignoring in particular prepayment risk. For details of this and a longer introduction to securitisation and tranching, see Chapter 10 of my book *Understanding Risk: The Theory and Practice of Financial Risk Management*, Chapman Hall 2008.

[186]This is a 'six pack' structure, one of the two major types of prime private label RMBS deal (the other was a structure with excess-spread credit enhancement). See *MBS Basics*, Nomura Fixed Income Research (March 2006).

[187]One of the early proponents of the safe asset hypothesis was W. Buiter: see *Lessons from the North Atlantic financial crisis* (2008) available at www.nber.org/~wbuiter/NAcrisis.pdf. Latterly the importance of the supply/demand dynamic for safe assets has been developed by a number of authors notably G. Gorton and collaborators, for instance in *The Safe-Asset Share*, prepared for AER Papers & Proceedings (2012) available via www.aeaweb.org.

[188]This process became particularly incestuous when one CDO of ABS bought the mezz tranche of another and vice versa. In this case neither tranche provided any subordination. This, and the general tendency for CDOs to buy mezz tranches, arguably created a false market in mezz securities since there were few 'real money' buyers bidding on these securities: see L. Cordell et al., *Collateral Damage: Sizing and assessing the subprime CDO crisis*, Federal Reserve Bank of Philadelphia Working Paper Number 11-30/R (May 2012) available at www.philadelphiafed.org/research-and-data/publications/working-papers/2011/wp11-30.pdf.

[189]R. Green, S. Wachter, *op. cit.*

[190]They did bear a small fraction of the risk. This was because mortgage servicing fees are typically a fixed fraction of the current loan balance, so originators sometimes suffered from fee income compression as default rates rose. Moreover they were (and are) subject to lawsuits from securitisation investors accusing them, for instance, of breaches in the representations and warrantees made in the securitisation process.

[191]This dramatically increased the incentive for appraisal fraud.

[192]Data from S. Chomsisengphet, A. Pennington-Cross, *The Evolution of the Subprime Mortgage Market*, Federal Reserve Bank of St. Louis Review Volume 88, No. 1 (2006) available at research.stlouisfed.org/publications/review/06/01/JanFeb2006Review.pdf.

[193]Non-recourse loans are the norm in some US states, including most of those that suffered the mortgage default rates during the crisis.

[194]See chapter one of my book *Unravelling the Credit Crunch* (Chapman Hall, 2009) for more on house prices and mortgage types.

[195] As so often, the market over-reacted; once the crisis had passed, many subprime RMBS rose substantially in price.

[196] See Figure 2 in A. Blundell-Wignall, P. Atkinson, *The Sub-prime Crisis: Causal Distortions and Regulatory Reform* (2010) available www.gem.sciences-po.fr/content/publications/pdf/Atkinson-Blundell_SubprimeCrisis032010.pdf.

[197] The ABX indices come with two characteristics. One is the six month period during which the underlying mortgages were originated. Thus the 06-02 index represents the prices of packages of mortgages originated during the second half of 2006. The second dimension is the credit rating of the risk, so the ABX AAA 06-02 is an index of packages of mortgages rated AAA when they were first sold. These indices are produced by Markit: see www.markit.com for more details.

[198] The problem was not just that losses were rising on the mortgage pools, but also that the spread account credit enhancement of many RMBS only worked if the collateral pool kept paying enough excess spread to fill the spread account. It was becoming obvious by mid-2007 that for many new RMBS that was not going to happen.

[199] See the document *Background information on suspension and reopening of ABS funds in August* (2007) available at media-cms.bnpparibas.com/file/76/1/5761.pdf.

[200] See Chapter II of the June 2008 ECB *Financial Stability Review* for a survey of these events.

[201] G. Gorton and A. Metrick's *Securitized Banking and the Run on Repo* available at papers.ssrn.com/sol3/papers.cfm?abstract_id=1440752 gives an account of the vulnerabilities repo funding created.

[202] A. Valukas, *In Re Lehman Brothers Holding Inc.*, United State Bankruptcy Court, Southern District of New York (2010), available at lehmanreport.jenner.com. Lehman's liquid asset pool decreased from $41B on 9th September to about $25B on 12th September, of which roughly $7B were not immediately convertible into cash, and $16B was locked up by Lehman's counterparties (mostly correspondent banks). This left only $2B of true cash liquidity. The situation was getting worse: Lehman was forecast to have a net cash outflow of at least $4B on the 15th, and it had exhausted its ability to borrow. It filed for bankruptcy that day.

[203] A more detailed US timeline from the St. Louis FED can be found at timeline.stlouisfed.org, while www.newyorkfed.org/research/global_economy/IRCTime linePublic.pdf discusses the non-US bailouts.

[204] Libor plus 850.

[205] For instance, the FED announced the Asset-Backed Commercial Paper Money Market Mutual Fund Liquidity Facility, broadened the range of collateral broker/dealers were allowed to post to the Primary Dealer Credit Facility, and expanded the Term Auction Facility.

[206] Note the slightly different use of the term 'collateral' here: these are assets which support the ABS, rather than credit support against a derivatives portfolio.

[207]See E. Buckberg et al., *Subprime and Synthetic CDOs: Structure, Risk, and Valuation* NERA Insights in Economics (June 2010) available at www.nera.com/nera-files/PUB_CDOs_Structure_Risk_Valuation_0610.pdf for more on cash and synthetic CDOs.

[208]For more details, see A. Rajan, G. McDermott, R. Roy, *The Structured Credit Handbook*, Wiley (2007).

[209]L. Cordell, Y. Huang, M. Williams in *Collateral Damage: Sizing and Assessing the Subprime CDO crisis*, Federal Reserve Bank of Philadelphia Working paper Number 11/30R (2012) available at www.philadelphiafed.org/research-and-data/publications/working-papers/2011/wp11-30.pdf say that synthetics were 31% of total issuance from 1999 to end 2007. It was closer to half in 2007.

[210]Technically, Abacus 2007-AC1.

[211]The amount comes from the SEC complaint *Securities and Exchange Commission v. Goldman, Sachs & Co. and Fabrice Tourre*, 10 Civ. 3229 (BJ) (S.D.N.Y. filed April 16, 2010) which can be found at www.sec.gov/litigation/litreleases/2010/lr21489.htm.

[212]The phrase comes from the SEC's Litigation Release No. 21592 *Goldman Sachs to pay record $550 million to settle SEC charges related to subprime mortgage CDO* (July 15, 2010) available at www.sec.gov/litigation/litreleases/2010/lr21592.htm.

[213]This is only an arbitrage if losses on the bond are certain to be offset by gains on the CDS. All too often on these trades it turned out that they weren't.

[214]See *Shareholder Report on UBS's Write-Downs* (2008) available via www.ubs.com for more details.

[215]CDS had some positive benefits, allowing risk to be distributed which, if it had not moved, would have further imperilled financial institutions. A system in which more institutions lose smaller amounts is more stable than one where there are isolated point failures. Ultimately, though, these benefits do not – for this author at least – amount to a comprehensive vindication of the pre-crisis CDS market and its arrangements. For further perspective, see R. Anderson, *Credit default swaps: what are the social benefits and costs?*, Banque de France Financial Stability Review No. 14 (July 2010).

[216]As we hinted in section 4.3.2 above, without trade reporting a counterparty can sell physically settled credit protection on more than the total notional of a bond outstanding providing that they use a number of different counterparties. In this case a credit event would lead to a squeeze on the deliverable bond. This is not just a theoretical issue: a small hedge fund, Amherst Holdings, did exactly this trade on subprime RMBS in 2009. Without trade reporting, the protection buyers have no way of monitoring this risk. Transparency is not just for regulators: it is sometimes needed in other areas of the market too.

[217]The details are in the FSA discussion paper *The prudential regime for trading activities*, DP 10/4 (August 2010) available at www.fsa.gov.uk/pubs/discussion/dp10_04.pdf. Note that this analysis will likely include some FSA-regulated subsidiaries of foreign banks and broker/dealers.

[218]Super senior CDOs with ABS underliers.

[219]As a counterparty deteriorates, the CVA increase. On average a historical CVA should converge on the loss given default, while a market-based one will converge on market estimates of LGD. If the counterparty fails, then the CVA losses are reclassified as default losses. If it continues to perform despite its distress, then the CVA will eventually decline, going to zero at portfolio maturity.

[220]To pick one case from many, see ABN Amro Bank N.V. et al. v. MBIA Inc., et al., No. 09-601475, New York Supreme Court. The majority of the banks in this case have now settled, reflecting an increasing trend on the part of both those insurers who are still standing and the dealers to put these events behind them.

[221]The ISDA Note *Counterparty Credit Risk Management in the US Over-the-Counter (OTC) Derivatives Markets, Part II: A Review of Monoline Exposures* (November 2011) available via www.isda.org has a detailed analysis of monoline CVA and default losses for twelve of the most active dealers.

[222]See D. Acemoğlu et al., *Systemic Risk and Stability in Financial Networks*, Manuscript, MIT (2012).

[223]The IMF's *Understanding Financial Interconnectedness* (October 2010) available at www.imf.org/external/np/pp/eng/2010/100410.pdf has a further discussion of this issue.

[224]The IMF, op. cit. discuss a particular form of direct interconnectedness via balance sheets, pointing out that large financial institutions not only have exposure via their assets (loans they have made), but also transmit that exposure via the issuance of liabilities which other institutions (among others) buy. The enormous balance sheets of the largest banks thus act as a form of direct connection between borrowers and lenders: indeed this is the basic function of banks.

[225]It is generally acknowledged that the central securities depositories are the epitome of 'too important to fail' institutions. See for instance the DTCC Press Release *DTCC Subsidiaries Receive 'Systemically Important' Designation* available at www.dtcc.com/news/newsletters/dtcc/2012/sep/subsidiaries_receive_designation.php.

[226]See section 6.5.3 for more details.

[227]A 'Lehman Risk Reduction Trading Session' was held on the Sunday before the firm's bankruptcy filing. This allowed participating dealers to reduce their counterparty exposure to Lehman. Arguably without this the impact of the failure would have been substantially greater.

[228]The Third Report of the CRMPG, *Containing Systemic Risk: The Road to Reform*, (6th August 2008) points out that dealers can create liquidity stress on their counterparties by two derivatives-related mechanisms. First by novation; and second by requesting close out of positions which are in-the-money to the counterparty and thus which require the return of collateral.

[229]For more details see D. Duffie's *The failure mechanics of dealer banks*, BIS Working Paper No. 301 (March 2010), available at www.bis.org/publ/work301.pdf, and in particular endnote 14.

[230]The IMF April 2010 financial stability review estimated total crisis related losses at $2.3T.

[231]A longer account can be found in D. Masciandaro, M. Quintyn, *Regulating the regulators: the changing face of financial supervision architectures before and after the crisis* CEPR/ESI 13th Annual Conference on 'Financial Supervision in an Uncertain World' (2009) available at www.cepr.org/meets/wkcn/1/1724/papers/masciandarofinal.pdf.

[232]Basel implementation is proceeding at a different pace in different jurisdictions: at the time of writing, for instance, the US has not yet implemented Basel II, while it has been in place in the EU for some years. The *Progress report on Basel III implementation* available at www.bis.org/publ/bcbs232.htm summarises the state of play.

[233]The 'big 5' pre-crisis broker/dealers were Bear Stearns, Lehman, Goldman Sachs, Merrill Lynch and Morgan Stanley.

[234]Chapter 6 of the Bank of England Financial Stability Report (October 2008) available at www.bankofengland.co.uk/publications/Documents/fsr/2008/fsrfull0810.pdf has a good discussion of historical capital levels and the growth of leverage in the years before the crisis. See also A. Demirguc-Kunt et al., *Bank Capital: Lessons from the Financial Crisis*, IMF Working Paper IMF Working Paper (December 2010) available at www.imf.org/external/pubs/ft/wp/2010/wp10286.pdf.

[235]The chairman of the SEC, Christopher Cox, acknowledged that the SEC's supervision of these five firms had been 'fundamentally flawed from the beginning' as he closed the program under which they had been supervised: see the SEC press release *The End of Consolidated Supervised Entities Program* is available at www.sec.gov/news/press/2008/2008-230.htm. To see Cox's point, notice that of the big five, one went bankrupt, two were forced to sell themselves to banks, and two became banks.

[236]Dick Fuld, CEO of Lehman Brothers before its bankruptcy, had the vast majority of his net worth in Lehman stock. This should have provided a very substantial incentive to be prudent, yet most observers agree that Fuld's actions were a major contributor towards Lehman's failure.

[237]See for instance D. Diamond, P. Dyvig, *Bank Runs, Deposit Insurance, and Liquidity*, Journal of Political Economy Volume 91, No. 3 (1983).

[238]A. Valukas, Bankruptcy Examiner for Lehman Brothers Holdings Inc., devotes an entire volume of his report into Lehman's valuation practices. See *Report of Anton R. Valukas, Examiner, Volume 2 of 9* (March 2010) available at jenner.com/lehman/VOLUME2.pdf.

[239]For instance through the use of financial guarantees or bond wraps rather than CDS.

[240]The financial stability board documents *Progress in the Implementation of the G-20 Recommendations for Strengthening Financial Stability* (starting April 2011 and available via www.financialstabilityboard.org) are quite interesting in that, reading them, one might think that the G-20 recommendations are more precise and thoroughgoing than they are. See for instance the G-20 Summit communiques for 2008, 2009 and 2010 available via www.g20.utoronto.ca.

[241]This observation applies just as much to credit markets broadly as to the OTC derivatives markets.

Part II

Reform and Its Consequences

5

Regulatory Responses to the Crisis

It is a very great thing to obey,
to live under a superior
and not to be one's own master
Thomas á Kempis

Introduction

The last chapter ended with a number of issues that supervisors thought caused the financial crisis or increased its intensity. Each of these vulnerabilities – lack of capital, liquidity risk, and so on – created substantial new regulation. This chapter reviews the major areas of rule making and sets out the principal new regulations in each of them.

5.1 Capital

The Basel Accords form a global framework for bank regulation. The first two Accords, in 1988 and 2004, defined the pre-crisis rules[242]: Basel III was introduced in response to the crisis, and changed the regulatory framework for banks in diverse ways.

5.1.1 Basel III's capital rules

The first and longest volume of Basel III relates to capital[243]. Specifically[244]

* It redefines how much capital banks have for regulatory purposes; and

* It redefines how much they need.

The new rules are scheduled for a phased introduction from 2013 until 2018, although it is doubtful if many major jurisdictions will be ready on 1st January 2013 with a full Basel 3 implementation. The rules dramatically increase the capital that a bank requires to support the same risks, as we discuss further in section 5.7. Moreover much more of that capital will have to be equity, while prior rules permitted substantial amounts of non-equity capital.

Some observers have suggested that Basel III does not go far enough in raising capital requirements[245], and others want to see a simplification of the rules for calculating the requirements[246]. Still, there is no doubt that Basel III has done much to ameliorate concerns that banks' quality and level of capital were too low.

5.1.2   Capital as a constraint

Regulatory capital was not a major constraint on many large financial institutions before the crisis. It was a cost, and it had to be borne in mind, but it was not often a major factor in banks' strategies. Basel III and related developments changed that by raising capital requirements so far that meeting them became a significant problem for many banks.

Supervisors have created this change, but it is capital markets investors who are enforcing it. Thus even though Basel III is not due for full implementation until 2019 (and its initial roll out in the EU and the US is delayed[247]), research on banks increasingly reports 'fully loaded Basel III' capital ratios because this is the number that investors are interested in. In other words, regardless of the implementation timetable, investors are taking the view that they want immediate Basel III compliance.

The struggle to meet the higher levels of required capital in Basel III is creating substantial change to banking. There are three ways to improve capital ratios:

1. Raise more capital, either by issuing securities or retaining earnings;

2. Reduce risk by selling assets or taking on less new business;

3. 'Mitigate' the impact of regulation through risk transmuting transactions or restructuring.

All of these are taking place. However, with bank returns on equity severely constrained by regulation, there is limited investor appetite to buy bank equity. Moreover shrinking assets risks losing market share, so banks are reluctant to do this. Nearly two thirds of the post-crisis improvement in capital ratios has therefore come from non-equity capital increase and mitigation[248].

It is important to note here that capital is not just a knob that regulators dial up or down. Overall levels of capital have gone up, but the *relative* capital requirements for different risks have changed dramatically too. This in turn creates a big incentive for banks to reduce risk in areas which are relatively expensive in capital terms. OTC derivatives trading is one of these areas so, as the IMF reports[249]:

> At least two large global banks have already announced that they will divest FICC [Fixed income, currency and commodities] business lines as they adapt to new capital requirements because they are not sufficiently competitive in the area. An unintended outcome of regulatory reform may be to concentrate FICC activities in banks with an already larger share of the business.

Increases in capital requirements are acting to reduce the diversity in OTC derivatives trading: the G14 is becoming the G12 (or perhaps even the G9 or 8).

5.1.3 Leverage requirements

Risk based capital requirements are vulnerable to risk estimation errors. In particular if regulators characterise any asset as very low risk then banks can have as much of it as they can fund. This can create vulnerability. Before the crisis, many of what we have called pseudo safe assets had a very low capital charge associated with them[250], allowing some financial institutions to accumulate vast positions[251].

Supervisors introduced a leverage limit in Basel III to mitigate this risk. This requirement constrain the ratio between capital and total assets, and thus acts to backstop risk-based capital requirements. The ratio is set at 3%, so institutions must have $3 of good quality capital[252] for every $100 of assets, whether low risk or not. OTC derivatives contribute to assets based on the net exposure plus an add-ons for potential future exposure[253].

5.2 Liquidity Risk

The Basel Committee proposes to address an excess of funding liquidity risk through the introduction of two new ratios which banks must meet. The 'Liquidity Coverage Ratio' (or 'LCR') is designed to ensure that banks can withstand a one month period of funding stress; while the 'Net Stable

Funding Ratio' (or 'NSFR') is designed to promote longer-term resilience by requiring banks to have funding for long term assets that will not disappear in a crisis.

5.2.1   The liquidity coverage ratio

The LCR ratio requirement ensures that banks can pass a liquidity stress test. Specifically banks must have a 'liquidity buffer' of high quality, unencumbered, liquid assets. These must be sufficient to meet likely cash outflows during a 30 day period of funding stress. The rules define how banks must calculate estimated cash outflows during this period, and what assets are sufficiently high quality and liquid[254] that they are permitted in the buffer. Cash, highly-rated government bonds and, to a lesser extent slightly lower quality government and the corporate and covered bonds are eligible for inclusion.

The LCR covers derivatives by assuming that 100% of net derivatives payables are drawn down during the stressed period. The rules also ensure that there is no double counting between collateral and the liquidity buffer: an asset can either reduce exposure, or be available to cover funding liquidity risk, but not both.

Trigger CSAs – a key factor in AIG's failure, as we saw in section 2.3.5 – are also addressed in the LCR. Banks must include in their calculation of cash outflows any amounts that would have to be posted on one, two or three notch downgrades.

We noted in section 3.4.2 that collateral price falls create liquidity risk in that the fall in value represents an extra amount that must be collateralised. This haircut risk is addressed in Basel III by the requirement that any piece of collateral held that the supervisors do not deem safe[255] is assumed to fall in value by 20% during the stress test. Sufficient liquid assets to meet this fall must therefore be kept.

5.2.2   The net stable funding ratio

The NSFR is, in the Basel Committee' words, 'structured to ensure that long term assets are funded with at least a minimum amount of stable liabilities'. It does this by defining the available amount of stable funding a bank has; the required amount of stable funding based on the bank's long term assets; and by requiring that the former is bigger than the latter. Stable funding is capital, long term debt, and stable deposits[256].

The required stable funding for an asset is defined via a range of 'RSF' factors. These range from zero for cash and short term unencumbered securities, to 85% for unencumbered loans to retail customers: the factors are based on supervisors' views of how much of the asset's value might be realised by sale or use as repo collateral during a stressed period.

There is an even more penal RSF than the 85% for retail loans, and that is 100% for 'other'. It seems (although it is not stated) that derivatives receivables count in this category; if so, Basel III will require that they must be fully funded from sources that supervisors consider stable.

5.2.3 Implementation of the Basel III liquidity requirements

The LCR and NSFR requirements are amongst the most controversial and ground-breaking parts of Basel III. While most commentators agree that something should be done to constrain bank liquidity risk, the details of the Basel proposals have attracted significant criticism. There were three main objections (and a host of smaller ones) to the original requirements:

1. The definition of which assets were high quality enough to meet outflows in the LCR was very constraining. In practice it provided a substantial incentive for banks to hold government bonds: assets that will also be in demand as collateral for OTC derivatives and secured funding[257]. Some countries did not have sufficient government bonds to meet this need[258]. Furthermore, there was a suspicion that others may be trying to stimulate demand for the large volumes of bonds needed to finance their deficits[259].

2. Banks had to comply with the LCR at all times. Therefore if there was a cash outflow, banks would not have been able to use the assets in the liquidity buffer to meet it as they would then be in breach of the LCR requirement. The regulation in effect tied up high quality assets without improving banks' liquidity position[260].

3. The details of the rules required banks to hold unnecessary amounts of surplus liquidity. This was inefficient given that central banks stand ready to provide extra liquidity against good collateral should a solvent bank require it[261].

These issues, combined with substantial industry pressure, created sufficient concern that the Basel Committee modified their position[262], expanding the class of assets which could be held in the liquidity buffer and modifying the stress test. It therefore remains to be seen whether the rest of the Basel III liquidity requirements will remain undisturbed before full implementation in 2018.

5.3 Pre– and Post-Trade Reporting

There are two kinds of information that potential participants in a financial market might wish to have:

1. 'Pre-trade' transparency refers to the availability of information about current market conditions. It could include the size and price of prospective trading interest, such as firm quotations in representative size; information on limit orders currently in force; or 'indicative' price quotes. Some markets have total transparency – the whole order book for a particular instrument is freely available – while others provide more limited information.

2. 'Post-trade transparency' refers to the dissemination of trade price and volume data for completed transactions. Typically this information is available soon after the trade is executed.

Basel III at least offers the framework for a global standard on capital and liquidity. There is no comparable framework for transparency: instead each jurisdiction has their own requirements, although there has been some cooperative work hosted by the Financial Stability Board among others[263]. We give short summaries of the current situation in the EU and the US for OTC derivatives. First, though, some remarks on the differing nature of equity and OTC derivatives markets.

5.3.1 Pre-trade transparency generally

Equity markets are usually organised rather differently from OTC derivatives markets. In them, market participants interact via an anonymous central order book. The best bid and offers are visible[264]; sometimes the whole order book is disclosed. There is thus a good measure of pre-trade transparency. This has historically not been the case for bilateral OTC derivatives markets where post-trade information was often scant.

However, the two markets are very different. Equity markets have a relatively small number of underlyings, and normal market size is quite small. In contrast, OTC derivatives offer a vast range of products (every maturity from a few months to fifty years in many currencies for the interest rate swap market alone, for instance). Trade sizes are much larger, yet the bid/offer spreads in many OTC products are tight. Thus there is little sign that the interest rate swap market, for instance, suffers from a lack of pre-trade transparency.

Central order books work well if there are enough orders to create a market, as there are in most equities. This is not the case, though, in

OTC derivatives. ISDA suggests that the OTC interest rate derivatives market globally consists of less than 6,000 trades per day: a large securities exchange would see a hundred times that volume[265]. It is by no means clear that the same arrangements are appropriate for markets that differ by two orders of magnitude in trade volumes.

The key issue here is that transparency is not free. If dealers are required to maintain quotes at all times, then they may only offer to trade a small range of liquid instruments; or they may widen bid/offer spreads as compensation for the risk of their quote being 'hit' at an inconvenient moment. This would be particularly damaging to the OTC market with its large range of less liquid (but still useful) instruments.

The contraction in the number of dealers created by higher capital requirements is exacerbating this risk: if most quotes, regardless of venue, are provided by a handful out of the ten or so leading dealers, then the end users of OTC derivatives are unlikely to be able to trade such a wide range of instruments on such a tight bid/offer spread as hitherto[266].

5.3.2 Pre-trade transparency in the EU and the US

EU rules on pre-trade transparency are defined by legislation relating to Markets in Financial Instruments. There are two EU directives, one current and one proposed, known as MiFID and MiFID II; and a regulation, MiFIR. We will refer to these (and more detailed implementing rules) collectively as the Markets in Financial Instruments Legislation or 'MiFIL'.

The United States Dodd Frank Act mandates some pre-trade transparency for OTC derivatives in the United States. Specifically, parts of title VII of Dodd Frank are the United States' analogues of the EU's MiFIL.

At the time of writing key aspects of MiFIL and the rules implementing Dodd Frank are not fixed[267]. However the broad sweep of both pieces of legislation can be discerned:

- A number of different classes of market are recognised[268].

- 'Sufficiently standardised' and liquid OTC derivatives will typically have to be traded on a recognised market, although there are (differing) exemptions for a limited range of market participants including smaller corporate end-users[269].

- Recognised markets will have to make public prices, and the depth of trading interest at those prices, for the orders or quotes that they advertise[270].

5.3.3 Post-trade transparency in the US and the EU

There is agreement in outline on post-trade transparency between the US, the EU, and indeed other jurisdictions[271]. A number of 'trade repositories' have been set up. These are large databases which contain details of all the trades reported to them. They provide summary market data publically[272], and allow qualified regulators deeper[273] access. Post-trade transparency requirements mandate reporting of most trades to a trade repository in a short period of time (such as 15 minutes). A delay is permitted for the reporting of larger (so-called 'block') trades. This gives dealers some time to hedge before it is publically known that they have a big position[274].

5.3.4 Standardisation

Transparency is clearly assisted by the existence of standard contracts: if there are hundreds of similar but not absolutely identical types of transaction, then information about prices may not be that useful as there are few direct comparisons. Standardisation is more subtle than this, though. It has three important aspects:

1. 'Contract standardisation' is the process of creating uniform terms for contracts with the same (or very similar) economics. The big and little bang events in credit derivatives described in chapter 2.5.2 are examples of this.

2. 'Operational standardisation' refers to the extent to which trade processing (including trade capture and revision, confirmation, settlement, close out, and other events) are managed in a common fashion to an agreed timetable[275].

3. 'Concentration in benchmarks' is the process of encouraging certain (hopefully) liquid contracts to be traded instead of customised ones.

Contract standardisation is self-evidently helpful: it assists trade processing, makes trade repository data more meaningful, and improves market liquidity. Operational standardisation is a club good which decreases operation risk and facilitates automated trade processing.

The benefits of concentration in benchmarks are less obvious. On the one hand, the existence of a large number of potential contracts (e.g. an interest rate swap maturing every day for the next fifty years) disperses liquidity: on the other, end-users have legitimate risk management requirements which are only perfectly met by one contract. If they are forced instead to trade a benchmark contract, then their costs may be very similar but they may well be left with substantial residual risk. A client wishing to hedge an eight year bond could find themselves only able to trade seven or ten year swaps, or facing higher costs on an eight year deal. Concentration in benchmarks either as an explicit policy or an accidental outcome of transparency requirements will likely reduce the usefulness of the OTC derivatives markets with few if any concomitant benefits for end-users[276].

5.4 Disclosure

An independent group recently drafted the following recommendations for financial institution disclosures[277]:

1.   Disclosures should be clear, balanced and understandable.

2.   Disclosures should be comprehensive and include all of the bank's key activities and risks.

3.   Disclosures should present relevant information.

4.   Disclosures should reflect how the bank manages its risks.

5.   Disclosures should be consistent over time.

6.   Disclosures should be comparable among banks.

7.   Disclosures should be provided on a timely basis.

These are laudable, and confidence in financial institutions would be higher and less easily lost if they were met. Sadly, though, despite the considerable length of many institutions' disclosures[278], investors often find large banks opaque and their risk profile mysterious.

This is not to say that no progress has been made in improving disclosure[279]: it has. Still, the four most systemically important banks[280] illustrate how much of a problem remains. Their average price/book ratio at the time of writing was less than 0.75. That means that the equity markets attribute on average a quarter less value to these big banks than accounting standards do. For these four institutions alone the total difference between investors' views and accounting value is over $100B. Moreover, this kind of gap has existed since the crisis. Investors simply do not believe that banks' financial statements accurately reflect their value: or, at least, they are nervous that there are risks in large banks which they do not understand.

5.5 Interconnectedness

We noted in section 4.4.2 that there are many forms of financial inter-connectedness. Of these, direct connections via OTC derivatives were far from the most significant. Still, authorities decided that this issue had to be addressed as part of the post-crisis reforms. In September 2009 in Pittsburgh, the G20 Leaders agreed[281] that all standardised OTC derivative contracts should in future be cleared through central counterparties. We begin by explaining what central clearing is and how it might help.

5.5.1 Central counterparties

A central counterparty ('CCP') interposes itself between two parties to a financial contract, becoming the buyer to the original seller, and the seller to the original buyer. This process is known as central clearing. Thus in a centrally cleared OTC derivative instead of the two counterparties facing each other directly (and being exposed to each other's counterparty risk), a CCP sits between them. The two parties are thus exposed to the CCP rather than to each other. Figure 5.1 illustrates the difference.

Figure 5.1: An illustration of the bilateral (top) and centrally cleared (bottom) models of OTC derivatives markets

5.5.2 Multilateral netting with CCPs

One advantage of an OTC derivatives CCP is that it facilitates multilat-eral netting between dealers. Thus if we had six dealers which were only exposed to each other (i.e. we ignore the client part of the picture), then the bilateral market could be depicted as in the top part of figure 5.2, but a centrally cleared market would look like the bottom illustration.

Consider dealer 1 in this figure. It has bilateral exposures to dealers 2, 3, 4, 5 and 6 separately. Each of these exposures could be margined or not; they could be under different CSAs; they will all require capital to support them. In the centrally cleared model in contrast, dealer 1 only has a single net exposure to the CCP, under a single agreement. The CCP will margin this exposure (something we discuss in section 6.1.2 below). It will offer

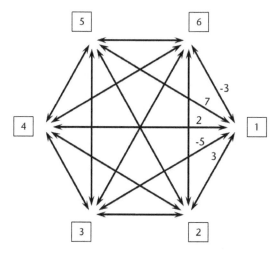

Figure 5.2: Conceptual schematic showing six bilateral OTC derivatives dealers (top) and the same six dealers clearing all trades at a single CCP (bottom). Potential multilateral netting for dealer 1 is also illustrated.

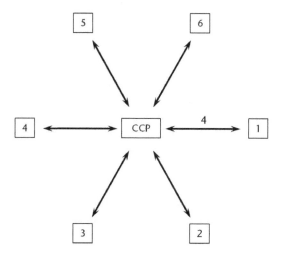

dealer 1 protection against the default of dealers 2 to 6 in that dealer 1 is not directly exposed to any of them. In this sense central clearing reduces counterparty credit risk.

The parties who face the CCP directly are known as 'clearing members'. These parties must agree to be bound by the CCP's rules in order to take advantage of central clearing and its concomitant benefits. A clearing house is therefore analogous to a club.

5.5.3 CCPs and interconnectedness

In a naïve sense CCPs reduce interconnectedness: there are fewer lines in the top of figure 5.2 than the bottom. The real question, though, is whether CCPs reduce system-wide counterparty credit risk. We will examine this in the next chapter. For now it suffices to remark that CCPs transform direct interconnectedness between bilateral OTC market participant into infrastructural interconnectedness: market participants are connected via CCPs.

A successful central counterparty, sitting at the centre of a web of connections, will clearly be a key piece of financial markets infrastructure[282]. Indeed, several OTC derivatives clearing houses have already been designated as systemically important financial market utilities[283], a status which subjects them to heightened prudential and supervisory provisions due to the systemic effects that their failure or disruption to their service could create.

5.5.4 Margin requirements for bilateral OTC derivatives

Regulators are interested in setting minimum margin standards for bilateral derivatives as these can constrain the extent of counterparty credit risk in the OTC derivatives system. At the time of writing, the standards have yet not been finalised, but there are proposed rules[284].

The supervisors make the point in their defence of minimum margin standards for OTC derivatives that margin is a 'defaulter pays' model, while capital is a 'survivor pays'. Supporting risk with capital gives diversification benefits, but this is imprudent unless such diversification is really present in stressed conditions. Moreover capital requirements are not designed to provide sufficient funds to cover the loss on the default of the counterparty, but rather the probability weighted loss given such default. As such the supervisors claim 'margin can be seen as offering enhanced protection against counterparty credit risk where it is effectively implemented'.

Their key suggestion given this context is that all financial firms (and systemically-important non-financial entities) must exchange IM and VM on non-cleared bilateral OTC derivatives. This margin must be sufficient to 'ensure that all exposures are covered fully with a high degree of confidence': it must also be in 'highly liquid' form. Moreover, it is proposed that IM should be on a gross basis, so both parties will have to post it to each other.

These proposals are controversial. There are a host of objections[285], many relating to compulsory IM. This would have a large liquidity cost to market participants in any case, and an absolutely enormous one if it could not be rehypothecated[286]. IM posting from regulated to unregulated financial institutions would also increase the connection between these two sectors, potentially increasing systemic risk. Moreover the costs of IM posting for end-users such as pension funds would be high. It remains to be seen how the supervisors will react to these comments.

5.5.5   Other policy measures to address interconnectedness

Supervisors have also taken or proposed a number of other measures to transform and somewhat mitigate interconnectedness, prominently:

- Higher capital requirements reduce direct interconnectedness by decreasing the amount of credit risk that can be taken with the same amount of capital[287];

- Proposals, as yet unimplemented, to address vulnerabilities in tri-party repo[288] and money market mutual funds[289];

- Unprecedented central bank interventions, both in terms of the amount of liquidity that has been provided and the means of its provision[290], have reduced interbank lending, replacing it with central bank funding. This has caused direct interconnectedness to decline at the expense of rising sovereign interconnectedness.

5.6   Resolution

Large financial institutions are, as the Governor of the Bank of England Mervyn King memorably put it, 'international in life but national in death'[291]. They also have many legal entities in a number of jurisdictions around the globe: a systemically important financial institution ('SIFI') might have hundreds of subsidiaries[292], and if the institution failed, each of these would need to file for bankruptcy in its particular jurisdiction. It is hard to imagine this process working well without pre-planning. Indeed, given that Lehman Brothers subsidiaries were still suing each other more than four years after the firm failed, it seems highly likely that a sudden SIFI failure would be destabilising.

The G20 recognised this, requiring jurisdictions to put in place on-going recovery and resolution planning processes[293]. There are a number of aspects to resolution. In broad summary:

- Supervisors need to have sufficient information to determine when a bank is failing, and the authority to intervene.

- This authority should allow the failing institution to be stabilised (either through funding or recapitalisation or both), with the provision for loss allocation. This may be in the form of the conversion of instruments into equity[294]; or the allocation of losses to equity or even debt holders. Thus some investors may be 'bailed in', with losses forced upon them[295].

- Authorities should be able to split the business into two or more parts.

- They may then transfer all or part of the bank's business to a private sector purchaser, transfer them to a government-owned bridge bank (perhaps as a prelude to a future sale), and/or put one or more of the bank's legal entities into administration[296].

- The viable parts of the business should be able to exit resolution in an orderly manner.

- There should be provisions which allow the institution to continue its business during resolution. This entails a stay on bankruptcy proceedings, and continuity of services (including payment, clearing and settlement functions).

- Resolution should be credible, legally certain, and it should seek to minimise the overall costs of the process.

As part of this process, many supervisors are requiring that some[297] large financial institutions prepare resolution programs, so called 'living wills'. These set out the key steps that would be required in resolving the firm; lay out the main subsidiaries, the businesses, financial condition and relationships; detail connections with major pieces of financial market infrastructure; and indicate which jurisdictions and regulators will need to be involved[298].

The effective resolution of a large financial institution will require different national supervisors to cooperate. However as New York FED President William Dudley put it recently[299]: 'regulatory coordination did not keep pace with the globalization of financial firms and markets [from the early 1980s to the crisis]'. Given that supervisors have little history of working well together in resolution, this remains a key practical issue[300].

One delicate issue in resolution regards OTC derivatives: clearly it may not promote financial stability if resolution triggers close out. Therefore typically the declaration that an institution is being resolved will include a short term[301] stay on close out. Authorities will also have the power to transfer contracts into new entities (such as a bridge bank) created in the process of resolution[302].

5.7 Risk Coverage

Basel III includes a substantial collection of new capital rules which extend and modify capital requirements for risks which were badly captured hitherto. These rules mostly relate to aspects of counterparty credit risk.

5.7.1 CVA risk

Section 4.4.1 discussed CVA risk: we saw that during the crisis uncollateralised trades with counterparties whose credit quality declined caused CVA to increase, resulting in losses. This risk is capitalised in Basel III. Firms are required to use one of two methods[303] to determine a CVA capital charge. As usual, the more advanced method is available only to sufficiently sophisticated banks[304]. It proceeds as follows:

- The firm must calculate a market-based CVA[305].

- The sensitivity of this CVA to a change in each counterparty's credit spread must be calculated.

- These sensitivities are then put into a value at risk ('VAR') model which analyses the effect of simultaneously moving the credit spreads of every counterparty under both normal and stressed conditions.

- Some hedges to counterparty credit are also included[306]. Thus for instance if a firm has a large uncollateralised exposure to a counterparty and so buys CDS protection on that counterparty, this CDS can be included in the model.

- The capital charge is given by the sum of the normal and stressed VAR losses.

This new capital charge dramatically increases the capital required for counterparty credit risk. The size of the increase depends on the precise portfolio, but a trebling of the capital required is a reasonable estimate[307].

5.7.2 The impact of the CVA rules

The CVA rules in the broad seem sensible: CVA risk caused big losses in the crisis; that risk was not capitalised; so something had to be done. Unfortunately a more detailed scrutiny reveals a number of issues:

- The main contributors to CVA are sovereigns (most of whom refuse to post collateral), and corporate end-users. The CVA charges will feed through into higher costs for these end users without much affecting inter-dealer trading: and thus without reducing interconnectedness. The impact of CVA capital requirements on the cost of corporate risk management is sufficiently worrying that the EU is contemplating exempting many transactions from CVA capital requirements[308].

- The CVA rules will strongly incentivise the market-based form of CVA against historical CVA. This in turn will lead to most large banks hedging CVA rather than treating it as banking-book style credit extension. Given that a fundamental role of a bank is to extend credit, this incentive is odd, especially when one remembers that the risk of most counterparties' default cannot be accurately hedged[309].

- The hedging of sovereign CVA will require dealers to buy sufficient sovereign CDS that spreads will be affected. This is an unhelpful incentive (as we discussed in section 3.2.3).

- These rules are strongly procyclical since credit spread volatility, and hence capital requirements, increase in a crisis.

There is also the philosophical objection that CVA risk, by its very nature, is transient. Dealers seldom novate client trades, so they only infrequently realise losses due to CVA risk. Client default risk is separately capitalised, so the CVA capital charge is not required to cover this risk, only the risk that a counterparty's credit spread increases *without it defaulting*. CVA capital requirements are therefore protection against the risk of unrealisable changes in fair value[310].

5.7.3 Other changes

Basel III also introduced a number of other rules, qualitative requirements and modifications to the capital framework. Two of the most important (in terms of impact) are:

1. Regulatory counterparty credit risk models (discussed in section 3.6.2) must use stressed market data in calculating EPE; and

2. Higher capital requirements are imposed for credit exposures to large financial institutions[311].

Concluding Remarks

The reader may be forgiven for a degree of confusion over which regulators proposed what, which rules are in consultation and which are final, and when compliance is required. There has been, as a recently popular phrase goes, 'a tsunami of regulation', often with multiple inconsistent measures seeking to address the same objective. Supervisors have written rules to, amongst other things:

- Increase capital requirements, and require that they are met with better quality capital;
- Regulate bank funding liquidity risk;
- Develop a resolution regime for financial institutions;
- Regulate OTC markets and increase pre-trade transparency;
- Require post-trade reporting to trade repositories;
- Mandate that some OTC derivatives trades are centrally cleared, with some exemptions; and
- Require minimum margin standards and increase capital requirements for uncleared OTC derivatives.

This regulatory zeal is understandable, but its haste and lack of coordination is unfortunate, as we discuss further in chapter 10. The new rules are also striking in their coverage: there is much on OTC derivatives, despite their minor role in the crisis, and rather little on residential mortgages or real estate lending generally. Perhaps now most of the post-crisis rules are complete it would be worthwhile to make a detailed comparison of regulatory efforts with the causes of the crisis.

Notes

[242] An exception is the United States, where Basel II has, at the time of writing, not yet been implemented.

[243] See *Basel III: A global regulatory framework for more resilient banks and banking systems* (December 2010) available via http://www.bis.org/publ/bcbs189_dec2010.htm.

[244] In what follows we will skirt around a lot of the detail of Basel III, dealing mostly with what is relevant to OTC derivatives. Thus for instance we have little to say about the definition of capital, and nothing about the countercyclical and capital conservation buffers. All of these details are in the Basel III documents (op. cit. and subsequently referenced).

[245] P. Alessandri, A. Haldane, *Banking on the state*, Bank of England (November 2009) available at www.bankofengland.co.uk/publications/Documents/speeches/2009/speech409.pdf is suggestive on this point.

[246] See for instance T. Hoenig's speech *Basel III Capital: A Well-Intended Illusion* (9th April 9 2013) available at www.fdic.gov/news/news/speeches/spapr0913.html.

[247] The US regulatory agencies announced in late 2012 that Basel III would not be implemented as planned on 1st January 2013: see Board of Governors of the Federal Reserve System, *Agencies Provide Guidance on Regulatory Capital Rulemakings*, Press Release, November 9th 2012 available at www.federalreserve.gov/newsevents/press/bcreg/20121109a.htm.

[248] EBA analysis of European bank capital plans reveals that capital improvements consist of 26% new capital and reserves, 28% conversion of hybrids and issuance of convertible bonds, 16% retaining earnings and 23% RWA reductions (notably on 9% internal model changes and 10% asset reductions). See page 7 of *European bank funding and deleveraging*, BIS Quarterly Review March 2012 available at www.bis.org/publ/qtrpdf/r_qt1203a.pdf.

[249] See the *Financial Stability Review*, October 2012, available at www.imf.org/External/Pubs/FT/GFSR/2012/02/index.htm.

[250] Their credit spreads were not very volatile so their contribution to trading book VAR was low.

[251] Citigroup's 2009 annual report states that the firm's gross ABS CDO super-senior exposure was $18.9B at year end 2008. In addition, the firm had $6.9B of exposure to the monolines (mostly protection bought on pseudo-safe assets).

[252] I.e. Tier 1 capital.

[253] The PFE add-on is calculated using the Current Exposure Method. Here, netting based on regulatory rather than accounting rules is used: this ensures consistency between jurisdictions despite differing accounting rules. See paragraph 160 et seq. in the Basel III text.

[254] See the Basel Committee's *Basel III: International framework for liquidity risk measurement, standards and monitoring* (December 2010) available at www.bis.org/publ/bcbs188.pdf.

[255] Unsafe collateral here is anything which is not 0% risk weighted under the Basel II standardised approach.

[256] Specifically, the amount of non-maturity deposits and/or term deposits that 'would be expected to stay with the institution for an extended period in an idiosyncratic stress event'. Similarly short term funding which would disappear in stress cannot be counted towards the stable funding amount.

[257] A. Levels and J. Capel analyse the supply and the demand for safe assets (taking into account Basel III and other regulatory initiatives) in *Is Collateral Becoming Scarce? Evidence for the euro area*, DNB occasional studies Volume 10 No. 1 (2012) available at www.dnb.nl/binaries/DNB_OS_1001_WEB_tcm46-268455.pdf. This work also attempts to quantify model risk in their estimates.

[258] A good example is Australia. Here the RBA proposes that banks can use a secured committed liquidity facility with them to meet their LCR requirements; in essence, the central bank will take whatever assets it deems acceptable and give banks enough cash to meet their LCR requirements. See APRA's Discussion Paper *Implementing Basel III liquidity reforms in Australia* (November 2011) available at www.apra.gov.au/adi/documents/adi_dp_iblr_november_2011.pdf.

[259] Carmen Reinhart has reintroduced the term 'financial repression' to describe the process by which governments force domestic savers to finance their deficits at artificially low rates. In an article with Jacob Funk Kirkegaard, *Financial repression: Then and now*, VoxEU (26th March 2012) available at www.voxeu.org/article/financial-repression-then-and-now she includes the Basel III liquidity requirements in these repressive policies.

[260] The Governor of the Bank of England, Mervyn King, recognised this, saying in 2012 that 'In current exceptional conditions, where central banks stand ready to provide extraordinary amounts of liquidity, against a wide range of collateral, the need for banks to hold large liquid asset buffers is much diminished, and I hope regulators around the world will take note'. (Speech at the Mansion House, 14th June 2012).

[261] See W. Buiter, *The role of central banks in financial stability: how has it changed?* CEPR discussion paper No. 8780 available at www.cepr.org/pubs/dps/DP8780.asp.

[262] See the Basel Committee's *Complete set of agreed changes to the formulation of the Liquidity Coverage Ratio published in December 2010* (January 2013, available at www.bis.org/press/p130106b.pdf.

[263] See *Implementing OTC Derivatives Market Reforms* (October 2010) available at www.financialstabilityboard.org/publications/r_101025.pdf.

[264] Although this may not be the case in some equity dark pools.

[265] The figures come from an ISDA note *MiFID/MiFIR and transparency for OTC derivatives* (February 2012).

[266] The FSB paper (op. cit.) is admirably balanced here. In contrast to other areas, where it recommends action, for pre-trade transparency it opines: 'Authorities should explore the benefits and costs of requiring public price and volume transparency of all trades, including for non-standardised or non-centrally cleared products that continue to be traded over-the-counter.' It would be interesting to review this cost/benefit analysis in order to understand how the trade venue requirements in EMIR and the Dodd Frank Act are justified.

[267] The US regulatory structure gives responsibility to both the SEC and the CFTC for implementing Title VII. Both agencies are in the process of rule making; these rules are broadly similar thus far, but not identical.

[268] Variously 'regulated markets', 'multilateral trading facilities', 'organised trading facilities' and 'systematic internalizers' in the EU, and 'designated contract markets' and 'swaps execution facilities' in the US: see chapter 7 for more details.

[269] The US draft rules require that any swap that clears must trade on an exchange or a SEF, and that SEFs/DCMs can 'self certify' other products as available to trade; the precise scope of the OTC derivatives trading requirements under MiFIL is not yet clear.

[270]This is currently in article 7 of the proposed MiFIR, and part of the CFTC's SEF requirements.

[271]See the CPSS/IOSCO *Report on OTC derivatives data reporting and aggregation requirements – final report* (January 2012) available at www.bis.org/publ/cpss100.htm.

[272]Some OTC derivatives trade reporting sites are live. See for instance rtdata.dtcc.com/gtr/dashboard.do for real time trade reporting from the United States.

[273]One of the problems with trade repositories is that confidentiality provisions are sufficiently constraining that often no supervisor can see the complete picture. A central bank might for instance have access to all the trades in their currency, and all the trades made by banks they supervise, but it might well not be able to see the full network.

[274]The Federal Reserve Bank of New York Staff Report, *An Analysis of OTC Interest Rate Derivatives Transactions: Implications for Public Reporting*, No. 557 (March 2012) available at www.newyorkfed.org/research/staff_reports/sr557.pdf, and previously referenced, contains useful background here.

[275]A further description can be found in the IOSCO, *Report on Trading of OTC Derivatives* (February 2011) available at www.iosco.org/library/pubdocs/pdf/IOSCOPD345.pdf.

[276]Dealers, who have much larger and more diversified portfolios, may be less inconvenienced if, say, swap liquidity was concentrated on IMM dates.

[277]Enhanced Disclosure Task Force, *Enhancing the Risk Disclosures of Banks* (October 2012) available at www.financialstabilityboard.org/publications/r_121029.pdf.

[278]To pick an example at random, HSBC's 2011 annual report is 436 pages long, and their Basel pillar 3 disclosures stretch to an additional 62 pages.

[279]See for instance the Financial Stability Board's *Thematic Review on Risk Disclosure Practices* (March 2011) available via www.financialstabilityboard.org/list/fsb_publications/tid_74/index.htm.

[280]These, according to the FSB in 2012, are Citibank, Deutsche Bank, HSBC and JPMorgan.

[281]This comes directly from *The Leaders's statement at the Pittsburgh summit* (September 2009) available at www.treasury.gov/resource-center/international/g7=g20/Documents/pittsburgh_summit_leaders_statement_250909.pdf.

[282]Paul Tucker, Deputy Governor Financial Stability at the Bank of England, gave his view on their importance this way: '... it is an understatement that it would be a disaster if a clearing house failed. Commentators have, indeed, been emphasising that CCPs are becoming systemic. To my own way of thinking, they have already been systemic for the markets they clear for a very long time.' (*Clearing houses as system risk managers*, Speech at the launch of the DTCC-CSFI Post Trade Fellowship

Launch, 1st June 2011, available at www.bankofengland.co.uk/publications/speeches/2011/speech501.pdf.)

[283] The designation is a US regulatory construct, and the two OTC derivatives CCP 'SIFMUs' at the time of writing are ICE and the CME. See www.treasury.gov/initiatives/fsoc/designations/Pages/default.aspx.

[284] This is a joint document from the Basel Committee and IOSCO, *Margin requirements for non-centrally-cleared derivatives* (July 2012) available at www.bis.org/publ/bcbs226.pdf, and presumably as such if implemented it would apply to both banks and broker/dealers.

[285] See for instance the various comment letters at www.bis.org/publ/bcbs226/comments.htm.

[286] See for instance the Office of the Comptroller of the Currency's *Unfunded Mandates Reform Act Impact Analysis for Swaps Margin and Capital Rule*, (15th April 2011) which looks at IM requirements for both cleared and bilateral trades.

[287] Rules ensuring a penal capital treatment when one financial institution holds material amounts of the capital of another, and restricting the total amount of exposure that a financial institution may have to another are particularly important here.

[288] See the New York FED, *Update on Tri-Party Repo Infrastructure Reform*, 18th July 2012, available at www.newyorkfed.org/newsevents/statements/2012/0718_2012.html.

[289] This has proved controversial, with some SEC Commissioners rejecting proposals from the Financial Stability Oversight Council. The current FSOC proposals are detailed in the press release *Financial Stability Oversight Council Releases Proposed Recommendations for Money Market Mutual Fund Reform*, 13th November 2012, available at www.treasury.gov/press-center/press-releases/Pages/tg1764.aspx.

[290] For more on central bank interventions post crisis see M. Joyce, *Quantitative easing and other unconventional monetary policies*, Bank of England Quarterly Bulletin Q1 2012 available at www.bankofengland.co.uk/publications/Documents/quarterlybulletin/qb120104.pdf or C. Borio, *Central banking post-crisis: What compass for uncharted waters?* BIS Working Paper No. 353 (September 2011) available at www.bis.org/publ/work353.pdf.

[291] This is in King's speech *Finance: A Return for Risk*, Working Compass of International Banks (17th March 2009).

[292] To pick one example, Goldman Sachs' SEC filings list over one hundred 'significant' subsidiaries as at the end of 2011 (see www.sec.gov/Archives/edgar/data/886982/000119312512085822/d276319dex211.htm).

[293] See the Financial Stability Board, *Key Attributes of Effective Resolution Regimes for Financial Institutions* (October 2011) available at www.financialstabilityboard.org/publications/r_111104cc.pdf.

[294] A novel class of capital instruments, contingent convertible bonds or 'Cocos', have been created for this purpose. CoCos convert into equity on resolution.

[295] There may also in some instances be the allocation of new equity in this process, so a senior debt holder who was owed $100 before resolution could conceivably find

themselves with a claim of $80 on a newly created institution ('the good bank'), and equity in the bad bank.

[296]B. Attinger's ECB Legal Working Paper, *Crisis Management and Bank Resolution*, No. 13 (December 2011) discusses the alternatives in more detail.

[297]For instance, section 165(d) of the Dodd Frank Act requires certain large bank holding companies and non-bank financial institutions develop resolution plans. The determination of who must do this will be made by the Financial Stability Oversight Council.

[298]A more comprehensive discussion of requirements can be found in, for instance, the FSA's *RRP Information Pack* available at www.fsa.gov.uk/pubs/discussion/fs12-01-info-pack.pdf.

[299]This is in Dudley's speech, *Solving the Too Big to Fail Problem*, 15th November 2012 available at www.newyorkfed.org/newsevents/speeches/2012/dud121115.html.

[300]It even seems to be difficult for two agencies in the same jurisdiction to work well together. The US House Staff Report on MF Global (November 2012) summarises a recent example of this as follows: 'The SEC and the CFTC failed to share critical information about MF Global with one another, leaving each regulator with an incomplete understanding of the company's financial health'. Given that many firms have extensive cross-jurisdictional derivatives portfolios, this failure to co-ordinate raises serious questions about how effective the resolution of a failing global bank will be.

[301]The FSB recommends two days.

[302]See Annex 8 to the Financial Stability Board's Consultative Document *Effective Resolution of Systemically Important Financial Institutions* (19th July 2011) available at www.financialstabilityboard.org/publications/r_110719.pdf for more of the thinking here. There is also the delicate issue that derivatives claims are *pari passu* with senior debt, so if a bank's senior debt holders are to be bailed in, the derivatives counterparties should be too. It is not however entirely clear how to do that while derivative contracts are still live.

[303]There is some variation within the advanced method so that, for instance, banks using the so-called 'shortcut' method are required to assume a constant EE profile in their CVA capital calculation.

[304]Specifically in order to use the advanced approach banks must have approval to use IMM models for CCR and approval to use a VAR model for specific risk.

[305]This CVA uses regulatory expected exposure (which may differ from the firm's internal estimate of EE).

[306]Single name CDS and contingent CDS are the only fully eligible hedges. Index CDS can be included under the assumption that they are only 50% effective unless a firm can convince its supervisor that it can capture the index/single name basis correctly.

[307]The Basel Committee's quantitative impact study on Basel III (available at www.bis.org/publ/bcbs186.pdf) makes it rather hard to estimate this number: they report that

the CVA change increases *total* credit risk RWAs by 11% for the largest banks, but this can only be translated into the impact on CCR capital requirements if you know the prior ratio of CCR capital to total credit risk capital. That in turn is disclosed neither by the Basel Committee nor by all banks. However if we take HSBC – which *does* disclose the breakdown of its regulatory capital in detail – as typical, then the ratio of CCR capital to total capital is 5%, meaning that if the CVA charge causes an increase of 11% in total credit risk capital, then the CVA charge is roughly double the bilateral capital charge, and total CCR capital increases by a factor of roughly three due to the Basel III CVA rules.

[308] At the time of writing, an end-user exemption from CVA capital charges is in the EU Parliament's text of CRD IV, the directive implementing Basel III in the EU. The European Commission is opposed to this exemption, so the final European rule will be the subject of negotiation between the Commission, the Parliament, and the Council of Ministers.

[309] As we mentioned in note 115, one reasonable estimate is that single name CDS are available on less than 10% of a typical dealer's counterparties.

[310] The validity of this objection to the Basel III CVA requirement depends on the definition of risk. If risk is defined as earnings volatility, then CVA risk creates earnings volatility and so it should be capitalised. If risk is defined as the potential for a realised loss, then CVA 'risk' is not a true risk and hence does not need to be supported by capital. I incline towards the former rather than the latter position, but I can appreciate both perspectives. Certainly if CVA changes flowed through the equity account rather than the P/L then the rationale for a capital charge would be weaker.

[311] This is implemented by increasing the correlation parameter in the Basel II IRB formula for these exposures.

6

OTC Derivatives Central Clearing

Mr Podsnap settled that whatever he put behind him
he put out of existence.
There was a dignified conclusiveness–
not to add a grand convenience–
in this way of getting rid of disagreeables
Charles Dickens

Introduction

We have seen in the last chapter how central clearing was mandated by the G20 after the Credit Crisis. In this chapter we look at what central clearing is and how it is practised[312].

We begin with a discussion of central counterparties. CCPs concentrate counterparty credit risk and so they need to protect themselves. We examine these protections, including CCP membership rules and margin. The latter is particularly important as it is the first line of defence that a CCP has against counterparty non-performance. We look at some of the later lines of defence, too, and why they are needed.

The risk that a CCP takes on depends on the transactions it clears. If all else is equal, highly liquid transactions are less risky than illiquid ones, as they can be closed out more quickly. Consideration of these issues suggests that not all OTC derivatives are clearable. We examine what features of a product are required for clearing, and estimate the fraction of OTC trades which are clearable.

Finally we turn to end users. Few if any of these will want to deal with CCPs directly, so they will be clients of parties that do. We set out the models of client clearing, and examine the choices available in protecting client margin.

6.1 OTC Derivatives Central Counterparties

The historical development of central clearing is insightful. As a Governor of the Federal Reserve System, Randall Kroszner explains[313]:

> *[CCPs] emerged gradually and slowly as a result of experience and experimentation.*

Kroszner sets out how, in the late nineteenth century the Chicago Board of Trade (a derivatives exchange) adopted a resolution stipulating that any member whose solvency was questioned must open its financial accounts to inspection. Soon it introduced margin requirements for exchange traded contracts, with tight time limits of how quickly a call had to be met. The exchange created what we would now call a 'central margin custodian': a body to calculate net margin requirements and settle contracts. Counterparty credit exposure above margin remained a bilateral matter. It was only in 1925 that a true CCP was created to act as a counterparty to all exchange-traded contracts in addition to its other functions.

The organisation of this early CCP (or 'clearing house') set the pattern for subsequent developments. It offered four levels of protection:

1. The CCP has certain membership standards for parties it will deal with, its 'clearing members' ('CM's). A rule book is published setting out how business is to be conducted. CMs must abide by these rules.

2. The CCP charges IM and VM to the CMs. In the event of clearing member default, the CCP takes responsibility for closing out the defaulter's trades. The margin posted at the CCP by the defaulter is available to meet the costs of this close out.

3. The CCP also requires its clearing members to provide an additional amount, their 'default fund' (or 'DF') contribution. If the losses of a close out exceeds the defaulter's margin, then the deficiency is charged first against their DF contribution, then if required against the whole fund. As such, each CM's obligations to the CCP are a joint liability of all CMs.

4. If the losses were so severe as to deplete the default fund then the CMs could be required to make additional contributions to the DF. This 'capital call' arrangement means that default funds can be topped up if there are multiple costly CM defaults during a short period of time.

The graduation of these arrangements is important. First, only admit parties which pass a membership test. Next, require them to support their own risk to some extent, so the first dollars of loss are borne by the defaulter. Then, because requiring everyone to completely support their risk individually is inefficient, mutualise losses at the next level. Finally, have a mechanism to recapitalise the CCP if the funds available for mutual co-insurance prove inadequate for the task. In the remainder of this section we discuss each of these features in more detail.

6.1.1 Clearing Membership

The need to close out clearing member portfolios if they default motivates CCP participation requirements. Most CCPs do not want members to fail too often, and so they require a certain level of financial resources for clearing members. Other requirements typically include:

* The ability to connect with the CCP's systems to process trades, move margin, and so on;

* Proven operational and trading experience and the willingness to contribute to the default management process;

* Willingness to participate in regular 'fire drills' to validate clearing member readiness.

6.1.2 CCP margin practices

CCPs have all of the counterparty credit risk of the trades that they clear, so a large CCP is exposed to a great deal of risk. It protects itself in a variety of ways. Margin is the most important of these. CCPs require clearing members to post both initial and variation margin. Margin is typically recalculated daily[314], there is no threshold, and clearing members often have a rather short period – perhaps hours – to meet a margin call.

The intent to centrally clear an OTC derivative is typically agreed between two parties during trade negotiations. The trade is created on a bilateral basis and submitted to the CCP for clearing. Once accepted by the CCP, both parties novate the trade to the clearing house. The CCP is therefore balanced on a market risk basis since it has both sides of the trade.

The fact that the CCP is balanced means that any VM movements simply flow through the CCP: whenever one party loses, and hence has to post more VM to the clearing house, there is a corresponding gainer, who receives it[315]. Therefore across the cleared system, CCP variation margin calls create no net change in liquidity[316].

CCPs also take initial margin. They estimate the amount each clearing member's portfolio might move between default and close out, and call for the resulting amount. Methodologies vary from CCP to CCP, but the general intent is clear: IM should protect a CCP against possible losses that might occur during close out to a high degree of confidence[317].

6.1.3 The default fund

Margin is taken on a counterparty-by-counterparty basis[318]. It would be highly inefficient for each counterparty to separately provide sufficient margin to protect the CCP against all close out losses[319]. Therefore the CCP takes a layer of mutualized capital: funds are provided by each clearing member, and these are available to absorb losses above IM if required. A given CM's required contribution to the default fund is estimated based on the risk of the portfolio it clears at the CCP, so CMs which bring more risk will have larger DF contributions.

Default fund amounts are typically much smaller than initial margin[320]. This reflects the fact that the default fund is shared: it is available to absorb excess losses, no matter from whom[321].

6.1.4 Capital calls

A costly default or series of defaults can potentially deplete the default fund to the point that it is no longer large enough to provide sufficient protection to the CCP. Therefore CCPs typically retain the right to call for additional default fund amounts. Sometimes this right is limited, for instance to the original default fund amount (so that a clearing member's total liability is twice the funded amount); in other instances, there is no cap[322].

It would be helpful if all OTC derivatives CCPs publicly disclosed both the current level of their financial resources and the level they estimate that they need, so that clearing members and other interested parties could assess the circumstances under which a capital call could take place.

6.1.5 CCP equity

The totality of CCP margin, default fund and other monies available to meet losses due to counterparty non-performance are known as the CCP's 'financial resources'. CCPs have equity, so this is part of their financial resources. Equity is important not least because CCPs can suffer losses for reasons other than non-performance, such as operational risk. Typically margin and default fund are only available to absorb default-related losses, so CCP equity is a vital protection against such problems.

The order in which different elements of a CCP's financial resources are accessed are known as the CCP's 'default waterfall'. Typically some CCP equity is at risk before the default fund and some after it, so the pattern of figure 6.1 is representative, although more elaborate arrangements are possible[323]. Loss mutualisation happens at level 5., with the defaulter or the CCP paying before that.

Level	Form of Protection
7.	The rest of CCP equity
6.	Capital calls on non-defaulting CMs
5.	Non-defaulting CM's default fund contributions
4.	Fixed amount of CCP equity
3.	Defaulter's default fund contribution
2.	Defaulter's initial margin
1.	Defaulter's variation margin

Figure 6.1: A typical CCP waterfall

Some CCPs clear more than one asset class. Members of such CCPs may not wish to be at risk from products that they do not participate in at all, so the waterfall is sometimes split into asset class-specific structures: the CDS waterfall, the IRS waterfall, and so on.

6.2 Clearing and Clearing Houses

It is obvious that the safety of clearing arrangements depends on CCPs being able to fulfil their functions to the maturity of the longest cleared contract. In order to gain some insight into the issues here, we start this section by looking at the historical clearing house failures. The risk profile of OTC derivatives CCPs is then discussed. This leads to the idea of a clearable product, i.e. one which a CCP can aspire to clear without running too much risk. The section ends with an extension of these ideas to mandatory clearing: when is it prudent not just to permit the clearing of a product, but also to require it?

6.2.1 Exchange-traded derivatives CCP failures

Many early CCPs grew up in securities and exchange-traded derivatives markets[324]. Securities CCPs primarily take settlement risk: they are only exposed to the credit of their counterparties for a short period, at most a few days. The vast preponderance of liquidity in the futures and exchange-traded options market is concentrated in short-dated contracts, so the maturity profile of the credit risk of exchange-traded derivatives CCPs typically peaks after a few weeks, and declines dramatically after a few months. Moreover, exchange traded contracts tend either to be very successful and hence highly liquid, or fairly illiquid; there is little middle ground. This means that exposures are highly concentrated in liquid contracts for these 'ET' CCPs.

These facts simplify the risk management problem for ET CCPs hugely. All the same, even exchange-traded derivatives clearing has risk. A number of CCPs clearing these markets have failed[325], prominently:

1. The Caisse de Liquidation, a French CCP, failed in 1974 after a period of high price volatility in the sugar market caused the Nataf Trading House, one of its clearing members, distress. Nataf had a large position in the market and could not meet margin calls, endangering the clearing house and causing the closure of the market.

2. The Kuala Lumpur Commodity Clearing House failed after only three years of operation, in 1983. Again, an inadequately margined large position at a clearing member combined with a large price move was to blame.

3. The final modern CCP failure occurred during the 1997 Hong Kong crisis. The futures market was closed for four days during the height of the crisis, and equities reopened heavily down. Margin calls were not met, and an emergency recapitalisation had to be effected to ensure that the Hong Kong Futures Exchange Clearing Corporation did not fail as a result.

The classic 'toxic' mixture for an ET derivatives CCP is market volatility, large positions, and inadequate margining. This cocktail has been mixed more than once because there is a great temptation for CCPs to reduce margin: lower margin encourages more trading, and hence more fees for the clearing house. Moreover one obvious way for two CCPs clearing the same or substantially similar markets to compete is on margin. There has historically been no internationally agreed standard for minimum clearing house margin, so it hardly a surprise that several clearing houses have failed due to inadequate margining. It also suggests that additional margin should be required once a CM's position becomes large or concentrated, as this situation poses the most risk to the CCP.

6.2.2 How OTC derivatives CCPs differ from other clearing houses

OTC derivatives are typically much longer maturity than exchange traded derivatives: thirty year interest rate or ten year credit default swaps are not uncommon. Therefore an OTC derivatives CCP ('OTC CCP') will take credit exposure for much longer periods than an ET CCP.

Another feature of OTC derivatives is the wide range of products traded. As we discussed in section 5.3.2, many of these are liquid in the sense that an end-user can get a quote on them in most market conditions, but not in the sense that there are market makers standing ready to provide liquidity come what may. OTC volumes are not concentrated in highly liquid products as they are in futures markets. This means that in stressed conditions closing out a large OTC derivatives portfolio may take some days. An OTC CCP therefore has to use a longer margin period of risk than is applicable to a CCP clearing only (or very largely) liquid futures[326].

Note too that the clearing members of a successful OTC CCP are likely to be systemically important institutions. The consequences of a special purpose CCP serving a single commodity market failing may be limited: this will not be true for a leading CDS or interest rate derivatives CCP. Not only are the risks bigger for OTC CCPs, the stakes are higher too. Moreover, these CCPs have had their growth artificially spurred by regulation. Instead of Kroszner's gradual development as a result of experience and experimentation, regulators have demanded a dramatic increase in the size and risk of OTC CCPs.

6.2.3 Clearable instruments

A key decision that an OTC CCP faces is what to clear. There are a number of requirements that a transaction must meet in order for it to be prudently clearable[327]:

- It has to have standard legal and economic terms, and a well-understood process to capture, confirm and process all trade details. The process should be automated as far as possible.

- There needs to be sufficient liquidity in the product that the CCP can reliably estimate VM requirements every day.

- The CCP must have a robust methodology for determining IM and DF on the product. Typically this implies not just a generally agreed risk methodology, but also that the product does not display substantial specific wrong-way risk[328]. It is also desirable that it does not jump substantially in value, as this can cause either under-margining or a prohibitively high level of margin.

• Product liquidity matters most where it is likely to be most problematic, in the difficult conditions after a clearing member default. It is here that a CCP will be closing out the defaulter's portfolio, so they need to be sure that liquidity will be present during this type of stress.

These criteria suggest that few if any OTC equity or commodity options should be cleared. This is because liquidity in options markets is typically concentrated around the at-the-money strike, and what this strike is moves. Thus a strike which may be liquid when an option is traded often becomes less so over time[329]. The situation is rather better for interest rate and related swaps. One estimate of which of these may potentially be clearable is given in figure 6.2[330]. This suggests that slightly more than half of all interest rate swaps are clearable.

Product	Sub-product	Fraction of total volume	Fraction clearing eligible
Single-currency swap	Fixed vs. float G4	57	70-80
	Fixed vs. float Other	15	30-40
	Float vs. float G4	3.3	20-30
	Float vs. float Other	0.5	10-20
OIS	G4	1.1	50-60
	Other	0.5	0-10
Cross-currency swap	Fixed vs. float	1.6	10-20
	Fixed vs. fixed	0.4	0-10
	Fixed vs. fixed	2.3	0-10
Inflation swap		1.2	0-10

Figure 6.2: An estimate of the proportion of OTC interest rate swaps which are clearable

Relatively few credit derivatives products are liquid. Thus, single name CDS on the most liquid few hundred names[331], excluding clearing members[332], and on some indices are clearable. It is notable that no CCP has suggested clearing CDS on ABS, simply because they meet few of the criteria to be clearable. The trades that brought AIG down, then, are not clearable[333].

The future illiquidity of far from the money options can be predicted. For some other OTC derivatives, though, the situation is less clear. They may be liquid for some years, but then be rendered illiquid, for instance by changes in the market[334]. Thus OTC derivatives CCPs may need to respond to the problem of falling liquidity for an already cleared class of product. Should these products be 'decleared' (i.e. revert back to bilateral trades); should initial margin be increased to reflect the longer MPOR; or should some other approach be taken?

6.2.4 The scope of mandatory clearing

Post-crisis regulatory reforms require that 'standardised OTC derivative contracts' with certain counterparties be cleared, as we discussed in section 5.5. The precise definitions of what must be cleared are not known at the time of writing, but it seems highly likely that only products which are clearable will have to be cleared. That is, the authorities will probably not ban trading by requiring clearing when it is not possible. Beyond this, the boundary is uncertain. It would be prudent to only mandate clearing of a product once multiple CCPs were available to clear it[335], so that the market would not be imperilled should a CCP withdraw from a product class or fail, but there is no guarantee of this.

The reader may wonder why the clearing mandate is so wide. It was not always thus: the original G-20 pronouncement only required clearing of all standardised *credit* derivatives. This made some sense[336], given the importance of credit instruments in the crisis. Why the mandate was so dramatically broadened remains shrouded in mystery[337].

The case of OTC FX derivatives gives rise to further questions about the rules mandating clearing. The US has exempted FX swaps and forwards[338], citing the fact that these derivatives are subject to a 'strong, comprehensive oversight framework'. That may well be, but it is also the case that the same could be argued of the interest rate swaps market.

6.3 Organisational and Legal Issues

We turn to the rules for dealing with a CCP. Different jurisdictions have different requirements, but many require that clearing members are organised as a certain kind of legal entity. Thus for instance clearing members of a US CCP must be FCMs[339]. We look at these constraints, and some additional ones imposed thanks to requirements about where clearing must take place.

This naturally leads to the question of the legal framework around cleared transactions: the documentation used, and the rights of set-off which are available. We end with the question of how many CCPs are optimal, and how many will be required to meet regulatory requirements.

6.3.1 Facing a CCP

The Dodd Frank Act requires that once the detailed rules are in force, eligible[340] clearable swaps must be cleared unless one of the parties to them is an exempt end-user. A party that has to clear in the US framework has two choices: it can either be an FCM[341], or it can sign an agreement with an FCM that can clear through a US CCP, and then use this FCM to process its transaction.

The situation in the EU is similar but not identical[342]. EMIR will apply to any entity established in the EU[343]. It will require eligible OTC derivatives[344] between covered counterparties[345] are cleared at a CCP which has been registered in the EU. If the party subject to the clearing mandate is not a member of such a CCP, it must use a clearing member who is.

These requirements, and similar ones in other jurisdictions, mean that OTC derivatives subject to mandatory clearing often have to be cleared at a CCP located in a particular jurisdiction. You cannot clear anywhere, in other words. Moreover, there are often restrictions on the nature of the clearing members: they may for instance have to be located in a particular country and registered as a particular type of entity.

6.3.2 Netting and standardisation of cleared positions

It is just as important for a CCP to establish the effectiveness of its netting as for any other counterparty. Therefore a CCP needs the legal framework of a master netting agreement, netting opinions, and so on. Typically CCPs use a modified version of the ISDA bilateral documentation, so this reduces the amount of work they have to do to establish a comparable degree of legal certainty to the bilateral market. However, there remains a degree of risk here due to the lack of bankruptcy case law regarding some clearing documentation.

A bigger issue arises in contract standardisation. The bilateral market has developed global standards for bilateral OTC derivatives. There is, for instance, a single mechanism for determining if a credit event has occurred on a credit derivative[346]. There is a risk that different CCPs will develop different approaches here, either from each other or from the bilateral market. If this happened it would mean that there was a substantial unhedgeable basis risk between two otherwise identical contracts cleared on different CCPs, or between a bilateral contract and the same contract cleared at a CCP. There is no obvious mechanism for coordinating CCPs' actions here.

6.3.3   Competition vs. netting

The greatest netting benefit from central clearing obviously comes from the use of a single CCP[347]. This is not the situation we will see. Instead:

- There will be multiple CCPs due to requirements that derivatives are cleared in particular jurisdictions.

- CCPs have specialised in serving specific assets classes so that, for instance, ICE[348] is a leading credit derivatives clearer, while LCH has a dominant position in interest rate derivatives.

- There are competing CCPs within an asset class and jurisdiction.

This means that the simple picture of figure 5.2 is not accurate. Instead we will see an architecture more like figure 6.3.

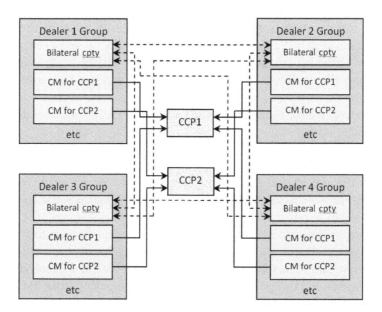

Figure 6.3: Conceptual schematic showing four financial institutions trading OTC derivatives some of which are bilateral, some cleared at one CCP, and some at another. Cleared trades are shown using solid lines; bilateral as dashed ones.

This architecture means the netting benefit of clearing is lower than it would be with a single global CCP (or indeed one CCP per asset class), and thus more collateral will be required.

The number of new and proposed OTC derivatives CCPs indicate that this problem could be significant. At the time of writing there are at least 30 new entrants to clearing, in addition to the established players CME, Eurex, ICE and LCH. It is likely that many CCPs will not be successful, due to the costs of competition: a successful CCP will have large existing portfolios with clearing members, and hence new trades will be added to already diversified portfolios. In contrast a new CCP will have no such benefits to offer[349], and thus even if its IM calculation is less prudent than the incumbent's, actual margin levels will be higher, at least in the start-up phase. CCPs are in this sense a natural monopoly[350].

There is one more issue which mitigates against dominant CCPs: regulation. Specifically, some central banks may not wish to see global CCPs develop, as such a CCP might require substantial multi-currency funding during stress. Central banks have already committed to providing liquidity to banks in such conditions; some of them are less sanguine about the desirability of being seen to provide liquidity to the global derivatives system[351]. Lending to an international CCP using central bank money would advantage its clearing members, many of whom would not be under the central banks' jurisdiction: not lending to it would risk a catastrophic collapse. The desire to avoid this Hobbesian choice provides some incentive for central banks to prefer local CCPs for local banks.

6.3.4 Back-loading

CCPs provide more netting benefits the more trades they clear. Therefore if the net impact of clearing is to reduce counterparty credit risk (something we discuss further in section 8.5), it makes sense to clear as many trades as possible. This naturally leads to 'back-loading', the process of taking previously executed bilateral trades, loading them into a suitable electronic platform and clearing them. This is possible if both parties agree to it: since the trades move out from the bilateral CSA into clearing documentation (and potentially increases one or both parties' IM and DF contributions), the process must be a joint one[352].

6.4 Client Clearing

Many OTC derivatives participants either cannot meet the requirements to be a clearing member or do not want to be one (not least because of the costs involved and the contingent liabilities that must be taken on). This section is about how these 'clients' access clearing and how the process works.

6.4.1   The principal to principal model

The typical paradigm used for client clearing outside the US is known as the 'principal to principal model'. Here the client faces the clearing member as principal and the CM in turn faces the CCP as principal.

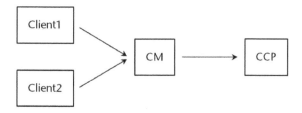

Figure 6.4: Schematic of the principal to principal model of client clearing

There are identical trades on either side of the CM, and no direct relationship between the CCP and the client (although in practice many of the terms of the client to CM trade will be determined by the rules that the CCP imposes for the CM to CCP trade[353]). Figure 6.4 depicts the situation.

When a client executes a trade, its dealer typically takes the other side of it. Once this trade is cleared, the dealer (or one of its affiliates) therefore acts both as clearing member, and as executing broker ('EB') for the trade. Thus client clearing in the principal to principal model is perhaps better visualised as in figure 6.5.

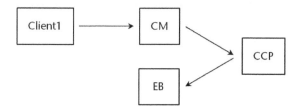

Figure 6.5: Schematic of the principal to principal model of client clearing including an executing broker

6.4.2   The agency model

The US uses a different paradigm known as the 'agency model'. Here the CM (which is an FCM in this setting) acts as agent for the client, introducing them to the CCP[354]. The CM also guarantees the client's performance to the CCP, so the CM is exposed to the credit of the client just as it is in the principal to principal model. Both models, then, involve credit risk management of client exposures by the clearing member.

6.4.3 Portability

A key feature of central clearing should be that cleared trades have standard terms. Margin, too, is determined by the CCP. Therefore any client's portfolio should be easily understandable and have a readily determined amount of margin. This means that in principle a client could move from one clearing member to another. This process is known as 'porting'. Figure 6.6 illustrates Client2 porting.

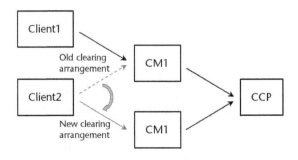

Figure 6.6: Schematic of client porting

6.4.4 Client margin and segregation

All market participants who submit trades for clearing will have margin requirements. The CCP wishes to ensure that it has enough margin for the party it is exposed to: the clearing member. Therefore it will call for margin based on its exposure. The clearing member, in turn, will want to margin each client, as it is exposed to each of them. However, different clients of the same clearing member will likely diversify each other. This gives rise to an opportunity whereby the CM can perhaps call for more margin from the clients than it needs to post on to the CCP. We begin by looking at two situations where client margin does not need to be fully segregated and so CMs can partially reuse client margin:

1. In an 'unsegregated model', the CCP margins the CM on the basis of the total portfolio the CM presents for clearing. Client trades are netted with the CM's own (proprietary or 'house') trades. This has the advantage that margin amounts are lower, and hence

there is less liquidity drain from clearing, but the disadvantage that there is no single account that contains the totality of a single client's margin (and nothing else). This makes portability more difficult, and clients are exposed to the risk that if the clearing member defaults, their margin may be used to cover the costs of closing out the clearing member's portfolio.

2. One way of preventing client exposure to clearing member default is to segregate the clearing member's house margin from that of its clients. The CCP separately margins the house and client accounts. This is known as 'omnibus' segregation, as all the clients' margin resides in one account. It has the advantage that the total amount of client margin is low, thanks to diversification between clients, but the disadvantage that clients are exposed to each other if their clearing member defaults[355]. This model is sometimes known as 'futures style', as it corresponds to the level of segregation for futures clients in the United States.

The alternative is a situation where client margin cannot be used by the clearing member. In 'full segregation' each client's margin is kept in a separate account at the CCP. A variant on full segregation is the 'legally segregated but operationally co-mingled' or 'LSOC' model. Here customers' margin is held in an omnibus account, but the CCP records which amounts are due to each client. The CCP can only access collateral attributed to the defaulting customer up to the value of the margin they have posted[356]; it cannot use margin attributed to other clients. In LSOC, then, clients face lower 'fellow client' risk than in less segregated models. LSOC is important because it is the segregation model mandated for OTC derivatives clearing in the United States[357].

Full segregation and LSOC assist portability in that the client can clearly identify the monies which represent their margin, and these can be moved to a new clearing member. However, a client would typically want to port due to concerns about or the actuality of default of its clearing member. In this situation it would need to have arrangements with the receiving clearing member already, as it is unlikely that a clearing member would accept a client (and their credit risk) without due diligence and without extensively negotiated documentation.

The practical implication of this is that clients who think that they might ever wish to port need to have arrangements with at least two clearing members. The position of 'backup' clearing member available to receive a porting client is not clearly an attractive one, as it involves contingent credit risk with no compensating return. This in turn means that clients will be encouraged to split their business between two or more clearing members, as no one will agree to be the backup. Then, at least, clients can port their business to the surviving CM(s) if one fails[358]. The resulting split netting sets are neither in the clients' nor the clearing members' best interests, but they seem to be a necessary price for potential portability.

6.4.5 *Financial architecture with client clearing*

Once we add clients to the picture, figure 6.3 becomes more complicated. In general clients will have some bilateral trades, some that are cleared at one CCP, some at another, and so on. Moreover they will likely face different legal entities for clearing at different CCPs. Figure 6.7 illustrates the situation.

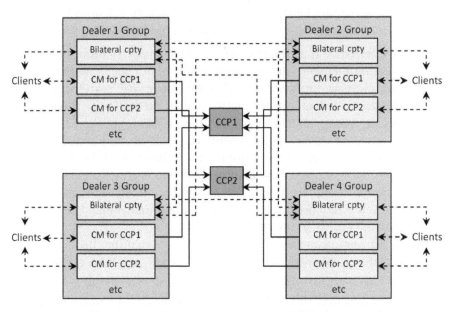

Figure 6.7: Conceptual schematic adding client clearing to our previous illustration of the architecture of OTC derivatives. As before, cleared trades are shown using solid lines; bilateral as dashed ones.

This only involves four dealers, two clearing houses and generic 'clients'. Still, it is noticeably more complex and more ridden with interconnections than the picture depicting the pre-reform OTC derivatives market (figure 1.9).

6.4.6 Indirect clearing

Smaller or more regional banks may not wish to become clearing members of global CCPs (something we discuss further in section 8.5.5). Instead, they may wish to access a clearing member as a client, but they may also have clients of their own. These clients-of-clients are known as 'indirect clients'[359]. Figure 6.8 illustrates the situation.

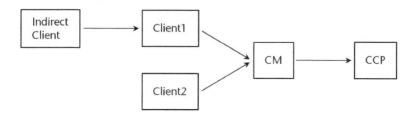

Figure 6.8: Schematic of indirect client clearing

One of the advantages of the agency model is that issues like this do not arise: there, CMs introduce and guarantee their clients to the CCP, but they do not intermediate them.

6.4.7 Interoperability

'Interoperability' is an arrangement whereby participants of one CCP can deal with another. It has been implemented for securities clearing houses, as it has numerous advantages, including lower costs (both in terms of CCP membership and IT costs for developing links to multiple CCPs[360]). In the OTC derivatives context, each clearing member would face their own CCP, and there would be a trade between the two CCPs. Each CCP guarantees both legs of the trade, so each guarantees the other to their local clearing member[361], as figure 6.9 depicts.

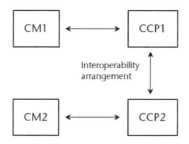

Figure 6.9: Schematic of CCP interoperability

Interoperability is more problematic for OTC derivatives CCPs, as it involves the two CCPs taking long term credit exposure to the other. CCPs could cross post margin, each acting as a client of the other; but this places CCPs in the unfamiliar position of posting, rather than being posted, IM[362]. Moreover interoperability can introduce operational and legal risks, both for the two clearing houses and for their clients and clearing members. This is especially true if the two CCPs are in different jurisdictions (which is typically when interoperability would be most useful). It is unclear, given these difficulties, if interoperability will be practical for OTC derivatives clearing houses.

6.4.8 Collateral transformation

Some clients will find it difficult to post margin as required by the CCP. Either they do not have sufficient cash to meet possible margin calls, or they cannot transfer funds fast enough to meet the clearing houses' standards, or both.

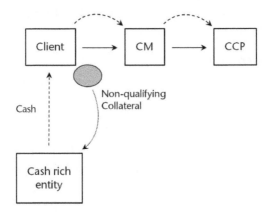

Figure 6.10: An illustration of collateral transformation

The solution to this problem is a process known as 'collateral transformation'. The client finds a party who has cash, and who is willing to let them borrow it for margin posting purposes while taking assets which are not acceptable at the CCP as collateral. This party might be their clearing member or it may be a third party. The cash provider usually mitigates its risk by demanding that the client over-collateralises its exposure: the value of the collateral required from the client is higher than cash provided. Figure 6.10 illustrates the general process.

It is important to note that collateral transformation is an example of one of the general functions of a bank: that of liquefying illiquid assets[363]. Therefore there is nothing inherently troubling in this process. It does, though, increase interconnectedness thanks to the transformation trade.

6.5 Margin and Default Management for Cleared OTC Derivatives Portfolios

The operation of CCPs is examined in more detail next. In particular, we look at margin levels; how margin is held; and at CCP default management procedures. The analysis of margin requirements for cleared portfolios leads to a discussion of the systemic consequences of CCP margin policies.

6.5.1 CCP collateral policies

CCPs take both IM and VM (as we discussed earlier in the chapter). VM flows through the CCP from the out-of-the-money to the in-the-money party, while IM is held against close out risk. There are various facets to this:

- The CCP will have its own model to calculate the required IM on a portfolio basis;

- This might for instance be a value-at-risk model producing a 99% loss for a holding period corresponding to the margin period of risk;

- The portfolio which is margined depends on the segregation style. For instance in omnibus segregation, the IM for a given clearing member will be the sum of the model estimates for the house and client accounts;

- Margin is called on at least a daily basis, or even (for some CCPs) at multiple points during the day;

- VM must typically be provided in cash[364]. Often IM can be posted in other forms, usually restricted to high quality liquid assets such as certain government bonds. The CCP will impose haircuts on non-cash collateral.

The requirement that VM is only posted in cash simplifies operational flows and valuation for CCPs[365]. It does however place a liquidity burden on margin posters.

6.5.2 Collateral ownership

A successful CCP will take a great deal of collateral. VM will pass through, but IM may accumulate at the CCP. What a CCP can do with these funds, and the risks that arise in that process, are key to both the risk and profitability of CCPs. As with bilateral transactions, there are two broad possibilities: title transfer or security interest. However because client margin can now reside at both the CCP and the clearing member, the situation is slightly more complicated. All of the following situations can occur:

1. All client margin may be the property of the clearing member;

2. Some client margin may be the property of the clearing member, and some the property of the CCP;

3. All client margin may be the property of the CCP; or

4. Client margin may reside at a third party custodian, with pledges granted to the clearing member and/or the CCP.

It will come as little surprise that CCPs usually prefer to own margin: having tens of billions of dollars to invest is more likely to lead to high earnings than not having those funds[366]. This means that a CCP typically has 'investment risk'. Not only might it lose money on invested margin[367], but it also runs liquidity risk in that if positions are terminated necessitating return of IM, the CCP may have to liquidate its investments to raise those funds.

It is not at all clear what we would want a CCP to do with the IM that it owns. Depositing it at a bank clearly leads to a substantial risk, especially if that bank is also a clearing member (or an affiliate of one). Government bonds may (or may not) be attractive from a credit risk perspective, but having CCPs compete for scarce safe assets is not necessarily helpful. The ideal situation would perhaps be for CCPs to deposit much of these funds with central banks, then invest the rest in a diversified portfolio of non-financial high quality liquid debt.

Some risks are reduced if CCPs do not own margin, but rather it is held at a third party custodian with a charge granted to the clearing house[368]. This reduces investment risk and users' exposure to the CCP without compromising clearing house safety.

6.5.3 CCP default management

When a clearing member defaults, the CCP becomes unbalanced. It has one side of the defaulter's trades but not the other. It therefore needs to replace these trades just as a bilateral counterparty would. CCPs typically retain considerable discretion over how they do this. For a small clearing member default, the process may be relatively simple; but for a large default, the CCP will have to replace a large number of contracts in a stressed market.

The typical process is to auction the defaulter's portfolio to the clearing members. The CCPs rule book typically requires CMs to participate in the auction, with the threat that the clearing house can 'force allocate' positions to clearing members if the auction fails. Some clearing houses, anticipating that smaller CMs may not be able to participate in large auctions (not least because the auction protocols may require a bidder to value and analyse the risk on hundreds of thousands of trades in a short period of time), permit CMs to out-source default management to third parties.

The London Clearing House's account[369] of closing out Lehman Brothers' cleared swaps portfolio gives an idea of the timeline. At the time of Lehman's default on 15th September 2008, this portfolio comprised over 66,000 trades. The CCP began by hedging the market risk of the portfolio (so that it would not be exposed to further market movements), then Lehman's portfolio was split into currencies and each hedged currency sub-portfolio was separately auctioned. These auctions took place between 24th September and 3rd October. The remaining clearing members were required both to contribute staff who assisted in the default management process and to participate in the auctions. All of the auctions were successful, and approximately two thirds of the defaulter's Initial Margin was returned to Lehman's Administrators. Given the turmoil in the markets at the time, this was a practical demonstration of the adequacy of the initial margin amounts required by the clearing house.

The flip side of the efficacy of initial margin in reducing counterparty credit risk is its impact on clearing members liquidity risk. At least variation margin is a wash across the system: initial margin is simply sucked from the clearing members into CCPs[370].

There are two aspects to this CCP-driven liquidity risk.

1. The overall average level of funds which will be required for margin once central clearing mandates are in place; and

2. The potential short term increase in margin during a stressed period.

We examine each of these in the last two subsections of this section.

6.5.4 Margin for cleared trades I: steady state

It is difficult to estimate the total amount of initial margin that will be required once OTC derivatives clearing mandates come into force because it will depend on the number and size of CCPs and the precise scope of the mandates, neither of which are known at the time of writing. Furthermore there will undoubtedly be changes in both end-user and dealer behaviour which will change the impact. Still, an order-of-magnitude estimate is possible: most commentators estimates are in the high hundreds of billions or low trillions of dollars[371].

There is also the issue of the extra VM that will be required in moving from loose CSAs to the tight collateral arrangements that characterise clearing. Again estimates are difficult, but low trillions of dollars are certainly possible[372].

These amounts are substantial. They are comparable in size, for instance, with a large quantitative easing in the US[373]. The impact of this increase in the liquidity required by the financial system is related to the question of what happens to margin: depending on CCP investment policies, it could be deposited back at banks, invested in the debt markets, or even deposited at central banks (as we mentioned in 6.5.2). Once the impact is known, central banks could mitigate any negative effects to the average money supply simply by printing money.

6.5.5 Margin for cleared trades II: stress

CCPs typically calculate initial margin using a portfolio risk model as discussed in section 6.4.6. The output of any risk model can change either because the data used to calibrate it changes, or model methodology changes are made. This can give rise to large changes in initial margin. Moreover CCPs typically reserve the right to make these changes then call for margin based on them in a short timeframe, giving rise to the risk of a 'systemic margin call' as all the CCP's clearing members are forced to simultaneously raise extra funds[374].

This initial-margin-related liquidity risk is much harder to control than the steady state component discussed above as it is inherently unpredictable. Moreover, 'losing' banks whose trades go against them will be subject to VM calls as well as IM increases. It is estimated that VM calls can, in a bad month, be substantial compared to banks' liquidity buffers[375]. These two effects mean that the liquidity impact of OTC derivatives central clearing policies will be significant on some dealers in times of stress.

6.6 Segregation for Cleared OTC Portfolios

Segregation is intended to protect margin from the default of various parties. However, exactly who is at risk for how much from the default of whom is subtle, and highly dependent on the precise segregation model.

In this section some of these issues are reviewed, and the risks of various approaches to segregation are summarised. We will assume that the architecture of two clients clearing under the principal to principal model illustrated in figure 6.4 applies. The following abbreviations are used:

- ‘COC’ is close out cost, and ‘COC1’ is the close out cost on Client1's portfolio. If close out requires that the terminating party pays out money, then we assume that the cost is positive, whereas if they receive money when replacing the portfolio, we assume that it is negative.

- ‘IM1’ is the initial margin Client1 has posted to its clearing member.

- ‘VM1’ is the variation margin on Client1's portfolio. We assume that this is positive if the CM has received cash and negative if the CM has paid cash to Client1.

- Analogously ‘CO2’, ‘IM2’ and ‘VM2’ pertain to Client2.

- ‘COCH’, ‘IMH’ and ‘VMH’ refer to the clearing member's house portfolio, while ‘IMC’ and ‘VMC’ refer to the margin amounts on net client portfolio[376].

Three models are examined: no segregation; omnibus or future style segregation; and full segregation.

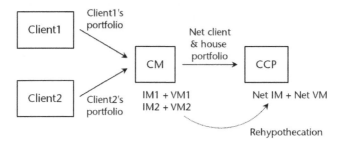

Figure 6.11: Margin holdings in an unsegregated model

6.6.1 No segregation, net margining

In this (unrealistically risky) model, each client posts margin separately to the CM, and CCP margins the CM on the net portfolio (i.e. on the combined Client1, Client2 and house position). Typically the CM will meet the CCP's margin requirements by rehypothecating some of the client's margin to the clearing house. (If the CM has chosen to margin the clients at a lower level than the CCP requires, it will have to fund the difference.) We assume in this situation that no one segregates anything. The situation is thus as in figure 6.11.

If we assume no involvement from third party custodians, and that only the party listed defaults. The first issue is who close out on various defaults. Figure 6.12 gives this information.

Defaulting party	Closing out parties
CCP	CM
CM	CCP, Client1, Client2
Client1	CM
Client1 and CM	CCP and Client2[377]

Figure 6.12: Parties closing out on various defaults

Each close out generates the risk of loss. Figure 6.13 summarises the amounts at stake. Here the loss given default for the party indicated is the maximum of the amounts shown and zero, assuming that there is no recovery.

The mechanics are best illustrated by an example. Consider the 'Loss to CM vs. CCP, CCP fails' entry in the table. In this situation, the CM closes out the net portfolio with the CCP. Suppose that the net VM at the CCP is positive. The portfolio at the last margin call therefore has a positive value to the CCP, meaning that the CM owes it money. Thus, provided the portfolio does not swing too much in value between default and close out, the CM will receive net money when the portfolio is closed out, meaning that the cost of close out, COC, on the net portfolio, is negative. Against that, the CM has posted IM and VM to the CCP. The net loss to the CM is therefore the margin posted minus the close out amount.

The symmetrical case is the CM failing, with the CCP closing out. This close out will have a positive cost to the CCP, under the same assumptions. Against this cost, it has the net IM and VM. The other points noted in the table are as follows:

	CCP	CM vs. CCP	CM vs. Client2	Client2
If the CCP fails[378]	N/A	Net IM + Net VM + COC on net portfolio	See note 1.	See note 2.
If the CM fails	COC on net portfolio – (Net IM + Net VM)	See note 3.	See note 4.	IM2 + VM2 + COC2
If Client1 fails	None	None	None	None
If Client2 fails	None	None	COC2 – (VM2 + IM2)	See note 5.
If Client1 and the CM fail	COC on net portfolio – (Net IM + Net VM)	See note 3.	See note 4.	IM2 + VM2 + COC2

Figure 6.13: Amounts at risk without segregation

Notes 1 and 2.   Both of these entries depend on whether the CM has guaranteed CCP performance to the clients. If it has, then the CM to client portfolios continue and no party suffers a loss from these trades. If the CM does not guarantee CCP performance, then presumably the clients would participate in the CM's losses on its exposure to the CCP, with the loss amount and offset against client margin depending on the details of the client clearing documentation.

Note 3.   Here the CCP closes out against the clearing member, and uses the net margin it holds against the close out costs on the net portfolio. Any excess after close out is returned to the estate of the defaulted clearing member.

Note 4.   In this situation Client2 closes out against their clearing member. The margin that Client2 has posted above COC2 is an exposure, as the next cell indicates.

Note 5.   Here, the clearing member closes out against Client2, using the margin that it holds from them against the close out cost. Any excess is returned to the client's estate.

6.6.2 Omnibus segregation

In this model, the CCP separately margins the net client and clearing member house portfolios. We assume that the CCP segregates the omnibus account for the benefit of clients, and that segregation works. As before, there are no custodians involved so the situation can be depicted as in figure 6.14.

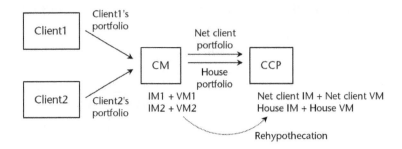

Figure 6.14: Margin holdings in an omnibus segregation model

Figure 6.15 reviews the amounts at risk from the default of various parties in this situation.

The key difference here is the very last cell. The CCP closes out the whole client portfolio, and has the whole amount of client margin available against the cost of this process. Therefore, Client2 has fellow client risk due to the possible excess costs of managing Client1's default. The other notes are as follows:

> Notes 6 and 7.   As in the unsegregated case, both of these entries depend on whether the CM has guaranteed CCP performance to the clients. Here though, in the unguaranteed case presumably the clients would only be at risk on the close out of the total client portfolio vs. total client margin at the CCP, rather than on the net client plus house portfolio vs. net client plus house margin.

> Note 8.   The CCP closes out the client and house portfolios separately. Client2 has direct exposure to the CM on that part of its margin which is not held in the omnibus account at the CCP. It is also at risk on being closed out by the CCP at a price different to the last mark-to market, and the subsequent use of omnibus account IM to cover this.

	CCP	CM vs. CCP	CM vs. Client2	Client2
If the CCP fails	N/A	IMH + VMH + COCH, IMC + VMC + COC1 + COC2	See note 6.	See note 7.
If the CM fails	COCH – (IMH + VMH), COC1 + COC2 – (IMC + VMC)		See note 4 .	IM2 + VM2 + COC2 – pro rata share of IMN: see note 8.
If Client1 fails	None	None	None	None
If Client2 fails	None	None	COC2 – VM2 – IM2	See note 5.
If Client1 and the CM fail	COCH – (IMH + VMH), COC1 + COC2 – (IMC + VMC)	See note 9.	See note 4.	IMC + VMC + COC1 + COC2 – pro rata share of IMN

Figure 6.15: Amounts at risk in omnibus segregation

Note 9.   Here the CCP separately closes out the clearing member house and client portfolios, and uses the net margin it holds against each to cover the respective close out costs. Any excess after close out is returned respectively to the estate of the defaulted clearing member and to the clients.

6.6.3 Full segregation

This approach requires the CCP to maintain separate accounts for each client's margin, as figure 6.16 depicts[379].

Figure 6.17 reviews the amounts at risk from the default of various parties in this new situation. Full segregation means that it is quite likely, at least, that clients can port if their CM fails. There is moreover lowered fellow client risk. The final note is:

Note 10.   In this case presumably the clearing house will separately close out the CM and the client. It will use IMH and VMH against the first cost; and IM1 and VM1 against the second.

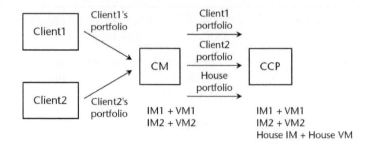

Figure 6.16: Margin holdings in the full segregation model

	CCP	CM vs. CCP	CM vs. Client2	Client2
If the CCP fails	N/A	IMH + VMH + COCH		See note 7.
If the CM fails	COCH – (IMH + VMH),		None	None
	In this case both clients can port			
If Client1 fails	None	None	None	None
If Client2 fails	None	None	COC2 – (VM2 + IM2)	See note 5.
If Client1 and the CM fail	COCH – (IMH + VMH), COC1 – (IM1 + VM1)	See note 10.	None, Client2 ports	

Figure 6.17: Amounts at risk in full segregation

It is clear from the account above that the choice of segregation model is subtle. Less segregation is cheaper, while higher levels of it are less exposed to the risk of clearing member default. If CCP failure or investment risk is a concern then the segregation of margin title-transferred to the CCP may not help: instead a third party approach whereby an independent custodian or CSD holds margin assets is required[380]. Alternatively, if a client has confidence in their clearing member but not the CCP, they could waive segregation entirely but require their CM to guarantee the clearing house's performance, thereby insulating themselves from it.

Summary

OTC derivatives central counterparties perform a number of functions. They interpose themselves between market participants, and guarantee each side of their trades. By doing this, they provide multilateral netting of cleared trades. They also impose a margin discipline; manage clearing member defaults; and facilitate client clearing.

CCPs take substantial amounts of counterparty credit risk. Against this, they have various defences including margin and a mutualised default fund. They restrict themselves to clearing liquid products; this provides some comfort that CCPs will be able to close out clearing member portfolios post default in a timely fashion.

A key issue for clients is the level of segregation their initial margin is subject to. Higher segregation standards reduce credit risk but increase the liquidity required by clearing. Better segregation also enhances portability and thus reduces clients' dependence on their clearing member(s).

Notes

[312]For more on the central clearing of OTC derivatives, see C. Pirrong, *The Economics of Central Clearing: Theory and Practice*, ISDA Discussion Paper (2011) available via www.isda.org.

[313]*Central Counterparty Clearing: History, Innovation, and Regulation* Speech by Randall Kroszner, 3rd April 2006 available at www.federalreserve.gov/newsevents/speech/kroszner20060403a.htm.

[314]VM requirements are typically calculated at least daily and sometimes more often, but IM may be calculated less often, perhaps weekly.

[315]Matters become a little more complex under trade compression, as there may be more than one gainer for every loser. However, the CCP remains flat.

[316]This is not quite true, as CCPs typically call for extra intra-day VM where required, but do not credit VM excesses where they occur until the next day. See section 8.4.1 for a further discussion of the liquidity risks created by CCPs.

[317]CPSS and IOSCO suggests that 'Initial margin should meet an established single-tailed confidence level of at least 99 percent with respect to the estimated distribution of future exposure' and that the MPOR should 'use a conservative estimate of the time horizons for the effective hedging or close out of the particular types of products cleared by the CCP'. There is however no requirement to use a ten day MPOR as there is in the Basel II requirements for bilateral OTC derivatives. See *Disclosure framework for financial market infrastructures* (Consultative report, April 2012) available at www.bis.org/publ/cpss101c.pdf.

[318]Strictly, on a clearing member-by-clearing member basis: some CCPs allow portfolio margining of those the clients of a given clearing member who consent to this co-mingling: we discuss this further in section 6.4.4.

[319]Margin reduces the risk of the poster's portfolio: it should therefore be based on the loss distribution of that CM's portfolio. DF reduces the risk of the total cleared portfolio: it therefore applies to the multivariate loss distribution of all cleared trades. The adequacy of DF therefore critically depends on the default comovement assumptions used to determine the multivariate loss distribution.

[320]Total DF for LCH in 2011 was roughly 1/20th of total initial margin according to its annual report (available at via www.lchclearnet.com).

[321]We discuss the issue of the sizing of default fund in chapter 8.

[322]This poses a serious problem for clearing members in that they cannot limit their liability. It also potentially creates an infinite capital requirement, which the Basel Committee deals with by requiring local supervisors to 'determine in its Pillar 2 assessments the amount of unfunded commitments' to which a capital requirement should apply (*Capital requirements for bank exposures to central counterparties*, July 2012, available at www.bis.org/publ/bcbs227.pdf).

[323]We have presented this with the riskiest layer at the bottom to emphasise the analogy with CDOs (which are usually presented that way). Note that we have not included loss allocation, discussed in section , in this figure.

[324]For more on the early history of clearing houses see J. Moser, *Contracting Innovations and the Evolution of Exchange Clearinghouses*, Federal Reserve Bank of Chicago (1998).

[325]This account is based on a longer discussion in B. Hills et al., *Central counterparty clearing houses and financial stability*, Bank of England Financial Stability Review (June 1999) available at www.bankofengland.co.uk/publications/Documents/fsr/1999/fsr06art6.pdf.

[326]Branding a transaction a 'future' is no guarantee of liquidity, even though many futures (and in particular many of the most-traded futures) are liquid. It is therefore surprising and imprudent that the regulatory margin period of risk on a future is one day in the US and two days under EMIR. This provides a substantial incentive to trade futures on swaps rather than the swaps themselves: the economics is very similar and the margin is rather lower. Market participants have not been idle in the face of this incentive, as we discuss further in chapter 10.

[327]A longer discussion can be found in C. Sidanius, A. Wetherilt, *Thoughts on determining central clearing eligibility of OTC derivatives*, Bank of England Financial Stability Paper No. 14 (March 2012) available at www.bankofengland.co.uk/publications/Documents/fsr/fs_paper14.pdf.

[328]For this reason prudent CDS CCPs do not clear swaps which reference their clearing members.

[329]This is less of a problem in interest rate markets than in equity or commodity markets due to mean reversion.

[330]This is from ISDA, and is quoted in C. Sidanius, A. Wetherilt, *op. cit.*

[331]At the time of writing, the leading CDS clearer, ICE, cleared CDS on 153 North American and 121 European names, as well as some sovereigns and indices: see www.theice.com/clear_credit.jhtml.

[332]The clearing of single name CDS by a CCP which have a clearing member as a reference introduces too much wrong way risk.

[333]It is rather unhelpful that some official papers on clearing, such as S. Cecchetti et al., *Central counterparties for over-the-counter derivatives*, BIS Quarterly Review, September 2009 mention AIG's distress as if it were a motivation for central clearing. AIG's failure is instructive in many regards, but central clearing would not have helped the firm or its counterparties. The same paper also suggests that central clearing assists regulators in providing transparency, when it is trade repositories that perform that function: again, central clearing is irrelevant.

[334]CDS on the ABX indices (as discussed in section 4.2.1) were liquid from roughly 2004 until the crisis; subsequently they became much less liquid.

[335]This 'mandatory products must have more than one clearer' principle would also assist in resolution (as the other CCP(s) could potentially take on trades from the distressed clearing house), and it could potentially allow CMs to move from one CCP to another. Any ability for clearing houses to claim patent or copyright protection on their contracts would be a countervailing and, in this context, unhelpful attribute.

[336]In August 2009, with the crisis less than a year old, the ECB articulated four conclusions from its review of the CDS market:

1. A comprehensive review of position transparency should be considered for the benefit of regulators and the market as a whole.

2. Regulatory attention may focus on how market participants can be encouraged to use the clearing services.

3. An impact assessment of bilateral collateral management processes should be conducted as quickly and comprehensively as possible and a roadmap for improvements should be established.

4. In the light of the issues raised by the current functioning of the CDS market and the shortcomings in risk management practices, the capital requirements for market risks have been revised in July 2009 within the Basel framework.

It is striking how much further than these sensible steps reform has gone.

[337]Some observers have suggested that the fact that Jackie Clegg, wife of Senator Chris Dodd (one of the two sponsors of the Dodd Frank Act), was a Director of the CME is not entirely irrelevant. Certainly derivatives exchanges with their own clearing houses, such as the CME (in the words of the LA Times) 'would likely benefit greatly' from post-crisis legislation. See *Chris Dodd's wife and derivatives trading*, LA Times, 19th March 2010 available at latimesblogs.latimes.com/money_co/2010/03/chris-dodds-wife-and-her-strange-entanglement-with-derivatives-trading-.html.

[338]See the US Treasury press release, *Final Determination on Foreign Exchange Swaps and Forwards*, 16th November 2012, available at www.treasury.gov/press-center/press-releases/Pages/tg1773.aspx.

[339]Futures Commission Merchants, discussed in section 2.4.3, are a class of entity which operates under CFTC regulation (although its 'line' regulator may be an SRO such as the NFA).

[340]I.e. a swap that is mandated to be cleared and is covered by US regulation. Given that there are extra-territorial aspects to this regulation, this may include transactions which are not obviously between two US parties. The rules here are in flux, with the CFTC having said that it will narrow its initial broad definition of US person, but has at the time of writing not proposed a final rule.

[341]There is also a requirement that certain types of derivatives market participants register with US regulators. For instance, the CFTC has identified two classes of dealer-like entity, swap dealers and major swap participants, who must register with them and comply with various other requirements. A swap dealer is anyone who holds themselves out or engages in activity that causes them to be commonly known as a dealer in swaps, makes a market in them or regularly trades them for their own account. A major swap participant is a party that maintains a substantial position in any of the major swap categories, excluding positions held for hedging commercial risk or certain employee benefit plans, or whose outstanding swaps create substantial counterparty exposure that could have serious adverse effects on the financial stability of the United States banking system or financial markets, or that is unregulated, highly leveraged and maintains a substantial position in any of the major swap categories. These definitions are supported by quantitative thresholds: see 77 FR 30596 available at www.cftc.gov/ucm/groups/public/@lrfederalregister/documents/file/2012-10562a.pdf.

[342]For a comparison of the clearing provisions of EMIR and Dodd Frank, see K. Janda, G. Rausser, *American and European Regulation of Over-the-Counter Derivative Securities* MRPA paper (2011) available at mpra.ub.uni-muenchen.de/35036/.

[343]And indirectly to some non-EU counterparties trading with or who have connections to EU parties.

[344]This will be defined by ESMA, likely at some point in 2013.

[345]Ditto, and likely including trades between two financial counterparties or between a financial counterparty and 'sufficiently big' non financial counterparties who cannot claim to be hedging 'commercial risk'.

[346]This is the ISDA Determinations Committee: see dc.isda.org.

[347]See D. Duffie, H. Zhu, *Does a Central Clearing Counterparty Reduce Counterparty Risk?*, Stanford University Graduate School of Business (March 2010) available at www.stanford.edu/~duffie/DuffieZhu.pdf.

[348]Or, to be specific, ICE Trust in the US and ICE Clear in the EU.

[349]This excludes the possibility that an ET CCP opens itself to OTC. In that case the potential benefit of cross-margining OTCs with futures could be significant.

[350]Thus credit risk management concerns would suggest that CCPs operate – and are regulated as – utilities. Clearing member ownership of CCPs (and if necessary regulation) could mitigate concerns over the extraction of monopoly profits.

[351]This may especially be the case if the central bank is not the supervisor of the CCP which could require liquidity, although memoranda of understanding and other co-operative measures may mitigate this risk.

[352]The economics of this are complex. First, since bilateral CSAs typically do not have identical margin arrangements to clearing, extra margin will be required. Second, since credit support affects valuation, the mark to market of trades will change when they are cleared. Third, regulatory capital requirements will likely decrease. Finally, both margin and capital requirements can change, which introduces further risk into the decision.

[353]This follows through into the documentation. Legal agreements can be implemented in various ways, but currently a modified ISDA master agreement is used for both the client to CM and CM to CCP trades.

[354]The term 'agency model' is ubiquitous in the US but OTC derivatives clearing is not a pure agency model in that the customer has few direct contractual remedies against the CCP, and the FCM both guarantees the client's performance and enforces the CCPs' rules upon them.

[355]CMs may margin clients separately in an omnibus structure, but only post the net amount to the CCP. The difference between the sum of each client's margin and the net amount required for the total client portfolio is then available to fund the CM. CMs can also call for more margin than the CCP requires: again this excess is available to them as funding.

[356]Thus in particular if a client has supplied more margin than has been called for, that amount is available to absorb losses on its default.

[357]See the Linklaters Note *CFTC Adopts 'LSOC' Model for Protection of Cleared Swaps Customers' Margin, Marking a Significant Departure From the Traditional U.S. Futures Model* (January 2012).

[358]Portability cannot be guaranteed in advance as one cannot know, for instance, that the receiving clearing member has sufficient capital (or indeed liquidity) to handle the ported portfolio. The standard is therefore 'highly likely' portability. See the Basel Committee's Consultative Document *Capitalisation of bank exposures to central counterparties* (November 2011) available at www.bis.org/publ/bcbs206.pdf, and its successor, BCBS 227, for more details.

[359]Multiple regulations can force this issue too. For instance, if local rules require, for instance, that a firm has to use a German entity to face German clients, but those German clients wish to trade at a US CCP, then since it is difficult for the German client-facing entity also to be an FCM (which it must be to be a clearing member under US rules), then indirect clearing is necessary. Regulation can cause other issues here too, for instance if there is a conflict of segregation requirements. Moreover, if

the client facilitating the indirect client is a bank, they will likely face higher capital requirements than would a clearing member facilitating a direct client.

[360]See the G30 Report *Global Clearing and Settlement – A Plan of Action* (2006) available at www.group30.org/images/PDF/ReportPDFs/Global_Clearing_and_Settlement_Plan_of_Action.pdf.

[361]For more details see N. Garvin, *Central Counterparty Interoperability*, Reserve Bank of Australia Bulletin (June 2012) available at www.rba.gov.au/publications/bulletin/2012/jun/pdf/bu-0612-7.pdf.

[362]There is also the senior/junior model of interoperability, whereby one CCP posts to the other but not vice versa. In a sense this is like an indirect client arrangement with the junior CCP acting as the clearing member; its clearing members as clients; and their clients as indirect clients.

[363]A classical bank is a vehicle for taking illiquid assets (loans) and turning them into liquid liabilities (deposits), thanks to the sprinkling of a little equity, and the magic of a deposit guarantee.

[364]This is further restricted to cash in a limited number of currencies. See for instance LCH's policy *Acceptable Collateral* available at www.lchclearnet.com/risk_management/ltd/acceptable_collateral.asp.

[365]As we discussed in section 3.1.3, CSAs affect the valuation of the portfolios they govern. A cash-only variation margin CSA leads to OIS-based pricing rather than something more complex. See the press release *LCH.Clearnet adopts OIS discounting for $218 trillion IRS portfolio* (17th June 2010, available at www.lchclearnet.com/media_centre/press_releases/2010-06-17.asp for more details.

[366]The Basel rules on bank exposures to CCPs somewhat mitigate the incentive clearing houses have to own IM. These reduce the capital required if IM is held remote from the bankruptcy of the CCP: see *Capital requirements for bank exposures to central counterparties*, July 2012, available at www.bis.org/publ/bcbs227.pdf.

[367]The CCP typically promises the collateral poster OIS on cash margin, just as a bilateral counterparty would, so it has to earn at least OIS on invested cash in order to break even. It is almost impossible to do this without taking credit risk and/or liquidity risk.

[368]A complete analysis here would include custody risks (created by the custodian and any sub-custodians) and transit risks (created as the collateral is passed). The safest model is probably one where the poster has an account at the central securities depository, and simply grants security interests from that without the collateral ever moving.

[369]See N. de Terán, *How the world's largest default was unravelled*, Financial News (13th October 2008).

[370]Or at least it is until CCPs invest it: if they simply deposit IM back with clearing members or buy debt issued by them, then while interconnectedness has increased, liquidity risk may be mitigated.

[371]There is relevant work here from Heller & Vause, Sidanius & Zikes, and Singh, amongst others. Singh also points out the related issue of the shortening of rehypothecation chains caused by OTC derivatives markets reforms. (See D. Heller, N. Vause, *Collateral requirements for mandatory central clearing of over-the-counter derivatives*, BIS Working Paper No. 373 (March 2012) available at www.bis.org/publ/work373.htm; C. Sidanius, F. Zikes, *OTC derivatives reform and collateral demand impact*, Bank of England Financial Stability Paper No. 18 (October 2012) available at www.bankofengland. co.uk/publications/Documents/fsr/fs_paper18.pdf; M. Singh, *Collateral, Netting and Systemic Risk in the OTC Derivatives Market*, IMF Working Paper WP/10/99 available at www.imf.org/external/pubs/ft/wp/2010/wp1099.pdf and *Making OTC Derivatives Safe – A Fresh Look*, IMF Working Paper WP/11/66 available at www.imf.org/external/pubs/ft/ wp/2011/wp1166.pdf).

[372]Op. cit. and Tabb Group, *Optimizing Collateral: In Search of a Margin Oasis* (June 2012).

[373]QE2 was $600B.

[374]My paper *The Systemic Risks of OTC Derivatives Central Clearing*, Journal of Risk Management in Financial Institutions Volume 5, No. 3 (June 2012) has more details on this and other systemic risks of CCPs.

[375]Heller & Vause state that 'One G14 dealer could expect CDS variation margin calls to drain 52% of its cash over one month with 0.5% probability': see D. Heller, N. Vause, *Collateral requirements for mandatory central clearing of over-the-counter derivatives*, BIS Working Paper No. 373 (March 2012) available at www.bis.org/publ/work373.htm.

[376]Note that the close out cost of the net client portfolio is just COC1 + COC2.

[377]We ignore here the issue of who closes out the CM to Client1 trade: that depends on who defaulted first.

[378]These items are somewhat conjectural as it is difficult to determine the legal position on CCP insolvency from the publically available documentation, and anyway given that LSOC and full segregation are relatively new legal concepts, there is little precedent to rely on. One example is illustrative: CME suggests that customer margin held for one FCM will 'never' be used to cover a deficiency caused by the failure of a different FCM (*CME Clearing Financial Safeguards*, available at www.cmegroup.com/ clearing/files/financialsafeguards.pdf), but is this true in the unlikely event that the CME itself fails too? In any case, large CCPs are likely to be resolved rather than allowed to fail, so this discussion may be moot.

[379]With more than two clients, we could have a situation where some clients have opted for full segregation but the others have chosen to use an omnibus account.

[380]Somewhat confusingly, market participants sometimes refer to 'fourth' or 'quad' party custodians. Here the first three parties aref the client, the CM, and the CCP. A fourth party custodial approach can provide margin to the CCP directly from the client's account, without the need to settle client-to-CM and CM-to-CCP transfers (with their concomitant operational and short term credit risks). In this case, though, the risks of the custodial arrangements themselves must be considered.

7

The Emerging OTC Market Infrastructure From Execution To Settlement

*Bill Hodgson**

Introduction

Since the emergence of trading in OTC derivative products, the infrastructure to support the market has moved towards greater automation and reduced cost. Progress was steady in the 1990s. However, in the early 2000s, CDS enjoyed a significant increase in secondary trading, causing a paperwork crisis. As discussed in section 1.3.5, this was mainly due to the manual approach used for completing assignments and novations. CDS automation had not kept pace with the growth of the market. The FED engaged with the largest banks, encouraging them to make material improvements to their back-office processing. A number of 'FED letters' defined a series of quantified targets for banks to reduce outstanding confirmations, and improve processing in most back-office areas. This substantially improved OTC derivatives market processing, leaving us with today's bilateral market[381].

The credit crisis and subsequent regulatory changes, due in part to the Dodd Frank Act and EMIR, have diverted the market into an alternative method of trading and processing OTC contracts. When complete, these

---

* Bill Hodgson is a leading expert on OTC derivatives trade processing. He is the owner of The OTC Space, an OTC derivatives consultancy: see http://theotcspace.com for more details.

will see the OTC market become traded on exchanges and new forms of
market. Traditional phone-based bilateral OTC trading will wither in most,
perhaps all jurisdictions. This chapter discusses the evolution of the new
processing ecosystem, and the practicalities of central clearing. Clearing
for interest rate swaps is the most mature, having been launched in 1998
by LCH.Clearnet, and is the basis for much of this chapter: clearing for
other products has similar procedures and concepts.

7.1   The Current Bilateral OTC Environment

We begin by discussing bilateral OTC trade flow in the post-FED letter
environment, and how it emerged from earlier trade processing initiatives.

7.1.1   Execution methods

Over time a variety of methods to execute an OTC trade have evolved,
providing different benefits, to suit various parties in the market. Figure 7.1 summarises the models in use.

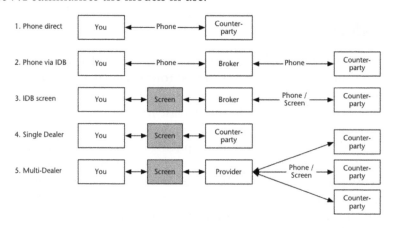

Figure 7.1: Bilateral execution models

These (as applied to the interest rate swap market) can be described as
follows:

1. *Direct bilateral by phone.* This method has been used by dealers
    since the inception of the OTC market. The parties have a brief
    conversation. The buyer shouts out the currency, notional and
    term, and the counterparty quotes a price. Each trader then
    enters the trade details into their trading system, and downstream
    processing takes place to confirm and complete the trade. Phone

lines are always recorded to provide a fall-back for resolving disputes should the electronic records prove to be inconsistent between the two parties.

2. *Via an inter-dealer broker ('IDB') by phone.* This is similar to the previous approach, but in this case the broker provides a price quote, without revealing the counterparty. The conversation proceeds until agreement is reached to execute at the quoted price. The IDB makes the choice on which counterparty to offer a price from, subject to the executing parties' credit constraints.

3. *Via an IDB but using a screen.* This is very similar to option 2 but the trader views a screen showing the best prices for a matrix of benchmark trades, varying by notional and maturity. The trader then requests a firm price and the IDB model continues as in the previous option.

4. *Single Dealer Platforms.* Some dealers, such as Barclays with BARX[382], provide their own screen of price quotes via data distributors, advertising indicative prices for a range of products. A trader makes a request for a firm price via the screen and can then execute directly with the provider. An advantage of this method over option 1 is full electronic disclosure of the details of the trade, avoiding confusion and ambiguity at the trade entry stage.

5. *Multi-dealer platforms.* Various data distributors offer screens which provide price quotes from multiple counterparties. These screens are popular with buy-side firms (such as Investment Managers, Pension Funds, Corporates or Hedge Funds) as they provide a single quick and easy way to understanding the range of prices and counterparties. The platform sometimes operate a Request For Quote ('RFQ') model, where the buyer will send out a request to execute a trade, and receive back price quotes, which the screen will sort from best to worst. The trader clicks the price to execute, and trade processing begins.

7.1.2 The early days of confirmation and trade processing

The early years of the OTC derivatives market was characterised by an army of back office staff sending and receiving faxes in an attempt to agree trade details in a world with few agreed standards. This process was not robust, so there was an obvious need to provide a more reliable and less error prone way of exchanging trade details. SWIFT[383] was an early mover in designing and delivering a method of matching Interest Rate Swaps. They developed a standard for the electronic exchange of trade details known as the MT360 format. This achieved some success, but the OTC derivatives market moved on, and soon a consortium of banks created a more capable replacement: the SwapsWire model.

The innovation SwapsWire brought was the idea that the trading desks had to own the problem of agreeing the trade details, and that agreement had to occur before the trade moved to the back-office. This paradigm eventually removed a layer of cost and caused the industry to focus almost entirely on electronic methods of communicating trades.

SwapsWire enacted a procedural change too. Instead of comparing and matching a pair of trade records, one from each party, a 'buyer submits' model was used, whereby the fixed payer entered the trade and sent it for review and agreement to the other party. The process became known as 'affirmation' compared to the traditional matching process of 'confirmation'.

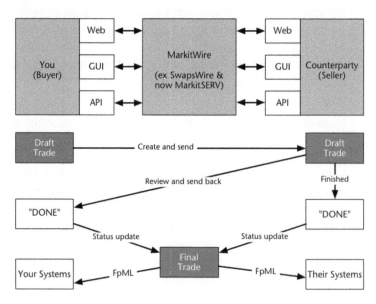

Figure 7.2: The affirmation process

The adoption of this model also meant the SwapsWire system could be programmed to provide an industry approved set of standards for many OTC trades, reducing the trade entry burden to only the key fields such as

Counterparty, Notional, Maturity, Floating Rate, Fixed Rate and Currency for instance. Figure 7.2 illustrates how the transaction flow becomes a 'bounce' between each party as they enter, revise, review, and re-enter the trade details. The process is complete once both parties click 'DONE'.

7.1.3 The credit derivatives model from DTCC

Around the same time as SwapsWire was expanding take-up, DTCC launched their own platform for automating the confirmation process for Credit Default Swaps. Despite the process change described above to move responsibility for confirmation into the Front Office, DTCC launched a matching process for CDS contracts which continued the back-office model. This came to market shortly before SwapsWire: the first mover advantage allowed this service to become standard across the credit derivatives business. Figure 7.3 illustrates the matching process in the DTCC's model.

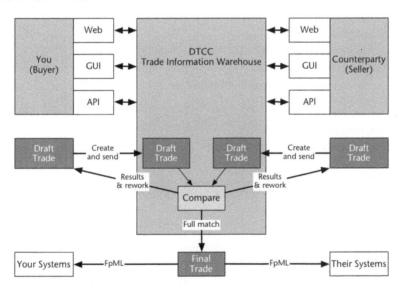

Figure 7.3: The match, compare and rework process in the credit business model

7.1.4 The evolution of FpML

Electronic publishing and the Internet brought new approaches to data representation, culminating in the first XML draft in 1996. By the early 2000s, this was gaining significant popularity. XML is a language for describing structured data[384], so it offered the possibility of developing a data standard for documenting OTC derivatives. JP Morgan provided this in 1997, applying XML to financial instruments to arrive at what we now know as Financial products Markup Language[385] or 'FpML'.

Figure 7.4 below shows a portion of an FpML document which defines the details necessary to calculate the interest payments on the floating leg of an interest rate swap. The items in bold are the data payload: the rest of the text structures the data and makes it machine-verifiable.

```
<calculationPeriodAmount>
   <calculation>
     <notionalSchedule>
       <notionalStepSchedule>
         <initialValue>267000000</initialValue>
         <currency currencyScheme=
            'http://www.fpml.org/ext/iso4217'>USD</currency>
       </notionalStepSchedule>
     </notionalSchedule>
   <floatingRateCalculation>
     <floatingRateIndex>USD-LIBOR-BBA</floatingRateIndex>
     <indexTenor>
       <periodMultiplier>3</periodMultiplier>
       <period>M</period>
     </indexTenor>
     <spreadSchedule>
       <initialValue>0.000</initialValue>
     </spreadSchedule>
   </floatingRateCalculation>
   <dayCountFraction>ACT/360</dayCountFraction>
   </calculation>
</calculationPeriodAmount>
```

Figure 7.4: An extract of the FpML description of an interest rate swap

The extract describes a swap where the floating leg will have payment calculations on a notional of $267m based on 3 month USD-LIBOR-BBA with a zero spread, using the ACT/360 daycount convention. More data is needed to define a complete OTC contract: the extract in figure 7.4 is part of a three page XML document which fully documents the swap.

FpML was adopted by SwapsWire and DTCC in the early 2000s for communicating and storing trade data. This encouraged the wider use of FpML throughout the industry, and it was latterly taken up by clearing houses.

7.1.5   Success at achieving electronic confirmation

ISDA conduct a survey amongst its members annually to gather data on the flow of trades through each firm's back office. The survey published in May 2012[386] asked firms to detail the percentage of trades confirmed using electronic means. Figure 7.5 summarises the answers to this question.

Bank size	Number of Respondents	Percentage by asset class				
		Rates	Credit	Equities	FX[387]	Commodity
Large	17	78%	99%	34%	67%	63%
Medium	18	51%	71%	14%	66%	60%
Small	25	49%	62%	5%	32%	47%

Figure 7.5: The fraction of the bilateral market which is electronically confirmed

This indicates that considerable progress has been made towards automation, but much remains to be done. For small banks, in four of the asset classes less than half of trades are electronically confirmed, and for equity derivatives products all sizes of bank have considerable challenges in increasing the level of automation. The survey does not give the reasons underlying these results, but it is fair to assume these include:

* Lack of investment in trade processing;
* Difficulties in representing trades electronically; and
* The complexity of the trades themselves.

7.1.6   The end-to-end functions of the trade information warehouse

The processing of most interest rate swaps follows the same pattern: they are agreed in SwapsWire, and subsequently each party independently performs the obligations of the trade, making payments as and when required. As part of the FED letter process it was necessary to apply the same degree of standardisation to the processing of CDS, unifying the conflicting approaches of different dealers. The DTCC extended their credit derivatives platform into a system which quickly became a market standard. The services available in it include:

* Payment generation, including those resulting from Assignments or Novations;
* Credit Event processing (i.e. taking the steps required when a CDS contract is triggered);

- Bilateral payment netting; and

- Actual settlement of the CDS contracts via CLS Bank (as discussed in section 2.1.2).

The end result of these improvements was dubbed the Trade Information Warehouse[388] (or 'TIW'). This platform enables firms to trade CDS, confirm them, and see them processed through to settlement and eventual maturity, on a single standard platform, with minimal amounts of involvement from the back office. Figure 7.6 shows the split in functions between the TIW and CLS.

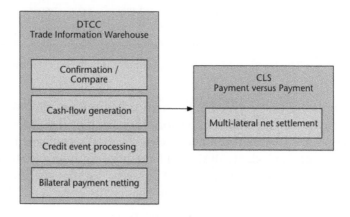

Figure 7.6: TIW and CLS functions in credit derivatives trade processing

7.1.7 *The evolution of trade processing*

A number of other firms have moved into the post-trade market. For example, in the confirmation space, TZero used the SwapsWire 'affirmation' model and provided an alternative front end into the DTCC matching service. This business was eventually sold to ICE and became ICELink[389]. It is now the official trade entry platform for ICE's central clearing business (while retaining a connection with the DTCC TIW).

Various parties also provide trading platforms for OTC products. These are typically connected to SwapsWire, since the major dealers prefer to keep the affirmation/confirmation step in one place, rather than see fragmentation of back office processes.

As time passed, SwapsWire and DTCC found themselves in competition in each of the Rates, Credit and Equities asset classes. Eventually users concluded that having two heavy weights competing kept direct costs low, but it also required design and implementation to support both platforms, increasing indirect costs. A proposal was made to merge the two affirmation and confirmation businesses. This was a clear monopoly, so US Department of Justice ('DOJ') approval was required. The DOJ was eventually persuaded of the efficiency benefits of the combination and allowed the merger to take place. The result is known as MarkitSERV[390]. This firm's infrastructure has now become the market standard platform for the affirmation of OTC derivatives trades, providing an integrated processing platform and increasing integration in the post-trade space.

7.1.8 Credit support management

One of the key back-office processes is the implementation of the credit support aspect of the ISDA documentation framework. The ISDA Credit Support Annexe enables parties to offset their credit exposures by delivering assets as collateral, as discussed in section 2.3.1. Firms negotiate and sign an ISDA CSA to capture as much of their trading activity as is desired. Those agreements are implemented somewhere outside the front office, often in Operations and sometimes in the Credit Risk department.

Typical inter-dealer CSA terms include many OTC asset classes, but often exclude some FX and Commodities trading (as these have their conventions and credit support arrangements). They are often relatively 'tight' (in the terminology of section 2.3.3), with a zero threshold, and small adjustments for rounding and minimum transfer amounts. However a zero threshold and daily margining is required to achieve optimal capital requirements, so for large dealers the efficient implementation of their CSAs is a challenge. The key steps to implement the credit support arrangements agreed in a CSA include:

- Gathering basic details of all trades within the scope of the CSA, from all internal processing systems;
- Capturing an end of day valuation for each trade;
- Applying the agreed upon exposure calculations to arrive (usually) at a single currency net exposure;
- Subtracting cash or securities already held;
- And then making a margin call on the other party where required.

In principal all this is not too difficult, but when banks with a large portfolio (perhaps 150,000 trades or more), global trading activity, and a variety of trading teams executing vanilla and exotic trades are involved, there are challenges.

These include:

- Gathering trade and valuation data from multiple systems in multiple time zones;

- Ensuring all trades are valued daily, preferably not on a spreadsheet, or by a single employee, or both;

- Executing data quality checks to catch missing or inaccurate information as some data feeds are prone to error;

- Processing large numbers of trades in a short daily time window;

- Building a system which can aggregate valuations across many CSAs for many group legal entities and counterparties;

- Providing a controlled workflow environment to track the issue and settlement of many daily margin calls for global teams;

- Designing a processing cycle which takes account of global time zones, with their own cycle of trading, pricing and book keeping.

One of the features of the CSA is the option to dispute a margin call. Given the bilateral nature of the OTC market, both parties need to be able to book and process large volumes of trades, and arrive at the same net value on a daily basis. This is problematic. Moreover, the typical CSA gives the receiver of a collateral call the right to dispute, and refuse to pay. In the early days disputes led to protracted investigations into the underlying causes of the dispute, without any guiding framework to govern the process.

Over time, mechanisms were designed under ISDA's auspices to prescribe the resolution process and obligate both parties to follow the procedural rules, with the penalty of 'losing' the dispute if they did not comply. This was a step forward, but collateral disputes remain relatively commonplace in the market, particularly in portfolios including highly structured trades, the problem being that a single problematic trade (i.e. one whose valuation has not been agreed) can taint the whole portfolio.

7.2 Trading in the Future Cleared OTC Environment

One result of the Dodd Frank Act is to require OTC 'swaps'[391] to be traded on one of two US derivatives execution venues (as we outlined in section 5.3.2). Either a Designated Contract Market ('DCM') or Swap Execution Facility ('SEF') will have to be used[392], subject to certain exceptions. The CFTC have defined under what circumstances a SEF or DCM can make a product 'available to trade'[393]. As one might expect, these are similar to the attributes required for clearing discussed in section 6.2.3. The following factors are required:

1. Whether there are ready and willing buyers and sellers;

2. The frequency or size of transactions on swap execution facilities, designated contract markets, or of bilateral transactions;

3. The trading volume on swap execution facilities, designated contract markets, or of bilateral transactions;

4. The number and types of market participants;

5. The bid/ask spread;

6. The usual number of resting firm or indicative bids and offers;

7. Whether a swap execution facility's trading system or platform will support trading in the swap; or

8. Any other factor that the swap execution facility may consider relevant.

The method by which trading will take place on a SEF or DCM is the subject of much debate. The two models likely to be offered are Request For Quote and Central Limit Order Book. We begin by looking at these, then turn to the consequences of the new execution methods.

7.2.1   Request for quote

The RFQ process is simple in concept: a party uses a screen to enter the details of the trade they wish to execute, then 'sends' it out for quotes to other parties within the trading platform. The requester receives price quotes. Typically the best price is highlighted and can be accepted with a single click or button push. The CFTC mandates that there must be at least two quotes provided[394]: at the time of writing the SEC requirement is less clear, but it seems likely that all users of a platform do not have to respond to an RFQ.

7.2.2   Central limit order book

Traditional exchanges use central order books, as discussed in section 5.3.1. The idea that the counterparty remains anonymous: rather, the platform select a counterparty based on the trading parties' price constraints. The trade is then sent for clearing almost immediately. At the time of writing one exchange, Tera Exchange, have announced they provide support for trading OTC derivatives using this model, but few other SEFs have intimated that they will support it.

7.2.3 Accepting trades for clearing

Once a trade is executed, it starts as a bilateral trade within the ISDA documentation framework. If it is then submitted for clearing: the CCP will check that it is clearable, complete margin checks, then begin the trade registration process.

Current CFTC rules require that clearing houses accept trades for clearing within 60 seconds[395]. This is burdensome in many ways. For instance, it requires the IM required for the portfolio including the new trade to be recalculated and this amount compared to the value of the IM held in less than a minute.

CME has demonstrated a rapid process here. It is claimed that the Javelin system platform in conjunction with CME clearing can process transactions from trading to cleared within 2 seconds[396], although this relies on an approach to measuring the risk of a trade (and hence calculating IM) using a percentage of notional or a few sensitivities, rather than performing a complete risk calculation.

Other CCPs are modifying their intraday registration process to meet the CFTC requirement, moving away from the idea of calling margin as needed. Rather, clearing members will have to over-collateralise their portfolios so that trades which increase IM can be cleared speedily. This increases both the credit and liquidity risk of the situation.

7.2.4 Block trading and block allocation

Many investment managers manage multiple funds with similar investment mandates. They often aggregate their trading activity into large trades, then allocate parts of the trade to different funds post-execution as illustrated in figure 7.7.

Large trades are also generated by various other activities, such as end users bond issuance (which creates the need to hedge substantial amounts of interest rate risk), and retail product issuance (creating the need for the issuer to hedge).

Block trading involves larger notionals and more risk, and so block trades have a greater impact on swap prices when executed. The CFTC has accepted that trading of large notional sizes needs to be given more privacy and that it may be executed off-platform to avoid unwanted price increases. It has also been in a dialogue with the industry over how to define a block.

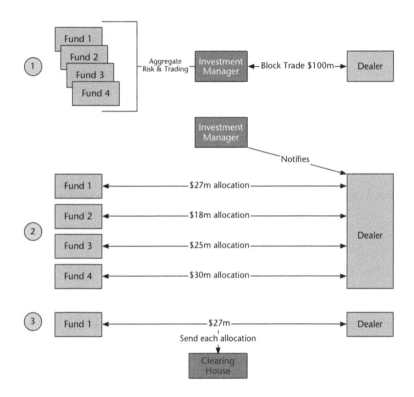

Figure 7.7: Block allocation in bilateral and cleared execution models

Any trade meeting the eventual definition of a block will not need to be traded on a SEF. Instead it will be possible to execute it bilaterally and then record the transaction (perhaps via a SEF). The reporting of a block trade to a Swap Data Repository need not be 'as soon as technologically possible' (as it is with smaller trades) but instead, as discussed in section 5.3.3, will have a more relaxed reporting deadline.

The trade allocation process introduces some issues when block trades are cleared. For instance, CCPs have thus far assumed in their workflow that allocations are complete, as this defines the legal entity who has traded (something that the clearing house needs to know, not least so that it can segregate margin properly). Fund managers and others executing on behalf of third parties will have to bear these issues in mind in the post mandatory clearing environment, especially when higher levels of segregation, with their accompanying need for the CCP to know the precise legal identity of the end client, are involved.

7.2.5 Push, ping and hub

A common feature of exchange trading is that members pre-fund their margin account so as to enable trades to be accepted for clearing immediately. In the OTC market the longer maturities and larger sizes mean the risk for each trade is potentially greater. This means:

- Large degrees of over-collateralisation are required to give 'head room' to trade;

- The process of calculating margin for the portfolio after a new trade is cleared is more complex; and

- The decision making required for both clearing members (deciding whether they can safely execute a new trade given the amount of extra margin they have available) and clearing houses is more difficult.

Trading venues would also like to avoid broken trades where either the CCP or the clearing member cannot accept a trade for clearing because sufficient margin is not available or because it breaks a credit limit. The CM has credit exposure to the client, as it guarantees them to the CCP, so its risk appetite acts as a constraint here. CMs tend to set credit limits for clients and to require that new trades do not exceed them. The problem is how these are allocated once multiple execution and clearing venues are involved. Three models are currently under discussion to manage this process (as depicted in figure 7.8):

1. *Push*, where the intermediary splits the credit limit of the client across multiple venues;

2. *Ping*, where each SEF uses a message to query the intermediary on their willingness to accept the trade; and

3. *Hub*, where an industry utility holds a central record of the limits, and then uses the Push or Ping model to control utilisation.

The disadvantage of the Push model is that the split of credit limit across each SEF is static, and hence waste is likely, unless the limit can be dynamically reallocated.

The Ping and Hub models require high speed messaging and decision making, which is expensive to implement and operationally risky.

At the time of writing, Markit are due to launch a Hub solution. There is aggressive competition for roles in the future OTC derivatives market infrastructure, so competitors such as ICE or Traiana may launch their

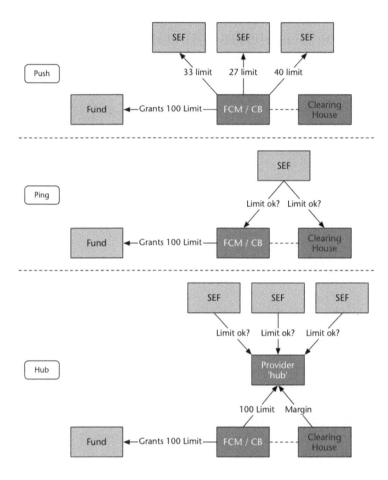

Figure 7.8: The three models of credit verification

own services too. In any event it seems that aggressive trade acceptance regulations have created the need for new infrastructure and, until this is fully functioning, the liquidity impact of clearing mandates will be higher due to the need for over-collateralisation.

7.3 CCP Processes for Clearing Members

The discussion of trade processing now continues with an overview of the processes by which clearing members interact with CCPs. This happens when new trades are submitted, when margin is called, and when a clearing member defaults.

7.3.1 Trading and acceptance for clearing

The steps involved in trading and clearing for direct members of a clearing house follow a series of generic steps. These are illustrated in figure 7.9 and discussed below:

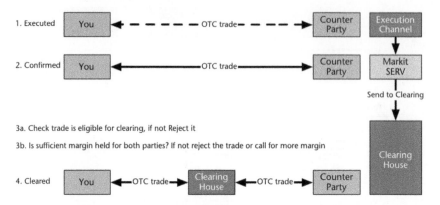

Figure 7.9: Schematic of central clearing for clearing members

1. *Execution*: Execute the trade using one of the execution methods mentioned earlier.

2. *Confirmation/Affirmation*: In time this step may prove unnecessary due electronic trading. For the moment firms have prevailed upon trading platforms to route trades into MarkitSERV to centralise the back-office processes for completing the agreement of the trade parameters.

3. *Submit for clearing*: In the future environment, firms will typically have pre-agreed the destination CCP, to meet the CFTC regulations for rapid clearing. The major dealers will be members at most or all OTC derivatives CCPs, so the decision on where to clear may depend on fees or other preferences rather than connectivity. For a client trade, the end user will choose where to clear and the CM will follow the client's instructions.

4. *Acceptance*: There is a difference of opinion in the CCP market as of writing as to whether to call for margin intraday. In current processing models, a CCP can measure the risk on a new trade and if needed call for top-up margin before trade registration. This margin call and settlement cycle could take up to an hour, significantly beyond the CFTC 60 second requirement. CCPs

are offering different approaches to address this issue, such as proactively suggesting margin top-ups but otherwise rejecting trades which would normally cause a margin call.

7.3.2   The daily processing cycle

CCPs have a daily processing cycle which aims to recalculate and call for all required margin amounts, and to settle net cash amounts, at least once per day. The typical process from the end of the business day is as follows:

1.   Close the customer accounts.

2.   Calculate the end of day VM and new IM amounts.

3.   Calculate all other trade related settlement amounts

4.   Produce reports, or data feeds to the members showing the net settlement amounts per currency.

5.   Before the system re-opens for business, require each member to settle their net amounts.

6.   Re-open the service and begin accepting trades again.

In an ideal world the period from closing the member's account at End of Day ('EOD') to re-opening should be as short as possible, so as to provide a global service: figure 7.10 shows a typical pattern. Receiving the margin call payments from the member is a dependency, as is delivering reports and data back to members. This is a major logistical challenge for large OTC derivatives clearing houses.

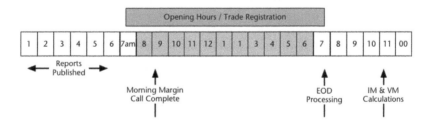

Figure 7.10: An illustration of a clearing house's daily processing cycle

CCPs settle net per currency to minimise the number of payments to be made. They must receive required amounts before allowing more trades into the members account. If this does not occur, then a default can be declared.

An example of this was the Lehman default at SwapClear discussed in section 6.5.3. Lehman was unable to pay the margin demanded on September 15th 2008, and by 11am it was declared in default within SwapClear by the CCP's Risk Committee.

7.3.3   The default management process for a clearing member

In the exchange traded futures market, the close out of a member's positions after default typically happens within one day: the CCP can usually terminate the positions quickly, due to the liquidity of the contracts[397]. Any parties to the other side of the trades see no more profits or losses as a result.

In the cleared OTC derivatives market, the norm has become a process whereby the defaulter's trades are put through an auction process. Non-defaulting clearing members are obliged by the clearing house rules to bid in this auction. If the auction fails, the clearing house can forcibly allocate the defaulter's portfolio at a price it sets, as we discussed in section 6.5.3.

The defaulter's IM and DF contributions are available to the CCP to service the defaulter's portfolio, and to hedge risk before the auction is carried out. The process of hedging followed by subsequent auction, while necessary given the less liquid nature of cleared OTC derivatives portfolios, can be extended. Thus, as we explained in section 3.3.2, a longer margin period of risk is appropriate for OTC derivatives portfolios, with 5 days having become the market standard.

The default management process at each CCP is partially visible from publically available rules, but the details often remain private to the members, as there are product specific and legal requirements which each has to negotiate. In outline the process has three phases:

1. Hedging risk in the portfolio to reduce swings in value[398];

2. Providing files of trades to the remaining members;

3. Running the auction and rebooking trades to winners.

This may take as long as three weeks if the defaulting clearing member has a large or concentrated portfolio. For instance, LCH.Clearnet reported[399] that in their handling of the Lehman default, 90% of the risk was removed from the defaulter's portfolio in the first week, and the auction process on all 66,000 trades was completed within 3 weeks, without loss to the default fund. Excess IM not required to fund the close out was returned to the defaulter's estate.

7.4 Clearing for Clients

For firms that choose not to join a CCP directly, or who do not meet the membership criteria, a model exists to give them access to clearing, by using an intermediary. This is client clearing, as we reviewed in section 6.4. In the US, the intermediary is a Futures Commission Merchant: outside the US they are often referred to either (as we have previously) as a Clearing Member or as a Clearing Broker ('CB').

7.4.1 The clearing process

The workflow to clear a client trade has converged upon an approach that remains close to the Exchange traded model but still allows for the possibility of a trade to fail to clear. The steps in the process in general are illustrated in figure 7.11. These are:

1. *Execution*: The trade is executed using one of the methods mentioned earlier.

2. *Confirmation/Affirmation*: This step is not necessary for a system with direct electronic connections to SwapClear and/or other CCPs: if this feature is not present, confirmation proceeds as in the dealer model.

3. *Submit for clearing*: The client will have elected which CCP and intermediary they wish the trade to be cleared by. When the trade arrives at the CCP an additional step is needed before acceptance.

4. *Intermediation*: The intermediary must have the credit line capacity to take on the client trade, and as described above must make a decision to accept the trade. Different CCPs have different approaches here. For instance, CME currently offer a model where they will carry out the credit decision on behalf of the intermediary by making a delegated calculation, using measures such as gross notional, net notional, PV01 or full IM recalculation[400].

5. *Margin check*: In theory a CCP will measure the additional exposure generated by a new trade. It should also monitor any build-up of exposure during the day due to market moves or changes in initial margin. What happens here is not standardised. Some CCPs seek to offset the risk of new trades by making a rapid margin call; others encourage firms to post additional funds to cover the potential increase in IM so a call is not necessary. Note that despite the CFTC's requirement to achieve registration

within 60 seconds of acceptance by the CB/FCM, there is no time limit on margin calls.

6. *Acceptance*: When all of the requisite checks have been passed, the CCP accepts the trade. In the agency model, the client now faces the CCP directly, while in the principal to principal model, it is the clearing member who faces the clearing house. The trade can now properly be described as cleared.

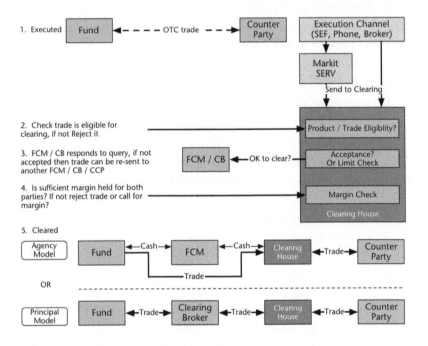

Figure 7.11: An illustration of client clearing

Once a client has trades in clearing, their settlement relationship is with their intermediary, who in turn settles on their behalf with the CCP. Should a CCP wish to make an intraday margin call, it is up to the intermediary to decide how to process that call for a client. Different client clearing agreements will require clearing members either to pass the call straight through to the client, or to pre-fund it.

It should be noted that each margin call takes time to meet. Therefore if the CM passes the call onto the client, funds potentially do not arrive in a segregated account until the client has settled with the CM, and the CM has then settled with the CCP.

7.4.2 Client default

One of the obligations on an FCM or CB is to take responsibility for the default of a client. Should a client default, the CCP will transfer the client portfolio (and associated margin) onto the books of the clearing member, who then has to carry the risk. In the US model not all FCMs will have trading capability, so some will rely upon another firm acting on their behalf to unwind the client trades, or net them off. Outside the US, many firms who offer a CB service are also large traders in their own names, so they have the capability in-house to wind down the client portfolio.

This obligation is the fundamental reason clearing members need to measure the build-up of risk in client portfolios: a default will have a direct effect on them.

7.4.3 Clearing member default in the principal-to-principal model

The process for the management of CM defaults will be managed by CCPs outside the United States. If each client of the defaulting clearing member has a backup or alternative CM, then the CCP will attempt to port clients, as we discussed in section 6.4.3.

This proceeds as follows. The CCP will provide backup CMs with the clients' trade portfolio. It will allow them time to make a credit decision, just as they would for individual trades, but with a longer timescale. If a backup CB accepts the client portfolio, then margin assets are refunded to the client (or in some cases bonds liquidated into cash, which in itself is an issue): this allows the client to meet the margin call from the replacement CM. The process is represented in figure 7.12.

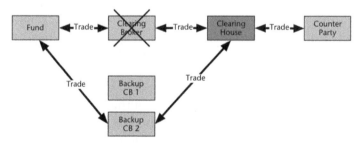

1. Primary CB is declared in default, accounts suspended
2. CCP provides Backup CB1 & Backup CB 2 with details of the Funds' Trade Portfolio
3. CB 2 agrees to accept the trades
4. CCP transfers the trade portfolio to the CB 2 account
5. CCP refunds the margin assets held by the Primary CB to the Fund
6. CB 2 calls the Fund for margin, which Fund meets, using the assets from step 5

Figure 7.12: Schematic of client porting on clearing member default

If porting is not possible then the CCP will close out the client portfolio, refunding any margin after close-out that is due to the client based on the segregation model that they have elected.

7.4.4 Clearing member default in the FCM model

The default management process is less clear in the US, as the CFTC have not (at time of writing) finalised the rules relating to clearing member default. However it is clear that after an FCM fails the Commission will be involved in making decisions on how to reallocate client portfolios to non-defaulting FCMs. It is reasonable to assume that the end result will be that client portfolios are transferred to other FCMs in a similar way to the non-US process, but with greater intervention from the regulator (who will presumably both be concerned with systemic risk, and with ensuring that the receiving FCM is not put at risk by the ported client).

7.5 Other Issues

Market participants will have to be aware of the processing requirements relating to margin under their chosen segregation model, and of the ability to simplify their cleared portfolio. We examine these issues next.

7.5.1 Higher levels of segregation outside the US

CCPs are still developing their segregation models outside the US, with few offerings at the time of writing which offer higher levels. One exception is Eurex, which does offer full segregation. This vertically integrated market and CCP group launched their IRS clearing service in 2012 with the promise that clients can elect to have all aspects of their business held apart from those of any other client or their clearing member. Full segregation increases operational costs by requiring cash and depository accounts for each client. It is illustrated in figure 7.13.

7.5.2 The omnibus model

A business model used globally is that of the intermediary calling for individual margin amounts for each client, but paying the CCP for a net margin amount by grouping trades in one account at the CCP. The effect of this omnibus segregation to retain excess margin assets within the FCM which can then be invested to make a return. The model is illustrated in figure 7.14, and an example of it follows.

- Net margin across co-mingled trades required by the CCP for Fund 1 and Fund 2: $100

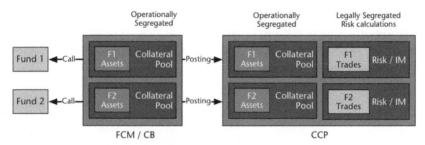

Figure 7.13: A depiction of full segregation (sometimes known as 'LSOS' for legal segregation and operational segregation).

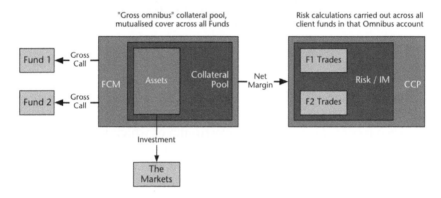

Figure 7.14: A schematic of the omnibus or futures model of segregation

* Margin on Fund 1 trades only: $60
* Margin on Fund 2 trades only: $75
* Total margin assets delivered to the CB/FCM: $135
* Margin assets delivered to the CCP by the CB/FCM: $100
* Monies available for reuse by the CB/FCM: $35

The downside of this arrangement for the client is that they do not know if their trades are being mingled with those of a loss making client at the same CM. If this second client defaults and bankrupts the clearing member, this could cause a margin deficiency for the non-defaulting client. (We discuss this 'fellow client' risk further in section 6.4.4.)

7.5.3 The legal segregation with operational co-mingling model

The CFTC have accepted and mandated a compromise between omnibus and full segregation. The legally segregated but operationally co-mingled

('LSOC') model[401] has some of the operational advantages of omnibus segregation, as there are a reduced number of cash or depository accounts. Legally, though, there is a higher degree of customer funds protection than in the omnibus model.

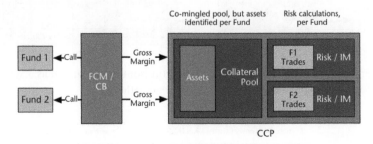

Figure 7.15: The proposed legally segregated operationally co-mingled or LSOC model

The LSOC model is illustrated in figure 7.15. Here, each Fund delivers bonds to the CCP, which will hold them in a single depository account, but keep records (assumed to be electronic) of which bond belongs to which Fund. The rules of the CCP will protect the assets of each Fund so that no client suffers losses in a clearing member or fellow client default.

7.5.4 'Trade netting' for cleared positions

The standardised nature of exchange traded derivatives (and their settlement model) mean that it is easy to trade in and out of a position. One key feature of this is that opposite trades cancel: if 10 futures are bought then 4 of the same contract are sold, the position is long 6. This type of cancellation is unusual in the OTC market as there are many more trade parameters which have to match before cancellation is possible[402].

CCPs have developed an approach to what they refer to as 'trade netting'. This process uses rules to define when one trade can reduce or eliminate the position in another. Trade netting[403] requires that all economic trade parameters are identical, that the cash-flow dates are aligned, and that the two trades are at the same price. Each CCP offers flexibility to include or exclude trades from the trade netting process.

Trade netting takes place in a single sided sense: one member can apply trade netting to their portfolio, without any action being required by the other (original) counterparty to the trade. The process ensures that the CCP remains flat of risk, as depicted in figure 7.16.

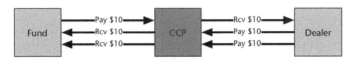

becomes after the application of one-sided trade netting

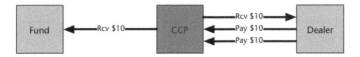

Figure 7.16: The effect of CCP-style 'trade netting'

Summary of the Differences between Cleared and Uncleared Environments

The new OTC trade processing environment will be quite different from that of the past, with many OTC products being cleared. Figure 7.17 summarises the changes.

	Before	*After*
Trading	Phone, IDB, Single Dealer Platforms	SEF mainly, with block trading a special case
Confirmation	Mainly via MarkitSERV	May remain as-is, challenged by direct links from SEFs to CCPs
Margining	Many bilateral CSAs have VM, fewer have IM	Cleared trades require VM, IM and Default Fund
Processing	Bilateral, decentralised	Highly automated via CCP
Settlement	Direct bilateral payments	Via CCPs' settlement infrastructure

Figure 7.17: Summary of the trade processing changes brought about by OTC derivatives clearing

We have seen that both levels of automation and the cost of margin will be at their highest levels ever once clearing mandates come into force. Meanwhile, bilateral trading will continue, in many cases with much the same operational environment as before. This represents a considerable challenge for the industry both in preparing for change, and in managing the two workflows.

Notes

[381]The Senior Supervisors Group, in their document *Risk Management Lessons from the Global Banking Crisis of 2008* (October 2009) noted that the industry's 'substantial efforts' here had 'significantly mitigated' systemic risk.

[382]See www.barx.com for more details.

[383]SWIFT is the Society for Worldwide Interbank Financial Telecommunication: see www.swift.com.

[384] XML is a type of mark-up language whereby the nature of data items is explicitly tagged. HTML is a member of the same family of languages.

[385]See www.fpml.org for more details.

[386]This survey is available via www2.isda.org/functional-areas/research/surveys/operations-benchmarking-surveys.

[387]This refers to FX Options.

[388]www.dtcc.com/products/derivserv/suite/ps_index.php has a fuller description.

[389]More details on this can be found at www.theice.com/ice_link.jhtml.

[390]A fuller account of MarkitSERV can be found at www.markitserv.com/ms-en.

[391]The term is a defined one.

[392]The CFTC define a DCM thus: 'DCMs are most like traditional futures exchanges, which may allow access to their facilities by all types of traders, including retail customers': see www.cftc.gov/IndustryOversight/TradingOrganizations/DCMs/index.htm. A swap execution facility is (at time of writing) more loosely defined as 'a trading system or platform in which multiple participants have the ability to execute or trade swaps by accepting bids and offers made by multiple participants in the facility or system, through any means of interstate commerce, including any trading facility, that: (1) Facilitates the execution of swaps between persons; and (2) Is not a designated contract market': see 77 FR 66288 available at www.cftc.gov/ucm/groups/public/@lrfederalregister/documents/file/2012-25764a.pdf.

[393]See the CFTC's proposed rule 17 CFR Parts 37 and 38, *Process for a Designated Contract Market or Swap Execution Facility To Make a Swap Available To Trade* (76 FR 77728, December 2011) available via www.cftc.gov/LawRegulation/DoddFrankAct/Rulemakings/DF_12_DCMRules/index.htm.

[394]This has proved one of the most controversial parts of the CFTC's rule making: the initial proposal was for five quotes, and the current requirement for two quotes rises to three after the first year.

[395]The language of the rule is 'quickly as would be technologically practicable if fully automated systems were used', with staff guidance that that means 60 seconds. See 77 FR 37803, *Customer Clearing Documentation, Timing of Acceptance for Clearing, and Clearing Member Risk Management* (April 2012) available at www.cftc.gov/ucm/groups/public/@lrfederalregister/documents/file/2012-7477a.pdf.

[396]The claim is from the Javelin press release *Javelin and CME Execute and Clear $4.1 Billion of Interest Rate Swaps in Real Time* (December 2011) available via www.thejavelin.com.

[397]This may not be the case if the defaulter has a large position relative to the market.

[398]It is difficult for clearing members to bid on a portfolio if its value is too volatile: they need to be able to estimate the value (& hence VM) and risk (& hence IM) of the portfolio before the auction, and be reasonably sure these estimates will not change too much as the auction proceeds. Therefore it is conventional to auction a hedged portfolio than an unhedged one, especially if the portfolio is large.

[399]The details are from LCH.Clearnet post *Managing the Lehman Brothers' Default* available at www.lchclearnet.com/swaps/swapclear_for_clearing_members/managing_the_lehman_brothers_default.asp.

[400]The level of margin, and who must provide it, depend on the segregation model. In a fully segregated situation, it is the client's account which must contain sufficient margin, while in an omnibus model, it is the clearing member's problem.

[401]The Davis Polk Client Memorandum *CFTC Adopts Final Rule on Protection of Cleared Swap Customer Collateral* (23rd January 2012) available via www.davispolk.com gives a further discussion of the LSOC regime.

[402]Thus for an interest rate swap, a new trade reduces the position in an old one only if it is with the same counterparty and has exactly the same terms (including maturity and start date).

[403]CCP trade netting is similar to trade compression within the cleared product set: the terminology is slightly unfortunate, as it is rather different from close out netting.

8

Risks in OTC Derivatives Central Clearing

They will attack us
When they learn that our leader
Is lying dead.
He who protected us
From those who would assail us
Who preserved the kingdom
After the heroes fell
Beowulf

Introduction

Chairman of the Federal Reserve Board Ben Bernanke said in 2011[404]:

> *Increased reliance on clearinghouses to address problems in*
> *other parts of the system increases further the need to ensure*
> *the safety of clearinghouses themselves.*

This is surely right[405]. Therefore it behoves us to examine the risks that assail clearing houses, and how CCPs might fail or become distressed.

The consideration of clearing house risk naturally leads to risk mitigation: what CCPs can do to protect themselves, and how regulators can enforce some of those protections. It is also important to consider the risks created by CCPs for other elements of the financial system. For instance, the possibility of CCP failure represents counterparty credit risk for its clearing members. These CCP-originated risks are increasing, and any analysis of the central clearing must include them.

We end the chapter with a discussion of the risks created by clearing mandates. As currently drawn, these create extra credit risk and liquidity risk, since they require an arbitrary risk-blind split of netting sets. The process is illustrated, facilitating a consideration of this and other supervisory choices in the next chapter.

8.1 Risks to CCPs

Financial institutions fail either because they sustain losses so large that they become insolvent, or because they can no longer finance themselves. For banks, liquidity risk typically causes failure before insolvency[406], but this may not be the case for CCPs. The obvious failure modes for an OTC derivatives CCP are:

- One or more clearing members default, give rise to losses comparable to[407] the CCP's financial resources;

- The CCP suffers substantial losses due to risks other than counterparty non-performance;

- A CCP cannot meet a demand for cash.

We examine each of these in subsequent subsections.

8.1.1 The counterparty credit risk loss distribution & CCP financial resources

The key job of a CCP is to take counterparty credit risk. Against this risk, it has financial resources (as described in section 6.1.5). The safety of the CCP therefore depends on the size of these financial resources compared to possible counterparty credit risk losses.

The counterparty credit risk loss distribution depends on the amounts that the CCP might lose were a clearing member to default, and the concentration of those defaults. Neither of those key parameters are known: the value of the portfolio of a defaulting clearing member at close out is uncertain, as are the default comovements of the CCP's clearing members. Still, the technology of chapter 3 could be used to analyse the problem. A margin period of risk could be picked and an EE profile for each clearing member could be estimated. Once the effect of margin was included, this would give the CCP a distribution of losses above margin for each clearing member[408].

Figure 8.1 illustrates the idea: here we see two loss distribution as estimated by a sophisticated CCP. Were the clearing member to default,

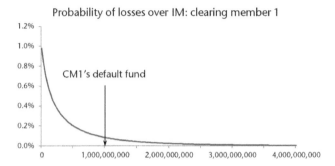

Figure 8.1: An illustration of the distribution of losses above IM for two different clearing members (above and below).

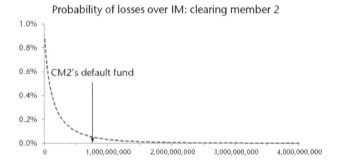

losses up to the clearing member's default fund contribution would be borne by the defaulter; non-defaulting clearing members' default fund contributions and CCP equity would be available to absorb losses above that. In the illustration the first clearing member has a riskier portfolio than the second, and so their default fund contributions are larger.

The next step would be to combine these loss distributions for different clearing members into a single counterparty credit risk loss distribution for the CCP[409].

Figure 8.2 illustrates the combined loss distribution[410]. The probability of failure of the CCP due to counterparty credit risk is given by the area to the right of the financial resources line: here losses are sufficiently big to overwhelm the clearing house's defences[411].

Estimations such as these are particularly sensitive to the relationship between clearing member defaults. As an illustration, consider figure 8.3. This shows the same analysis with the only difference being that multiple clearing member defaults are a little more likely. The area to the right of the Total financial resources line is twice as large, representing a higher

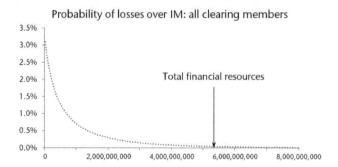

Figure 8.2: An illustration of the combined loss distribution.

probability that the CCP's financial resources will be exhausted[412]. It is hard to know which of these lines is right, as there is no easy way to measure clearing member default comovement[413].

We recommend that clearing houses conduct counterparty credit risk analysis in this type of framework for three reasons:

1. The data and modelling required to complete an analysis like this is much the same as that required for IMM models. These are both the regulatory standard for banks and are (close to[414]) the state-of-the-art in counterparty credit risk. Given that the major rationale of a clearing house is to take counterparty credit risk, it is appropriate that leading CCPs use leading approaches to counterparty credit risk management.

2. It would be helpful to be able to compare bank and CCP counterparty credit risk taking on the same terms. Furthermore, the disclosure by a CCP of its estimate of the probability of losses greater than financial resources would provide useful information to the market on its safety.

3. It is important that CCPs and their users understand the sensitivity of CCP IM and default estimates to clearing member credit quality and to the relationship between clearing members. Models like this, unlike the usual clearing house approach discussed in the next section, allow these sensitivities to be understood.

8.1.2 Default n

CCPs do not typically look at counterparty credit risk this way. Instead, they prefer to use the ideas of 'default 1' and 'default 2'. That is, they

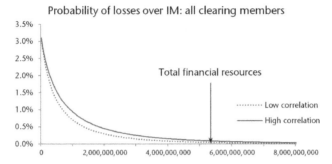

Figure 8.3: An illustration of the combined loss distribution under different clearing member default comovement assumptions.

seek to be robust under either the default of their largest clearing member, or their two largest clearing members. In order to do this, they estimate the potential clearing member losses in 'extreme but plausible' market conditions[415]. The biggest or biggest two of these are selected[416]. The CCP is then required to have sufficient financial resources to cover the losses caused by this default event.

This requirement illustrates another key issue in assessing the loss distribution of a CCP: that of the market data used to estimate the loss distribution. This must include stressed periods so that the loss distribution will not underestimate the kinds of losses that occur in a crisis. It is, after all, in just such situations that a clearing member is likely to fail.

If a CCP which was robust under default 2 actually suffered a large loss, then it might not have sufficient DF, and so it would have to make a capital call to top up its financial resources.

8.1.3 Operational risks and other causes of loss

CCPs are subject to operational risk, like any other financial institution. Moreover, since CCPs handle large amounts of money[417], some of which they invest, the risks are not inconsequential. As an illustration of this, consider the following uncongenial possibilities:

• After a large clearing member defaults, the relevant bankruptcy court rules that the CCP does not have the right of set-off against the clearing member, given the documentation that has been signed;

- ✦ A CCP suffers from an initially hidden systems problem which results in its trade population becoming unbalanced. As a result it is exposed to substantial market risks;

- ✦ Cash transferred to a CCP to meet initial margin requirements is invested by the CCP's treasury operation. This operation suffers a large rogue trader loss.

Typically none of these risks would be protected by a CCP's default waterfall, so the only element of financial resources available to support them would be CCP equity[418]. Moreover, the losses sustained from events like this could easily be much larger than a clearing house's equity capital so they could potentially cause a CCP to fail.

8.1.4 CCP liquidity risks

Liquidity risk arises at a CCP when it invests margin in assets which may not be liquidatable should margin have to be returned. Clearing houses therefore need to monitor and manage liquidity risks. This includes both ordinary and stressed conditions, especially since asset liquidity is likely to be lowest in a crisis. They should also have access to external liquidity[419].

8.2 CCP Risk I: Mitigation

There are a number of protections available to CCPs which could mitigate their business risks. These include limits on who may be a clearing member; effective governance; financial resources; and loss allocation mechanisms. We examine each of these in a subsequent subsection.

8.2.1 Membership and governance

CCP membership requirements and governance are an important defence: if a CCP were only to admit as clearing members firms which do not default, then it would be very stable. High membership standards help to reduce the risk that clearing members pose to their CCP.

Clear, transparent and equitable governance arrangements are also important. A key part of these is the CCP's risk committee. This is a body including representatives of clearing members and clients[420], together with independent board members, which should decide key risk issues such as the level of financial resources, the design of the waterfall, margin modelling, default procedures, clearing member membership rules and which products are to be cleared.

8.2.2 Assessing the adequacy of financial resources

Financial resources form a key protection against the principal risk CCPs face, counterparty credit risk. Therefore it is vital that they are sufficient. There are a number of important mitigants here:

* The models used to estimate margin amounts and default fund contributions must be thoroughly tested with both a range of real-world and hypothetical portfolios to ensure that they do in fact calculate the intended quantity for reasonably varied portfolios.

* There should be extensive testing of margin and default fund amounts against losses in both normal and stressed markets. This testing should be sufficient, in a statistical sense, to give confidence that the models do in fact meet the standards they aspire to in a range of market conditions[421].

* CCPs should conduct stress tests to validate their risk measures and procedures in times of crisis. This could for instance include very large market moves, multiple clearing member defaults, and extreme market illiquidity.

These tests should be reviewed regularly to ensure that they remain relevant, and redesigned when appropriate. Moreover CCPs which rely on a default n assumption should review their population of clearing members and market information on their comovement to ascertain whether this (necessarily jejune) assumption remains valid.

8.2.3 Credit risk beyond the waterfall

CCPs have a range of potential techniques available to mitigate counterparty credit risk losses beyond the funds available. These include capital calls (discussed in section 6.1.4), forced allocation of a defaulter's portfolio (which was touched upon in section 6.5.3) and 'loss allocation'. This last is a technique whereby a CCP enforces losses on its clearing members. For instance, it might 'haircut' margin, promising only to return a certain fraction of the amounts posted to it[422]. Another possibility is to 'force allocate' or put the portfolio of a defaulting clearing member (or members) at a price determined by the CCP to surviving CMs. This avoids the possibility of the CCP taking losses on closing out the portfolio. It also both provides a response should no clearing member provide an acceptable bid in a post-default auction, and strongly encourages clearing members to participate in such an auction.

It is important to note that techniques such as loss allocation or portfolio puts should only be used after a CCP's default waterfall has been exhausted, or is very near to exhaustion, and thus they are essentially CCP resolution tools. In particular, CCPs should be required to bear very substantial equity losses before forcing risk back onto their members: this provides them with an incentive to avoid big losses.

8.3 CCP Risk II: Externalities

We now turn to clearing houses' external relations. Specifically, we look at how OTC derivatives CCPs keep the confidence of their clearing members; how they are regulated; what they must publically disclose; and how they might be resolved should they become distressed.

8.3.1 Confidence and the adequacy of CCP financial resources

Clearing houses have to keep the confidence of their clearing members, for if confidence is lost, clearing will cease[423]. It is difficult to determine in the abstract how much a CCP can lose and still keep confidence, not least because much would depend on the regulatory response. But it is obvious that there is a tipping point after which a CCP would be unattractive as a clearer of new trades even if it was still solvent. This indicates that CCP financial resources perform at least five functions:

1. Absorbing losses caused by clearing member failure;

2. Absorbing other losses;

3. Giving the CCP 'skin in the game' so that it is incentivised to minimise losses;

4. Keeping confidence in the CCP; and

5. Funding the CCP during wind-down.

Typically 1. is mostly met by initial margin and the default fund; 2. and 3. by CCP equity[424]; and 4. and 5. by equity, the default fund, and capital calls. Of these requirements, 1., 2. and 5. are quantitative: it is possible to make reasonable estimates of the resources needed to meet them. 3. and 4. are more judgemental, since incentive and confidence are difficult to model. It is clear, though, that some resources are needed to meet these needs, since a CCP which suffered sufficient losses that the quantitative elements of financial resources were fully allocated would not be a going concern.

8.3.2 CCP regulation

This brings us to the current state of CCP regulation[425]. As OTC derivatives central clearing has grown in size, so regulation has evolved[426]. It continues to develop, but several facets of the new regime are clear:

- A CCP authorisation regime, whereby a CCP's supervisor has criteria for the admission of clearing houses as a regulated body (and for the withdrawal of authorisation);

- An international recognition process whereby authorities can deem other jurisdictions' CCPs adequately supervised;

- Requirements for CCP ownership, governance, record keeping, disclosure, and regulatory reporting;

- The requirement for non-discriminatory access to CCPs, so that there are clearly articulated membership standards, and bodies meeting them are permitted to clear if they agree to standard terms;

- Rules on segregation, portability and interoperability;

- Minimum standards for margin and default funds;

- Limitations on acceptable collateral and on CCPs' liquidity risk management;

- Rules on how defaults are managed;

- Statutes which allow for CCP resolution and define CCPs' access to central bank liquidity.

We touch on a number of these aspects in subsequent subsections.

8.3.3 Access to central clearing

OTC derivatives clearing houses enjoy a natural monopoly: successful ones are likely to grow, since they can offer netting benefits for new transactions with previously cleared portfolios[427]. This means that absent fragmentation caused by regulation, there will be at most a small number of CCPs per asset class. In turn, a dominant 'downstream' position potentially allows a CCP to extract 'upstream' revenues by only providing access to markets who will pay. A swaps marketplace that is not permitted access to clearing would be a losing proposition. Therefore some measure of protection is required to stop dominant CCPs exerting quasi-monopoly power over marketplaces.

Similar arguments apply to clearing member access[428]: CCPs should be permitted to set standards for clearing member strength and capabilities, but they should not be permitted to block access to qualified firms for anti-competitive reasons.

8.3.4 Transparency

Big OTC derivatives CCPs are vital pieces of markets infrastructure in the post-crisis financial system. Dealers will have substantial exposures to the CCPs they use through initial margin and default fund contributions. Therefore it is important that CCP safety can be assessed by market participants. This requires disclosure.

There has been some regulation in this area[429], but it falls short of what is required for third parties to be able to make an accurate assessment of CCP safety. Systemically important[430] OTC derivatives CCPs should disclose:

* Membership requirements and clearing members;

* Precise details of the CCP's methodology for calculating initial margin and default fund contributions;

* Actual amounts of margin and default fund held, the clearing house's capacity to make capital calls and/or allocate losses, and the level of its equity before and after supervisory deductions;

* Details of back and stress testing carried out, with their results;

* An analysis of the probability and extent of losses in excess of the CCP's financial resources;

* Analysis of the enforceability of the CCP's rules (including close out netting) in all relevant jurisdictions, and with details of any conflicts of law or of regulatory jurisdiction;

* Disclosure of the clearing houses' default procedures and water-fall[431];

* Information on the CCP's segregation arrangements, including a clear discussion of when margin is at risk from CCP failure, from clearing member failure, from 'fellow client' risk, and from custodial risks;

* Estimates of the CCP's operational and other non-default-related risks, and the capital allocated to mitigating them.

This is not a complete list: we have simply set out a few of the more important pieces of information that would be required to make an independent credit assessment of an OTC derivatives CCP. Of course, supervisors' assessments are important here too, and these should also be publically available[432].

8.3.5 CCP resolution

If a CCP becomes distressed, then regulators may wish to step in. There are many forms this intervention could take, ranging from liquefying the CCP (perhaps by lending central bank money against collateral), through forced recapitalisation and/or loss allocation, to winding-down or sale of the CCP[433].

The situation here is similar to the one for banks discussed in section 5.6. Supervisors need information which would allow them to determine when a CCP is close to failure, and intervention authority. This should allow for a range of different approaches, including potentially splitting the CCP into 'new CCP' and 'run off CCP' vehicles. Contract continuity is particularly important during OTC derivatives CCP resolution, so the legislative framework must be highly robust in this area.

The loss allocation techniques discussed previously (in section 8.2.3) potentially offer an alternative to CCP bankruptcy or state recapitalisation[434]. However, it is important to note that a single large financial institution might be the member of multiple CCPs: its failure would therefore cause CM default at multiple CCPs. If several CCPs inflict losses on substantially the same group of financial institutions in a short period of time, then a crisis may be exacerbated. Thus while loss allocation may be a useful technique should a CCP suffer losses that are only marginally in excess of its financial resources, it may be destabilising for larger losses[435]: potentially more destabilising than CCP bankruptcy. Flexibility is key here. Supervisors should have the ability to use a range of resolution techniques[436], including an orderly bankruptcy filing.

8.4 Risks from CCPs

Clearing houses do not just have risk; they also cause it. Specifically, they create new risks for the rest of the financial system. These threats include systemic risk, liquidity risk and credit risk. Liquidity risk arises from margin calls, default fund reassessments, and capital calls. Credit risk arises through the risk of CCP failure, the risk of loss allocation, and capital call risk. We discuss these issues next.

8.4.1   Margin as a systemic risk

Most margin models produce higher IM requirements during conditions of market stress: they are somewhat procyclical. This can result in substantial liquidity stress as clearing members are forced by the exigencies of margin requirements to post increasing amounts to CCPs. For instance, the Brady Taskforce, reporting the events of October 1987, relates the following[437]:

> OCC [Options Clearing Corporation, a US CCP] members also faced substantial morning and intraday margin calls to cover the deterioration in the positions of put options sellers, both proprietary and customer. On October 19, the OCC issued four intraday margin calls that collected $1.0 billion from clearinghouse members. In many cases, the OCC clearing members, such as large investment banks, also belong to the CME. Like the CME clearinghouse, the OCC does not pay out excess margin funds on an intraday basis. Thus, OCC and CME clearing members were required to deposit $3.0 billion on Monday, October 19. Some of these deposits were to cover options losses that were offset by futures profits, which resulted in further strains on liquidity.

This kind of widespread liquidity stress in difficult conditions can justifiably be called a systemic risk.

8.4.2   CCP calls as a liquidity risk

It can be seen that the impact on the financial system of these procyclical margin practices can be destabilising. The effect on individual clearing members can be significant, too. Today, it is entirely conceivable that a dealer might face a multi-billion dollar margin call[438], with mere hours to meet it or be placed in default by the CCP.

Similar issues apply to default fund reassessments and capital calls: both of these can draw down substantial liquidity from clearing members during a period of stress.

8.4.3   The credit risks of clearing houses

The failure of a CCP could create very substantial credit risk. Clearing members might have to close out their cleared trades; their initial margin and default fund contributions would be at risk; and, depending on the resolution mechanism chosen, they might face additional capital calls or loss allocations or both. The potential loss amounts are enormous. It is therefore much to be hoped that CCP resolution will reduce the potential for large losses and provide certainty of outcome[439].

8.4.4 Investment risks

Cash transferred to the CCP to meet margin or default fund requirements is often invested by the CCP, as discussed in section 6.5.2. This creates two risks:

1. The risk that the CCP follows its investment policy but nevertheless suffers losses; and

2. The risk that funds are not invested as mandated, and losses result.

The members of the CCP's risk committee can control the first risk by setting an investment policy. Moreover, supervisors can and should require that CCPs carry capital to support investment risks. The second is a type of operational risk, and hence suggests that CCPs should also be required to keep capital to support operational risk.

Note that in either case, a relatively small loss on investments can snowball into a much larger one for clearing members. This is because once the investment loss has sufficiently depleted CCP equity, the clearing house will fail, potentially causing much larger close out losses. CCP resolution procedures therefore need to deal not just with stress caused by counterparty credit risk, but also with other causes of clearing house non-viability.

8.5 Risks from Mandatory Clearing

The regulations mandating clearing introduce risks to the financial system which would not be present if the central clearing of OTC derivatives was optional. Mandatory clearing splits netting sets, so that what was once a 'glued together' bilateral portfolio is cleaved into the part which must be cleared, and the rest. Typically the rest will include trades which cannot be cleared, so the original netting set must be split into a cleared and uncleared piece (although there may be some choice about how this is done if there are trades which are clearable but not mandated to be cleared). Thus for instance the netting set between A and B depicted in figure 2.1 might be split as shown in figure 8.4.

We begin by looking at the impact of this splitting of netting sets in more detail.

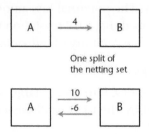

Figure 8.4: A splitting of the netting set between A and B

8.5.1 Split netting sets: valuation

Figure 8.4 depicted one split of a netting set. Originally the portfolio value was 4: when the netting set is split into clearable and unclearable pieces, the two fragments are worth 10 and -6 respectively. Let us assume that both A and B are clearing members, and that the bilateral CSA between A and B is tight. Then before clearing, A would post 4 of variation margin to B. When clearing is imposed, as in figure 8.5, A posts 10 of VM to the CCP, which the CCP passes on to B. B posts 6 of bilateral variation margin to A, and both A and B post IM to the CCP.

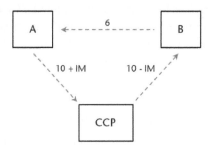

Figure 8.5: Margin movements after a bisection of the netting set

At first sight, this is not too bad. If we ignore IM, then both parties have the same net liquidity position as before: A is long 4 of margin and B is short 4. From B's perspective, it pays 10 to the CCP while receiving 6 from A. Of course there may be timing differences, so that the 10 may well have to be paid before the 6 is received, but perhaps this can be anticipated.

8.5.2 Split netting sets: multiple CCPs

The situation gets worse once we remember that a single CCP cannot currently clear all asset classes. Therefore, even ignoring jurisdictional issues, the two counterparties will likely have to use more than one clearing house. The 10 of cleared exposure therefore itself has to be split, say into 14 of interest rate derivatives exposure cleared at **CCP1** and -4 of CDS exposure cleared at **CCP2**. Figure 8.6 illustrates the new situation.

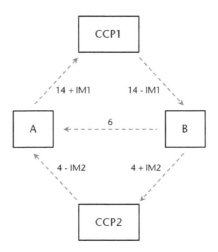

Figure 8.6: Margin movements after a trisection of the netting set

It can be seen that gross VM amount have increased again: from 4 in the bilateral case; to 16 with one CCP; and now 24 with two CCPs. These amounts have to be funded, as simultaneous margin movements are unlikely.

8.5.3 Split netting sets: risk

If we turn to the risk of the netting set, the situation worsens. If A and B are both dealers subject to the Basel Capital Accords then they will manage their bilateral netting set so that the effective EPE is small, as that produces the lowest capital requirements. Essentially they try to arrange their trades with each other such that the bilateral portfolio cannot change too much in value during the MPOR (as well as signing a tight CSA to minimise uncollateralised current exposure). Splitting the netting set will result in new bilateral and cleared portfolios which do not necessarily enjoy low effective EPEs. Indeed, since exotic (unclearable) derivatives are typically hedged with simpler (clearable) ones, the two portfolios might both have more risk than that of the original pre-mandatory-clearing portfolio. Figure 8.7 illustrates the phenomenon.

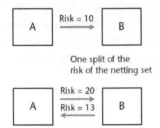

Figure 8.7: A splitting of the risk of the netting set between A and B

This means that even if A and B posted each other IM on their bilateral trades before clearing was imposed (something that would be unusual), that bilateral IM might be much lower than either the IM they had to post at the CCP post clearing or the IM they would post each other on the bilateral portfolio post split. Figure 8.8 illustrates the IM postings made by A and B based on our hypothetical split.

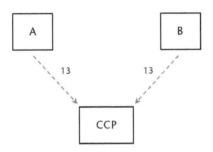

Figure 8.8: IM posting after a bisection of the netting set

This issue is mitigated by the multilateral netting benefits of clearing. After all, A and B do not deal only with each other, but also with other counterparties, some of whom may use the same CCP. Thus it is not the risk of A's cleared portfolio with B that matters, but the risk of its whole cleared portfolio at the CCP. This will hopefully contain trades which diversify the risk of the cleared portion of the portfolio with B.

8.5.4 Split netting sets: risk with two CCPs

In the last section, we saw that IM went up from 20 (if both parties posted bilaterally) to a gross of 66 once a single clearing house is introduced. This falls to 0 vs. 26 if there is no bilateral IM. Multiple clearing houses make the situation worse. Thus for instance if the cleared portfolio is split between CCP1 (which clears interest rate derivatives, say), and CCP2 (which clears CDS), we would have two lots of IM; one posted to each CCP.

We illustrate the situation by assuming that the 13 of risk for the cleared netting set illustrated in figure 8.7 is split into 12 of risk at CCP1 and 5 at CCP2[440]. The IM postings would then be as shown in figure 8.9.

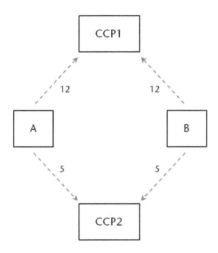

Figure 8.9: IM posting after a trisection of the netting set

Unequivocally, then, the more CCPs we have, the worse the issues around the splitting of nettings sets are. Gross VM amounts go up; IM goes up; the number of payments made go up; and of course the number of entities that the parties are exposed to the failure of goes up too.

8.5.5 *Joining the club*

Clearing mandates force each bank to decide between being a clearing member and being a client of a clearing member. Each choice has potential disadvantages:

- Clearing members have to post default fund, and this is at risk from mutualisation. Therefore even if a bank is eligible to be a clearing member, it is not clear that it would want to join the club as this would expose it to the risk of the other clearing members failing.

- On the other hand, clients of clearing members will probably enjoy less control over clearing houses, they will probably have higher capital requirements (unless they can 'look through' their clearing member to the CCP for capital purposes[441]), and they will probably enjoy a lower netting benefit[442].

This is an invidious choice in that it encourages concentration: only the largest dealers may decide to be clearing members, while medium-sized banks may withdraw partially or completely from dealing OTC derivatives.

8.5.6 *Risk transformation and the support for risk*

Clearing houses concentrate counterparty credit risk. They reduce the total amount of this risk thanks to multilateral netting: but they also increase it thanks to the splitting of netting sets. The former effect is probably more important than the latter, although data (as we discuss further in section 10.4.2) is sketchy. It is important to note that the financial resources that CCPs use to support this risk come almost entirely from within the existing system of OTC derivatives market participants. That is, they have not been required to raise substantial[443] amounts of *new* capital to support counterparty credit risk[444]. This is interesting, in that two policy choices are available to reduce the danger that a risk poses to the financial system without causing problems elsewhere:

1. Pool or diversify it to reduce the total amount of risk; or

2. Require that the financial system raises new capital to support it.

Central clearing attempts to use the first but not the second of these mechanisms.

Summary

If we step back from the detail, central clearing transforms risk in a simple way. It turns the low probability, medium severity risk of loss from bilateral counterparty default into the lower probability much higher severity risk of loss from CCP stress. Central clearing represents a trade-off between loss frequency and loss severity.

CCPs also introduce extra liquidity risk, thanks to their margin requirements. This effect is substantial, and procyclical CCP margin requirements represent a potent systemic risk to the post-clearing financial system.

Finally, mandatory clearing as implemented reduces the efficacy of multilateral netting. It increases both initial margin and gross variation margin flows compared to the uncleared market.

Notes

[404] B. Bernanke, *Clearinghouses, Financial Stability, and Financial Reform*, Speech at 2011 Financial Markets Conference, Stone Mountain, Georgia, April 4th 2011, available at www.federalreserve.gov/newsevents/speech/bernanke20110404a.htm.

[405] The need for highly robust CCPs is generally recognised in the official sector. For instance, the CPSS/IOSCO *Recommendations for Central Counterparties*, Consultative Report (March 2004) available at www.bis.org/publ/cpss61.pdf says 'Although a CCP has the potential to reduce risks to market participants significantly, it also concentrates risks and responsibilities for risk management. Therefore, the effectiveness of a CCP's risk control and the adequacy of its financial resources are critical aspects of the infrastructure of the markets it serves.' An update to this document, that has much of relevance to standards for clearing houses, is CPSS/IOSCO's *Principles for financial market infrastructures* (Consultative report, March 2011) available at www.bis.org/publ/cpss94.pdf.

[406] The failures of RBS or Washington Mutual are good examples.

[407] A CCP does not have to suffer credit losses which reduce its resources to zero to fail. Clearing members would likely start to withdraw from a CCP due to fears of an eventual default – or large capital call – well before that.

[408] Strictly, for each separately margined account, so under futures style segregation, we would have separate loss distributions for client and house accounts at each clearing member.

[409] In previous work, I made the analogy between CCP safety and CDO pricing. Essentially a CCP's financial resources (margin, default fund, equity etc.) correspond to the liabilities of a CDO. The CCP can take (unknown) losses given by the default of clearing members and the subsequent costs of closing out their portfolios. The safety of the CCP corresponds to asking what the probability that the tranches corresponding to the CCP's equity are exhausted is: see D. Murphy, *The systemic risks of OTC derivatives central clearing*, Journal of Risk Management in Financial Institutions, Volume 5, No. 3 (June 2012).

[410] We have illustrated the situation with IM given by the 99th percentile loss at the MPOR.

[411] The probability of losses this far into the tail is heavily dependent on the default comovement assumptions made about the clearing members.

[412] This indicates that if clearing member default comovement is higher, a much higher default fund is required to provide the same degree of CCP safety.

[413] If the Basel Committee's AVC multiplier is to be believed, default correlations for large financial institutions are 25% larger than for typical corporates. Still, taking 1.25x an implied correlation backed out e.g. from a traded index would likely not be a good approach, not least because such a correlation might be greater than one.

[414]This is perhaps a little generous to IMM models, given that they do not have default comovement modelling. Still, given IMM infrastructure, it would be relatively easy to model a bank's portfolio of counterparty credit risk as a CDO.

[415]The language is from the CPSS/IOSCO report *Principles for financial market infrastructures* (April 2012) available at www.bis.org/publ/cpss101.htm. The requirement is for CCPs that are 'involved in activities with a more-complex risk profile' or that are 'systemically important in multiple jurisdictions'.

[416]'Biggest' here means the clearing member(s) with the largest losses over IM.

[417]Tens of billions of dollars worth of initial margin; hundreds of billions of variation margin.

[418]To pick two examples at random, according to their Annual Reports, JP Morgan's capital for operational risk *alone* at $8.5B was more than twice the IntercontinentalExchange's total capital *for all non-default risks across all of its businesses* of $3.2B.

[419]The IMF in *Making Over-the-counter Derivatives safer: the role of central counterparties*, Chapter 3 of the April 2010 Global Financial Stability Report suggest that all CCPs should have access to liquidity facilities from private sector institutions who are not (or are not affiliated with) clearing members. This would allow them to cover temporary shortfalls from liquidity-challenged but otherwise solvent CMs. They note however that the small number of global settlement banks could create risk concentrations (especially if these are also CCP liquidity providers), and so suggest that systemically important CCPs should have access to emergency central bank liquidity.

[420]EMIR requires that CCP risk committees have a significant degree of independence: CCP staff can attend, but only in a non-voting capacity, for instance, and CCP management have to inform their regulator if the CCP's Board decides not to follow the risk committee's advice on any particular issue. These requirements aim to ensure that the CCP's risk decisions are aligned with the interests of its users. (The EMIR text, *Regulation (EU) No. 648/2012 of the European Parliament and of the Council of 4 July 2012 on OTC derivatives, central counterparties and trade repositories* is available via ec.europa.eu/internal_market/financial-markets/derivatives/index_en.htm.)

[421]This means amongst other things that if IM is claimed to be based on a 99th percentile five day loss, then in no more than, say, nine five day periods in a thousand should the losses on any clearing member portfolio be bigger than IM. The standard here is the Basel Committee's *Sound practices for back testing counterparty credit risk models* (December 2010) available at www.bis.org/publ/bcbs185.htm.

[422]One approach would be as follows. There is a default. To the extent that defaulting CM(s) with out-of-the-money positions have been unable to pay VM to the CCP, and so the CCP does not have sufficient amounts to pay VM to in-the-money CMs, the flows due to those in-the-money CMs are 'haircut'.

[423]Most CCP rule books have a provision to allow clearing members to leave, although the alternative, sometimes dubbed 'Hotel California', has also been discussed. Typically leavers must first flatten their portfolios, then wait for some period, perhaps 30 days, before they can resign their membership. They are then no longer liable for capital

calls, loss allocation or portfolio puts. There are a variety of reasons which might motivate clearing members to resign including loss of confidence in CCP stability, a change in membership criteria, changes in CM and/or client profiles, changes in balance of products cleared, changes in the level of legal protection offered to margin, or changes in financial resources or the default waterfall. Clients may also decide to use alternative clearing houses for these or other reasons. In any case, the key issue is when various monies (IM, DF etc.) have to be returned, and when the CM is off risk at the CCP.

[424]We discuss CCP equity requirements further in the next chapter.

[425]The IMF give a longer discussion of CCP regulation in *Making Over-the-counter Derivatives safer: the role of central counterparties*, Chapter 3 of the April 2010 Global Financial Stability Report.

[426]Compare, for instance, the 2004 CPSS/IOSCO *Recommendations for Central Counterparties* with the 2012 *Principles for financial market infrastructures* from the same two bodies.

[427]For similar reasons already successful exchange traded derivatives CCPs have innate advantages in the OTC derivatives central clearing business.

[428]A fuller discussion of CCP access issues can be found in J. Slive et al., *Access to Central Clearing Services for Over-the-Counter Derivatives* Bank of Canada Financial System Review (June 2011) available at www.bankofcanada.ca/wp-content/uploads/2011/06/fsr_0611.pdf.

[429]See for instance the CPSS IOSCO *Disclosure framework for financial market infrastructures* Consultative report (April 2012) available at www.bis.org/publ/cpss101c.pdf.

[430]It is vital that systemically important institutions are not just safe, but seen to be safe: therefore higher disclosure standards are necessary for systemic institutions, as the negative externality of a loss of confidence in them is much bigger than it would be for a smaller clearing house.

[431]It is important for market confidence that it is clear when and by whom default is declared; what actions may be taken post-default; and what impact this has on non-defaulting members (including when their funds are at risk and the impact, if any, of the default on the CCP's normal operations).

[432]A key issue in the regulatory capital treatment of cleared trades is whether the clearing CCP is 'CPSS IOSCO compliant', i.e. compliant with the CPSS/IOSCO principles. This determination is made by supervisors. For an example of this type of regulatory disclosure, see FSA's *Assessment of LCH.Clearnet Limited against the CPSS-IOSCO recommendations for Central Counterparties* available at www.fsa.gov.uk/pubs/other/lchclearnet.pdf.

[433]The CPSS IOSCO document here is *Recovery and resolution of financial market infrastructures* Consultative report (July 2012) available at www.bis.org/publ/cpss103.pdf.

[434]There is understandable hostility to any taxpayer backstop from the official sector. See for instance paragraph 2.25 of HM Treasury's *Financial sector resolution: summary*

of responses (October 2012) available at www.hm-treasury.gov.uk/d/condoc_financial_
sector_resolution_broadening_regime_responses.pdf.

[435]Given the choice between having to resolve a CCP and having to resolve several
systemically important clearing members, the latter is not clearly preferable. There is a
problem, though, in that the supervisor who would have to resolve the CCP is not
necessarily the same as the one(s) who would have to resolve the clearing members.

[436]One interesting idea in this context is the use of interoperability as a resolution
tool. If safe interoperability between OTC derivatives CCPs could be established, then
it may sometimes be possible to transfer the transactions of a failing CCP, together
with the associated collateral, to a sound partner. Without interoperability – or at least
the kind of standardisation required for interoperability – that kind of transfer would
be much more difficult.

[437]See *Report of the Presidential Task Force on Market Mechanisms*, United States
Treasury Department (1988) available at archive.org/stream/reportofpresiden01unit/
reportofpresiden01unit_djvu.txt. Similar issues occurred in 2008, as N. Chande et
al. in *Central Counterparties and Systemic Risk* Bank of Canada Financial System Review
(December 2010) report.

[438]D. Heller, N. Vause in *Collateral requirements for mandatory central clearing of over-
the-counter derivatives*, BIS Working Paper No. 373 (March 2012) available at www.bis.
org/publ/work373.pdf give a total VM movement for IRS in a stressed scenario of nearly
$100B. Given most of this would come from members of the G-14, 'several billion'
seems a conservative estimate of a stressed VM drawdown at a large dealer.

[439]It is vitally important that market participants know whether CCP distress will
require close out or not as soon as possible. Any uncertainty here could be profoundly
destabilising to the derivatives market, and indeed to the wider financial system.

[440]This is equivalent to assuming that the two asset class portfolios are uncorrelated.

[441]This is only possible if (a) the cleared trades are identified as client transactions
and the collateral held to support them is not at risk from the default of either the
clearing member or other clients and (b) there is 'highly likely' portability. See the
Basel Committee's Capital requirements for bank exposures to central counterparties
(July 2012) available at www.bis.org/publ/bcbs227.pdf.

[442]Due to the need, for the sake of portability, to have multiple clearing members.

[443]I.e. tens or hundreds of billions of dollars.

[444]As the banks have, thanks to the changes to the capital required to support bilateral
OTC derivatives in Basel III discussed in section 5.7.

9

Design Choices in Central Clearing and Their Consequences

Edwin Budding & David Murphy

> *One cannot launch a new history—*
> *the idea is altogether inconceivable;*
> *there would be no continuity, no tradition.*
> *Tradition cannot be invented or learned.*
> *Without it one has, at best,*
> *not history but 'progress'—*
> *the mechanical movement of a clock hand,*
> *not the immaculate progression of connected events.*
> Osip Mandelstam

Introduction

Central clearing can be implemented in many different ways. For instance, there could be one CCP or many; initial margin can be high or low; and clearing mandates can be wide or narrow. Each design choice has consequences. We will examine some of the principal choices in this chapter, looking not just at the options selected in practice, but also at their alternatives. For each choice, we will set out what it is, and the pros and cons of the various alternatives.

We trisect our discussion into choices relating to the level of financial resources and the design of waterfalls; those which concern CCP organisation; and those which shape clearing mandates.

A number of paradigms which organise the various choices, such as that between more and less mutual arrangements, are also examined. The final section of the chapter then looks at the various functions of an OTC derivatives CCP. We show how these can be deconstructed and, in many cases, carried out in the bilateral market without the need for central clearing.

9.1 Financial Resources

There are a huge range of questions which must be answered when CCP capital structure is designed including:

- How is initial margin determined?

- How are default fund contributions determined?

- Once a defaulting clearing member's margin and default fund contributions are exhausted, whose funds are used to absorb any remaining losses?

- When (if ever) will the clearing house be allowed to fail?

- How much equity does the CCP have and when is it at risk?

- How are non-default losses, such as those caused by operational or investment risk, absorbed?

- When are capital calls made, how are they determined, and what limit (if any) is there on their size?

We begin by looking at the level of initial margin and default fund, as bearing counterparty credit risk is the key function of a CCP. After this, more extreme losses are considered.

9.1.1 The level of initial margin and default fund

Since DF is almost always above IM in the CCP default waterfall, higher levels of DF can compensate for lower levels of IM and vice versa (assuming financial resources are fixed). Therefore we pose the choices relating to these two elements of financial resources in one section. First, initial margin:

Choice 1: Should initial margin be set at a higher[445] or a lower level?

High levels of initial margin imply excessive costs for all. They also encourage 'innovative' ways of sourcing collateral[446] and may leave CCPs with higher levels of investment risk. In contrast, low levels mean that CCPs are risky, capital calls are more likely, and that the under-resourced CCP will have a competitive advantage[447] compared with any prudent peers it may have.

Choice 2:   Should default fund be set at a high or a low level?

Higher levels of default fund allow CCPs to be robust even if clearing member default comovement is elevated: they are more crisis-proof. This comes at a significant cost to clearing members, though, as they have to provide these funds, and take the risk that they will be used to absorb the losses of others.

There is an interaction between IM and DF in that some degree of imprudence or model risk in IM can, at least from the CCP's perspective, be compensated for by higher DF, and vice versa. Using DF in place of IM, though, requires clearing members to subsidise the risk of their clients, since only CMs pay DF (while everyone pays margin)[448].

DF Level *IM Level*	High	Low
High	CCPs are very robust against credit risk losses	CCPs can still be safe, CMs do not subsidise clients
Low	CCPs can still be safe, client clearing is cheaper	Lower costs for all

Figure 9.1: The pros (above) and cons (below) of differing initial margin and default fund levels

DF Level *IM Level*	High	Low
High	Egregious cost, increased liquidity risk	Residual risk[449] may be significant
Low	Low incentive for counterparty due diligence	High CCP solvency risk, greater chance of loss allocation

When DF is high, incentives may be blunted due to over-mutualisation. This is especially the case if IM is too low: in this case, the defaulter's DF can be absorbed even without a really unusual loss event, and in this case, everyone's DF is at risk. This means that there is little incentive to do due diligence on cleared OTC derivatives counterparties, as the consequences of a bad loss are visited on all clearing members[450]. Figure 9.1 summarises the advantages and disadvantages of differing margin and default fund levels, and the interaction between the various choices.

9.1.2   The market risk sensitivity of financial resources

The next design decision concerns the nature of the methodology used to calculate IM:

Choice 3:   Should initial margin models be highly risk sensitive?

The problem here is procyclicality: if financial resources models are highly risk sensitive, then by definition risk as measured by the model increases in a stressed period. This means that IM assessments go up, drawing liquidity down just when institutions can afford it the least. If financial resources models are less sensitive, then to avoid DF breaches they must require high levels of margin at all times. This means that market participants pay more than they need to most of the time in exchange for less liquidity risk.

Figure 9.2 illustrates the issues here[451]. The procyclical model produces margin requirements which vary substantially. There are two less procyclical models, but of these only the one which produces high, stable requirements is prudent. Essentially we are faced with the choice between

- Risk sensitivity, lower average margin requirements, but procyclical liquidity risk; or

- Stable low margin requirements which reduce costs for end-users but which increase the risk that CCPs will not be robust when clearing members default, and which supervisors are therefore likely to reject; or

- Stable high margin requirements which make CCPs credible counterparties but which also make it uneconomic for some end users to hedge their business risks.

9.1.3   The credit risk sensitivity of financial resources

A related question is whether financial resources should depend on the credit quality of counterparties:

Choice 4:   Should initial margin and default fund models be credit risk sensitive?

Most CCPs do not have credit-risk-sensitive margining[452]. However there is no reason in principle why this could not be applied. The table in figure 9.3 summarises the issues.

Notice that if CCPs charged IM based on the market credit spread of their counterparties, then they could incorporate all the information available

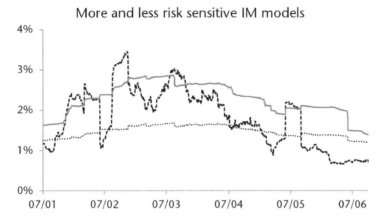

Figure 9.2: Initial margin requirements calculated using a risk sensitive model (the dashed black line), a reasonably prudent but less procyclical model (the solid grey line), and a less prudent but not procyclical model (the dotted line).

	High credit sensitivity
Pro	No implicit subsidy of bad credits by good ones, CCP financial resources rise in a crisis, strong incentive for CMs to preserve good credit quality, defaulter pays
Con	Highly procyclical
	Low or no credit sensitivity
Pro	Not procyclical, encourages smaller firms to become CMs
Con	Bad credits subsidised by good ones, no disincentive to or extra protection from worsening CMs

Figure 9.3: The pros and cons of credit-sensitive IM

in such spreads into their margin levels (whether relevant or not)[453]. This would at least not suffer from the cliff effects[454] and lag which would be associated with a margin based on credit ratings, although it would result in much more variability of margin levels. This kind of credit-risk-sensitive IM would share many of the characteristics of a market-based unilateral CVA[455].

9.1.4   Degree of mutualisation

The waterfall design we outlined in section 6.1.5 is common to many CCPs, and still more use minor variants of it. Nevertheless, this is not the only choice. The questions here include:

Choice 5:   Should lower levels of mutualisation, perhaps based on the level of trading with the defaulter, precede or replace full loss mutualisation?

The idea here is that loss mutualisation does not promote counterparty due diligence. Perhaps it would be better to encourage parties to make accurate credit assessments by giving them an incentive. Thus rather than complete mutualisation at level 5 in the waterfall, we could have non-defaulting CM's default fund contributions at risk only to the extent that they had dealt with the defaulter. CMs who correctly foresaw trouble and spurned trading opportunities with the eventual defaulter would not run the risk of loss mutualisation (or perhaps would only be at risk after the default funds of the defaulter's trading partners were exhausted). This would remove the moral hazard whereby no clearing member can avoid the costs of another's default so that they are less incentivised to take steps to prevent it.

This design decision brings up the same question as in choice 4: to what extent should there be an egalitarian treatment of all clearing members? Clearly higher levels of equality make it easier for smaller firms to become clearing members, and hence discourage market concentration. This is a good thing. But smaller firms may be worse credits; they may have fewer resources to contribute to default management; and they may have less effective risk management generally. The right balance between encouraging a diverse 'ecology' of market participants and discouraging prudent clearing members by making them bear costs created by the imprudent is not clear. Indeed, we could phrase the general issue as:

Choice 6:   To what extent should all clearing members be treated equally[456]?

A lower level of mutualisation (i.e. less equality) means that the default fund benefits from less diversification, and hence default funds might have to be higher to achieve the same degree of safety. In turn this could affect the affordability of clearing. On the other hand, since higher DF levels make CCPs robust even in high default comovement environments, that is not necessarily wholly bad.

9.1.5 CCP equity

The regulatory framework for banks has constraints on capital as a key element. This suggests that one should consider:

Choice 7:   What methodology should be used to set minimum capital requirements for CCPs?

In order to answer this, we need to consider the roles of CCP equity. These include at least the following, as we discussed in the previous chapter:

* Absorbing non-default losses (e.g. due to operational risk);

* Giving the CCP 'skin in the game'[457];

* Keeping confidence in the CCP;

* Absorbing default losses at certain stage(s) in the default waterfall; and

* Funding the CCP through resolution and possible wind-down.

Given this, the right blend between a fixed minimum capital level[458] and a risk-based add-on is unclear. Moreover, there is a trade-off between rather high standards, which make CCPs safer but which discourage CCP competition[459]; and somewhat lower ones, which give CCPs less ability to withstand losses before failing but which may make a challenge to incumbent CCPs more likely.

9.1.6 Capital calls and loss allocation

We have already discussed losses beyond default fund in section 8.2.3. The essential issue here is who bears 'far tail' credit risk losses, and how. Some of the key questions are:

* Should far tail losses be absorbed by CCP members through a loss allocation or capital call mechanism?

* Should CCPs be allowed to fail?

* Do systemic risk considerations mean that some CCP failures may require central bank intervention?

Thus we have:

Choice 8:   How should losses beyond a CCP's allocated financial resources be borne?

Figure 9.4 sets out some of the issues here[460].

	Pro	*Con*
Unlimited capital call	CCP only fails when all CMs do	Pushes CCP tail risk back onto CMs[461]
Haircutting VM	Parties who gained, pay; encourages CMs to reduce their cleared risk	
Haircutting IM	Parties who took most risk pay	Risk may be unrelated to defaulter(s)
Bankruptcy	Risk of this encourages CMs to do due diligence on CCPs	Likely to be destabilising, total cost likely to be larger
Nationalisation	Contract continuity, reduction of systemic risk	Cost to taxpayer, moral hazard

Figure 9.4: The pros and cons of far tail CCP loss allocation mechanisms

9.2 CCP Organisation

In the last section we saw that there are credible alternatives to the usual way that CCPs protect themselves and allocate default losses. Here we turn to similar choices relating to the organisation of CCP. Specifically we examine possibilities relating to CCP ownership; competition issues; CCP governance arrangements; the criteria for membership of CCPs; and segregation.

9.2.1 Governance and ownership

There are two main models of the arrangement of clearing and settlement services[462]:

* In the 'vertical' clearing model, an exchange (or some other form of market) owns the clearing house that clears its trades, and this CCP only clears trades made on its parent's market; whereas

* In the 'horizontal' model, clearing houses are separately owned and potentially able to clear trades made on multiple markets. There may be competition between CCPs in this model.

This gives rise to:

Choice 9:   Should OTC derivatives CCPs follow the vertical model, the horizontal model, or should both be permitted?

The debate about which model is best is a complex and at times vociferous one. We summarise some of the main issues in figure 9.5.

	Pro	*Con*
Vertical Model	Allows economies of scale to be captured, allows CCP to be customised to a given market's products	Potential for monopoly rents, opaque pricing of clearing, new entrants are discouraged
Horizontal Model	Users can select best service at each stage, harder for CCPs to extract monopoly profits	Significant IT cost & risk from connections to multiple CCPs, multiple CCPs are inefficient, CCP ownership issues[463]

Figure 9.5: The pros and cons of various models of clearing

9.2.2 The many or the few

A related debate concerns CCP competition. Even with one jurisdiction, should there be multiple competing CCPs, or are clearing houses in fact utilities where there are substantial cost savings if a single body serves multiple execution venues[464]? Hence[465]:

Choice 10:   Should OTC derivatives CCPs be utilities or should there be competition between different for-profit CCPs?

Clearly the vertical model from the last section requires multiple CCPs[466], whereas horizontal arrangements allow for but do not require a common clearer. Figure 9.6 illustrates the alternatives here.

If one were a client wanting to trade a single swap with no pre-existing portfolio, then CCP competition would be desirable as that would be more likely to lead to lower clearing fees. Large clearing members, in contrast, would tend to prefer a single utility CCP as that brings the most multilateral netting benefits[467]. Indeed, the benefit of being able to offer netting with already cleared trades is a substantial selling point for incumbent CCPs and justifies the suggestion that OTC derivatives clearing is a natural monopoly[468]. Natural monopolies typically have to be regulated, though[469], so clearing model which uses utility CCPs would require that the cost as well as the safety of central clearing attracts supervisory attention.

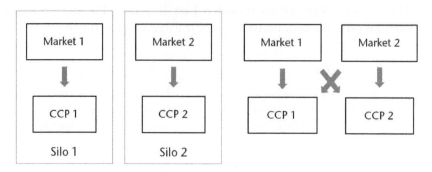

Figure 9.6: An illustration of the vertical model of clearing (above left); the horizontal model with CCP competition (above right) and the utility clearing model (below)

Neither the horizontal nor vertical models preclude CCP interoperability. However, vertical structures are typically less conducive to interoperability and are likely to result in more fragmentation of OTC derivatives clearing.

9.2.3 The governance of OTC derivatives clearing houses

Many of the concerns articulated in the last section relate to the possibility that clearing houses might charge higher fees for clearing than is economically efficient, or otherwise abuse their power. These concerns can, to a certain extent, be mitigated by governance. That is, CCP owners' freedom of action can be reduced by requiring that they take account of the views of users to some degree. One example is the composition of the CCP risk committee discussed in section 8.2.1, but the issue is larger than this: potentially CCPs could be required to include users in service pricing as well as risk decisions. This would intrude on the power of owners, but in a fashion that is commonplace among regulated utilities. Hence:

Choice 11:   To what extent should OTC derivatives CCPs be required to take account of the views of their users?

9.2.4 *Clearing membership*

Consider the following (caricature) alternatives:

- Big Boys CCP permits only the top ten global derivatives dealers to apply for membership. Members must have a net worth of at least \$25B; they must have over five years proven expertise in trading equity, credit, interest rate and FX derivatives; and they must have successfully managed at least 100 client defaults.

- Small-is-beautiful CCP permits any firm with a net worth of at least \$10M to apply for membership. Members must either attest that they have default management expertise or sign a contract with an agreed expert clearing member which 'outsources' participation in default management.

These are two very different concepts of a clearing house. The first is a piece of infrastructure which primarily addresses inter-dealer transactions; the latter is a much wider conception of a CCP. The contrast suggests:

Choice 12:   How high should the bar be set on CCP membership?

A high bar results in fewer potential members, and hence could lead to market concentration and/or high fees due to the lack of competition among clearing members. It does however mean that CMs are likely to be safer[470]; that they are more likely to be able to successfully participate in default management; and that they are more likely to be able to meet a capital call.

If a wider range of potential clearing members are allowed, then competition is promoted. Moreover, it could be argued that it is unfair both to mandate clearing and for there not to be any CCPs which allow medium sized or smaller banks to become clearing members, so fairness might suggest a low bar. On the other hand, wider membership means that there could be members who cannot actively participate in default management; that there is a wide range of different credit qualities of member (and thus there are lower quality members who pose higher risks to the CCP); and that some members may have more difficulty in meeting large VM or IM calls and/or capital calls. None of these are desirable.

This choice interacts with others, too. If IM is high, then having a wide range of credit quality among CMs may not matter that much. On the other hand, if IM is low and credit-risk-insensitive, then there is significant subsidy from better to worse CMs through the default fund. Losses beyond margin are also significantly more likely. Thus there are really three concepts:

1. A CCP which primarily admits large dealers as members, and which does not need to distinguish between member quality as they are all similar;

2. A CCP which admits a much wider range of clearing members and which treats them all identically; and

3. A CCP which admits a much wider range of clearing members and which varies IM and perhaps DF depending on clearing member credit quality.

The second alternative might be unattractive to large banks; were they to join such a CCP as clearing members, they might well bear a disproportionate burden. Without any big firms as CMs, though, such a CCP might find it hard to attract enough business to survive. Thus CCPs need to carefully balance having a larger number of diverse CMs with having a smaller number of higher quality CMs.

The bar for clearing membership also interacts with the choice of default fund level. Figure 9.7 sets out the issues here.

	High CM Bar	Low CM Bar
High DF	Only SIFIs can be CMs and they bear most of the tail risk	Tail risk loss absorption is spread over more firms
Low DF	Reduces costs for CMs, but high IM is needed to make CCPs safe	Financial stability depends critically on the prudence of CCP's IM methodology

Figure 9.7: The interaction between default fund levels and the bar for clearing membership

A key issue here is whether having a small group of high credit quality CMs makes the financial system more stable, or whether it creates too much concentration and contagion risk.

9.2.5 Segregation and portability

We set out the issue of the level of segregation of margin in section 6.4.4, and include it here for completeness: in brief, higher levels of segregation offer more protection to margin and facilitate portability. On the other hand, they cost more and create more liquidity risk[471].

Choice 13: What level(s) of margin segregation should CCPs be required to provide?

9.3 Clearing Mandates

Supervisors clearly intend to encourage clearing. They have decreed that there should be a capital advantage to central clearing[472] and that certain products must be cleared unless they are traded with an exempt party. However this still leaves some choices concerning clearing mandates. Specifically, what must be cleared; who must clear; and where must clearing happen?

9.3.1 The definition of the clearing mandate: products

We have already set out some of the issues around the definition of clearable products in section 6.2.3. Similar issues apply with greater force in the definition of mandatory clearable products[473].

There is another dimension to this issue, too:

Choice 14:   Should the clearing mandate be defined by products or as an overall constraint?

That is, rather than saying that certain products should be cleared, supervisors could simply require that, for instance, x% of OTC derivatives traded by a dealer are cleared, or that y% of their OTC derivatives risk[474] is cleared. This approach would have several advantages:

- It would not impose an arbitrary split of netting sets (as discussed in section 8.5.3), instead allowing dealers to keep non-clearable and clearable trades together where this was justified for risk management purposes and provided that they cleared 'enough' trades;

- It would ensure that the required percentage of inter-dealer trades was cleared. Dealers could not evade clearing by structuring trades to fall just outside the clearing mandate;

- Clearing mandates do not have to be revised as products innovation occurs[475]; and

- It would give CCPs greater freedom to decide which products they should clear. Moreover, the incentive to clear products which are not prudently clearable would decline as there would be no danger that, having seen that a product is being cleared (albeit not safely so), supervisors would mandate that it must be cleared[476].

The disadvantages include:

- Dealers might simply engage in more trading (and more clearing) in order to meet the required threshold;

- Supervisors would lose control over which trades were cleared (although they would all still have to be reported); and

- There would be no standard set of mandated clearable products which new CCPs could aspire to clear.

9.3.2   The definition of the clearing mandate: exempt parties

Most supervisors accept that there should be some parties who are exempt from the clearing mandate. The definition of which parties, exactly, has been highly controversial. It has been variously suggested[477] that all of the following should be exempt:

- Governments, multilateral and para-statal agencies, regional and municipal entities and their affiliates;

- Pension funds;

- Cooperative and not-for-profit corporations;

- Corporate end users of OTC derivatives and non-financial entities generally;

- Smaller financial institutions;

- Transactions between affiliates.

Indeed, it almost seems that no one who is not a G14 dealer thinks that they should have to clear. This suggests:

Choice 15:   Should the exemptions from the clearing mandate be widely or narrowly drawn?

Figure 9.8 summarises the situation.

9.3.3   The definition of the clearing mandate: location & local compliance

Product-specific clearing mandates can split netting sets in a way that increases risk: so too can the requirement to not just to clear, but to clear in a specific jurisdiction. A market participant can find that it has to clear one set of derivatives in the EU; another set in the US; a third in Japan; and so on. Supervisors could recognise each other's regimes to reduce this unhelpful phenomenon. For instance, the EU authorities could view clearing at an authorised US clearing house as sufficient to meet the requirements of EMIR; and vice versa.

Exemption	Pro	Con
Wide	Deals with dealers (who pose most systemic risk), does not impose costs on others	Reduces CCP profitability, opens the door for new dealers to become systemic
Narrow	Arbitrage of mandate less easy, more OTC derivatives cleared (probably)	Many non-systemic parties suffer higher costs with little regulatory benefit

Figure 9.8: The pros and cons of wide and narrow exemptions to the clearing mandate

There is little sign of willingness to permit jurisdictional substitution on the grounds that it would likely facilitate regulatory arbitrage, but one can easily envisage a rules which permitted this 'substituted compliance'[478]. Therefore we have:

Choice 16:   Should authorities have a wide or narrow definition of substituted compliance?

Figure 9.9 sets out some of the implications of this choice.

	Pro	Con
Wide definition	Pragmatic approach, less extra-territorial	Regulatory arbitrage is easier, encourages a race to the bottom
Narrow definition or ban	Strong jurisdictions can enforce consistency & protect themselves against laxer ones	Extra-territorial, higher costs for global dealers, detracts from regulatory cooperation

Figure 9.9: The pros and cons of different approaches to substituted compliance

9.3.4   The definition of the clearing mandate: size

It is self-evident that requiring that more products are cleared increases the size of clearing houses. As financial institutions get larger, they can become too big to fail, though; or, in the derivatives context, too interconnected to fail. Thus there is a trade-off between the extent of clearing mandates and the risk of CCPs[479].

9.4 Opposing Paradigms

There are a number of principles which serve to organise the choices of the previous sections. These represent the irreducible trade-offs in the design of OTC derivatives clearing. One obvious such public policy choice is cost vs. safety. Another, as we have emphasised earlier in the book, is credit risk vs. liquidity risk. In this section we examine a third trade-off, which we dub communism vs. capitalism. First, an explanation of these terms:

9.4.1 The terms 'communism' and 'capitalism'

We use the term 'communism' to refer to arrangements whereby parties are treated in the same manner. Thus for instance charging the same initial margin for the same portfolio regardless of the counterparty is in our terms communist; while counterparty credit quality-sensitive margin is 'capitalist'.

Another key distinction is that in arrangements which we dub 'capitalist', parties typically bear all (or at least more) of the consequences of their decisions, while in communism losses, or profits, or both, are widely shared. Thus for instance the typically CCP default fund is communist, in that losses are shared mutually. On the other hand, arrangements where loss allocation depends on the degree of trading with the defaulter are more capitalist. Strictly capitalist arrangements therefore tend to have better incentive structures than strictly communist ones, but lower loss absorption, as parties who did not trade with the defaulter do not bear losses.

9.4.2 Communist and capitalist arrangements compared

Figure 9.10 compares some of the key features of the communist and capitalist paradigms.

It should be noted that there is no political tone – and still less one of approval of some arrangements or disapproval of others – implied by our terminology. There is a natural tension between more and less mutual arrangements in many areas of finance, and OTC derivatives clearing is simply one example of this phenomenon[484]. Moreover, of course, clearing arrangements can be more communist in one dimension and more capitalist in another: there is nothing contradictory about combining, for instance, a high membership bar with equal loss allocation and credit-insensitive margin. Indeed, this can be thought of as communism for the few rather than the many.

Feature	Capitalism	Communism
Slogan	To each, their own[480]	They shared with one another everything that they had[481]
Key property	Good incentives	Fairness
Moral hazard	Less	More
Membership	High bar	Lower or no bar
Credit-sensitive initial margin	Yes	No
Loss allocation	Based on trading with defaulter	Mutual[482]
CCP failure	Once limit on loss allocation reached	Only after all CMs fail
Capital use	Less efficient (as less mutualised)	More efficient
Large dealers	Matter more, as only they have the resources required to compete[483]	Matter less: it is easier for a smaller firm to compete
Market share	Concentrated in a few dealers	Spread over more dealers

Figure 9.10: Capitalist vs. communist clearing paradigms

9.4.3 Client specificities

The communism vs. capitalism distinction extends to the market, and to clients, thanks to two different conceptions of trading:

* In a fully communist market, market makers would be compelled to engage in trades should clients so wish, clients would trade anonymously, client terms would be standardised, and CCPs would be compelled to clear clearable trades regardless of counterparty. In contrast

* In a fully capitalist market, trading would be optional, all market participants' identities would be disclosed, client terms would be individually negotiated, and CCPs could reject clearable trades should they so desire.

9.5 Deconstructing an OTC Derivatives CCP

An OTC derivatives CCP performs the following functions:

1. It facilitates multilateral netting by acting as a counterparty to trades;

2. It calculates initial and variation margin requirements on cleared products;

3. It calls for and settles margin. In addition it may hold some margin amounts either on its own account, on behalf of its customers, or both;

4. It calculates default fund requirements for clearing members and holds this fund as a layer of mutual trade insurance;

5. It guarantees cleared transactions to the extent of its financial resources;

6. It manages member defaults;

7. It facilitates client porting; and

8. If necessary it may make capital calls on or allocate losses to clearing members (or both).

Most of these roles could be performed in the bilateral market: indeed, many of them could be implemented alongside central clearing. In this section we examine how this could work. Our aim is simply to illustrate that central clearing as currently implemented is not the only way of achieving CCP functionality. The alternatives may in some cases be less effective or more costly, but they do exist. We will look at each function in a subsequent subsection.

9.5.1 Multilateral netting

We first observe that the real advantage of multilateral netting is in close out. Therefore the point at which we need netting is at, or just before the point of close out. This can be achieved in the bilateral market by encouraging and organising novation post default. That is, before close out, the counterparties of a defaulting firm could novate trades between themselves in order to achieve the greatest degree of netting[485].

This is a different form of multilateral netting to that facilitated by central clearing. Rather than netting A's cleared exposures to B and C, it allows B and C to net their exposures to A after (or just before) A's default. Figure 9.11 illustrates the difference.

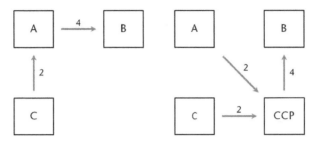

Figure 9.11: An illustration of the nettings of exposures to different counterparties in clearing (above) and via post-default novation (below).

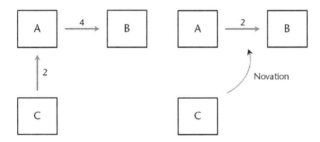

This form of netting can be less effective than that facilitated by clearing, in that it requires those market participants with exposure to participate in the novation process. Moreover, those parties who are owed by the defaulter can only monetise that amount to the extent that they can novate their trades to a party who owes the defaulter[486]. Still, this process can facilitate some degree of multilateral netting without the need for a clearing house.

9.5.2 Calculating margin

Supervisors already propose setting minimum standards for bilateral margining[487], so they clearly see no difficulty in implementing these in the bilateral market: neither do we.

9.5.3 Holding and settling margin

The function of settling margin movements could be performed by a utility. This body would facilitate efficient variation margin movements for the bilateral market. It could also hold initial margin as a custodian. Since it would not act as a counterparty, and hence would not need IM to protect itself, it could support a wide range of terms including no IM, unilateral IM and asymmetric IM as well as symmetric bilateral IM. The central margin custodian would therefore be a piece of financial market infrastructure which facilitates VM movements, invests cash transferred to meet IM requirements, and sets haircuts for non-cash collateral. It would be a regulated entity, and its investment policy would be highly conservative[488], making it substantially safer than an OTC derivatives CCP.

9.5.4 Mutual guarantee fund determination and management

It would be straightforward to set up a company which acted as a guarantor for bilateral OTC derivatives. This company would calculate a guarantee fee based on the current and potential future exposure of the guaranteed portfolio and the credit support arrangements present[489]. Dealers and other systemically important firms could be required to participate in the scheme; others could be permitted access at their discretion. The guarantor could be either a private body or a multilateral agency[490]. It would invest guarantee fees in suitably liquid and high quality securities. It could even, in analogy to a CCP's capital calls, have a layer of contingent capital which could be called on if needed.

9.5.5 Mutual guarantee protection

The guarantor described in the last section would pay users based on their close out losses. The guarantee could be either full (and hence capable of causing failure of the guarantor in extreme circumstances) or capped. In order to mitigate the liquidity risk of defaults, payment should be very prompt post default.

9.5.6 Default management

The process of gathering information on the portfolio of a defaulter, immediately hedging it, then auctioning the hedged portfolio does not require a CCP. This could be done either by the bilateral guarantor discussed above (and indeed participation in such a process could be made a criterion for membership of the guarantor), or by a separate industry body.

There are three further features of CCP default management which are worthy of comment here:

1. CCPs guarantee contract continuity to the non-defaulting party.

2. By imposing uniform rules on clearing members, and uniform documentation of both clearing relationships and cleared con-

tracts, CCPs standardise both counterparty terms and contract terms. This makes it easier to replace a failing counterparty[491].

3. Clearing house close out establishes a binding close out amount for cleared trades. The intent is evidently that there will be less dispute over these determinations of close out amounts than has sometimes been the case for bilateral close outs[492].

The proposed guarantor could achieve the first two of these in the bilateral market[493]. The third would require wider cooperation, but there is no reason to believe that a process similar to that which led to the standard CSA could not provide the required standardisation.

9.5.7 Portability

Clients benefit substantially from the ability to port cleared trades. This could be achieved in the bilateral market too, if client margin was segregated at a central margin custodian[494], trades were guaranteed (so that clients were compensated for any losses due to counterparty default), and terms were standardised.

9.5.8 Loss allocation beyond the guarantee fund

Far tail loss allocation is potentially the hardest part of a CCP's job since it is likely to be controversial. The only circumstances under which it would be attempted for a systemically important CCP are highly stressed conditions after the failure of at least one, and likely several banks. There is no difficulty in principle with a guarantor signing contracts allowing it to allocate losses to surviving members just as a CCP would[495]; the problem in practice will be making the loss allocation stick.

Summary: central clearing without central clearers

The analysis above suggests that most of the benefits of central clearing do not require the use of CCPs. The combination of a central margin custodian and a guarantee fund could have substantially mitigated the systemic risk of the bilateral OTC derivatives market. Indeed, the OTC market might even have created either or both of these pieces of infrastructure had central clearing not been mandated. We do not claim that the resulting situation would clearly have been better than central clearing as imposed, because such a claim could only be made after an extensive study. Equally though, the proponents of central clearing cannot claim that the CCP-based approach is better. It is striking that so many policy decisions have been taken when there are credible alternatives available and with little cost/benefit analysis (albeit that such analysis would be highly contestable[496]). Rule writing has been so voluminous and so hasty that there was no time to explore the road less travelled even if it might have been smoother, more direct, faster and graced with better views.

Notes

[445]E.g. based on a 99% 5 day VAR.

[446]Such as collateral transformation trades.

[447]Some users will prefer to use the CCP with the lowest level of margin, especially in a market that they perceive to be benign.

[448]That said, the DF sizing issue is relevant to existing and potential clients too as CMs will attempt to recoup any costs incurred in providing client clearing though higher clearing fees.

[449]Since there is not much DF, credit losses larger than margin may well breach CCP financial resources. Multiple CM defaults will probably pose substantial risk to the CCP unless IM is very large.

[450]We discuss this further in section 9.1.4 below. The problem arises because CCPs make derivatives receivables a joint and several liability of clearing members (at least to the extent of DF), so 'free riding' is rational. For more on free riding, see M. Olson, *The logic of collective action*, Schocken Books (1968) or G. Hardin, *The tragedy of the commons*, Science Volume 162 (1968).

[451]The risk sensitive IM is a VAR based on 90 days' worth of data; the prudent but less procyclical one is a blend of VARs using longer and shorter data series; while the less prudent one is based on a one year VAR at a lower confidence interval. For a further discussion, see N. Chande et al., *Central Counterparties and Systemic Risk* Bank of Canada Financial System Review (December 2010).

[452]This is not quite true: clearing houses generally have the right to impose higher margin requirements should they so desire. These, together with other constraints such as pre-notification of trades, are usually only imposed on highly stressed firms. For examples of this, see for instance the discussion of 'near misses' in the presentation *LCH.Clearnet's Default History* available via www.lchclearnet.com.

[453]This raises the possibility of CCPs charging a credit fee akin to a CVA rather than IM. This fee could then be spent on buying CDS protection on clearing members. Perfect hedging would not be possible, but the idea of CCPs dynamically hedging their counterparty credit risk portfolio is an interesting one.

[454]Some CCPs increase margin if a clearing member is downgraded. Thus for instance at the time of writing, LCH.Clearnet increases IM by 10% at BBB- and by 100% at BB+: see www.lchclearnet.com/membership/sa/market_capital_requirements.asp. Policies like

this help to protect the CCP, but they introduce exactly the kind of credit-contingent liquidity risk that caused AIG to fail (as we discussed in section 2.3.5).

[455]This suggests the possibility of bilateral margining. That is, CCPs could post IM to their clearing members (or rather to their custodians: we envisage a third party gross IM arrangement). This would provide clearing members with some protection against the failure of CCPs. Indeed, rather than having CCPs that are very safe but whose failure is catastrophic, we could consider CCPs which are less safe but which can fail without systemic consequences.

[456]High levels of loss mutualisation and a fully equitable treatment of all clearing members in effect means that OTC derivatives liabilities are close to being a joint and several liability of all clearing members, as discussed in note 450 above. This protects tax payers, but at the cost of removing most incentives for counterparty due diligence.

[457]I.e. aligning CCP risk management incentives with those of CMs via its inclusion in the default waterfall. This also mitigates the risk of CCPs setting IM or DF levels too low to attract business.

[458]One of us has previously suggested \$2B as a minimum equity capital level for systemically important CCPs partly motivated by the size of typical firm-threatening operational risk losses. See D. Murphy, *The systemic risks of OTC derivatives central clearing*, Journal of Risk Management in Financial Institutions, Volume 5, No. 3 (June 2012).

[459]Competition implies fragmentation, but it also has benefits. Notably, the concentration risk created by a single clearer is mitigated. Furthermore, competition will likely create pressure on clearing fees, an issue we consider further in section 9.2 below.

[460]Another one is fairness. It seems inimical for a CM who joins just before a large loss to bear as much of it as the clearing members that created the problems. We discuss the issue of equality of treatment further in section 9.4 below.

[461]If CCPs cannot fail unless their CMs do, then in effect most far tail credit risk is still born by the same banks. The systemically important clearing members will be much the same banks as were systemically important bilateral dealers. As we discussed in section 8.5.6, central clearing only helps to the extent that (i) it brings substantial *new* capital to market or (ii) that it reduces total system-wide counterparty credit risk thanks to multilateral netting. Moreover, the benefits of CCPs in, for instance, imposing a margin discipline or managing defaults could equally be obtained in the bilateral market: see section 9.5 for more details.

[462]For a further analysis, see Committee on Payment and Settlement Systems, *Market structure developments in the clearing industry: implications for financial stability* (November 2010) available at www.bis.org/publ/cpss92.pdf.

[463]If CCPs are wholly or largely owned by their clearing members, then the same global dealers who dominated the bilateral system will control CCPs. For more on this argument, see C. Pirrong, *Clearing Up Misconceptions on Clearing*, Cato Institute (Fall 2008) available at www.cato.org/pubs/regulation/regv31n3/v31n3-4.pdf. One response might be that between the Charybdis of vertical silos and the Scylla of CM-owned

CCPs, a not-for-profit global utility CCP similar to CLS looks like plain sailing. Various authors have suggested exploring this approach: see for instance M. Singh, *Making OTC Derivatives Safe – A Fresh Look*, IMF Working Paper WP/11/66 (March 2011) available at www.imf.org/external/pubs/ft/wp/2011/wp1166.pdf.

[464]This model has been successful in the US, where the OCC acts as a utility clearer for options and the DTCC for securities. For more on CCPs as natural monopolies and related issues, see R. Bliss, C. Papathanassiou, *Derivatives clearing, central counterparties and novation: The economic implications*, Joint Conference of the ECB and the FRBC on the role of Central Counterparties (2006) available at www.ecb.int/events/pdf/conferences/ccp/BlissPapathanassiou2.pdf.

[465]It is interesting that one of the early papers suggesting the creation of an OTC derivatives CCP, G. Rausser et al., *Centralized Clearing for Over-the-Counter Derivatives* (2009) available at papers.ssrn.com/sol3/papers.cfm?abstract_id=1475351 states 'Government backing is an essential ingredient, since it is the guarantor of last resort. Compensation to the government for providing such insurance, should be explicitly recognised by forming a public-private partnership.' In other words, some early proponents of mandatory central clearing were clearly envisaging that CCPs would be utilities. This argument is continued in S. Cecchetti et al., *Central counterparties for over-the-counter derivatives*, BIS Quarterly Review, September 2009 who state 'The need to insure continued operation in the face of a systemic event, in which a number of participants collapse simultaneously, suggests that CCPs may require public sector support... to minimise market-wide uncertainty during periods of stress, there may be a case for making the nature of any support clear ex ante.'

[466]Or at least it does if there is more than one market. In passing we note that the OTC derivatives market is less liquid than many leading equity markets, at least in terms of numbers of trades, so the liquidity fragmentation that has accompanied the growth of competition in equity execution would be even more damaging to OTC derivatives than it has been for stocks.

[467]Global CCPs are also likely to have more clearing member and more resources: both important benefits in managing defaults.

[468]The concept of a natural monopoly comes from W. Baumol, *On the Proper Cost Tests for Natural Monopoly in a Multiproduct Industry*, American Economic Review Volume 809 (1977). In an area where a single institution can serve the entire market at a lower per-unit cost than can two or more institutions, or to which new entrants are incapable of survival, the dominant institution is known as a 'natural' monopoly. Clearing is notable in this context in that

(a)   the cost to the CCP of clearing extra trades is often very low, providing infrastructure capacity is not exceeded, but

(b)   the benefits to a clearing member increase due to multilateral netting so

(c)   CCPs can charge 'per trade' fees, despite their sub-linear cost function.

[469]See P. Joskow, *Regulation of Natural Monopolies*, Handbook of Law and Economics (Polinsky & Shavell, Eds., 2007).

[470]Not least because they are likely to be too big to fail banks.

[471]There may be an offset here, though, in that if clients can port, then it has been suggested that their risk need not be accounted for in the calculation of clearing member DF. Given the lack of experience of porting OTC derivatives clients in stress, though, this seems imprudent.

[472]See the G-20 *Leaders's statement at the Pittsburgh summit* (September 2009) available at www.treasury.gov/resource-center/international/g7=g20/Documents/pittsburgh_summit_leaders_statement_250909.pdf.

[473]C. Pirrong, in *The Inefficiency of Clearing Mandates* (Cato Institute Policy Analysis No. 665, 21st July 2010), available at www.cato.org/pubs/pas/PA665.pdf makes a case against clearing mandates.

[474]The mandate could for instance be defined by the requirement that the ratio of the 5 day 99% VARs of the uncleared to the cleared portfolio for every dealer is less than some threshold.

[475]C. Culp, in *OTC-Cleared Derivatives: Benefits, Costs, and Implications of the Dodd-Frank Wall Street Reform and Consumer Protection Act*, Journal of Applied Finance (2010) notes this issue and comments that product innovation is often ahead of product regulation.

[476]This is a type of 'rogue CCP' risk.

[477]This is not all, either. For a description of various exemptions, see F. Carruzzo, *The End-User Clearing Exception*, Swiss Derivatives Review Volume 45 (Spring 2011) available via www.kramerlevin.com. Both the CFTC and ESMA websites detail comments the respective agency has received: see for instance the comments on ESMA's EMIR draft technical standards available via www.esma.europa.eu.

[478]Substituted compliance means that non-US market participants are permitted to conduct business which may touch on the US (where 'touch' is, of course, defined by US rules) by complying with their home regulations, provided that these are judged to be comparable to US ones. See for instance the CFTC Press Release *CFTC Approves Proposed Interpretive Guidance on Cross-Border Application of the Swaps Provisions of the Dodd-Frank Act*, 29th June 2012 available at www.cftc.gov/PressRoom/PressReleases/pr6293-12.

[479]Culp, *op. cit.*, comments that the growth of large clearing houses gives rise to moral hazard in that OTC derivatives market participants may manage their risks less prudently if they consider a CCP likely to be bailed out. It is worthy of note here that even if market participants do not do this, clearing mandates may force them to use CCPs that they do not consider to be safe counterparties. Of course, CDS referencing CCPs are not readily available, so dealers cannot easily buy protection on clearing houses.

[480]Cicero, *de Natura Deorum* III, 38.

[481]*Acts* 4:32. This was one off the inspirations for the Diggers, an influential group of 17th century agrarian communists. See G. Kennedy, *Diggers, Levellers, and Agrarian Capitalism: Radical Political Thought in Seventeenth Century England*, Lexington Books (2002).

[482]Any arrangement which includes loss mutualisation is to some extent 'communist' in our terms.

[483]Larger dealers have the resources to do counterparty due diligence; they can meet a high membership bar; and they have sufficient capital to bear default losses beyond the defaulters' IM and DF.

[484]There is a rich history of economic thought on the optimal organisation of the firm which includes many examples of debate dating back to Adam Smith. See for instance D. Kantarelis, *Theories of the Firm*, Interscience (2009).

[485]This has in fact occurred immediately after the bankruptcy of several derivatives market participants. However, in the chaos likely to occur after a SIFI bankruptcy, it may be difficult for market participants to arrange this trading bilaterally, so some organisation of this process and the rules surrounding it would be helpful. Thus there could be a formal process for auctioning derivatives claims, similar to the auction which determines CDS settlements.

[486]There is also the potential problem that the price of the novation has to be agreed: those owing money to the defaulter will seek to buy claims on the defaulter (which are worth recovery to the asset holder but par to them) cheaply.

[487]See the discussion in section 5.5.4 and the joint BCBS/IOSCO document referred to therein.

[488]Perhaps central margin custodians investments could be limited to making central bank deposits. Central banks could also gain considerable insight into conditions in the OTC derivatives market through requiring that the central margin custodian deposited their cash with them.

[489]If the guaranteed party benefited from IM posted, then either the guaranteed amount would be losses over IM, or the guaranteed's claim over IM could be passed on to the guarantor.

[490]This suggests another unexplored avenue: a single global OTC derivatives CCP run under the auspices of a multilateral body such as the BIS or the IMF, and with a liquidity backstop provided by them.

[491]The analogy has been made between replacing one train operating company by another while the trains still run. However, as the controversy over the award of Virgin Train's franchise on the UK West Coast Main Line to First Great Western indicates, sometimes replacing one operator with another is not as simple as it first seems. See for instance the Guardian story *West coast mainline fiasco may claim further victims*, 4th October 2012, available at www.guardian.co.uk/uk/2012/oct/04/west-coast-mainline-fiasco-victims.

[492]For more on this, see S. Noh, *Lesson from Lehman Brothers for Hedge Fund Managers: The Effect of a Bankruptcy Filing on the Value of the Debtor's Derivative Book*, The Hedge

Fund Law Report, Volume 5, No. 27 (July 2012) available via www.shearman.com. This paper refers to a study by Lehman's bankruptcy trustee which estimated that the cost to Lehman of being closed-out vs. immediately pre-default mark to market was $50B. Given that initial margin has to cover this gap, this implies that a prudent margining system would have demanded that Lehman post at least $50B of IM.

[493] On default of its counterparty, the client would novate its trade to the guarantor. The guarantor would net this trade with others novated to it and close out the net portfolio, providing in the process an industry-wide standard for close out amounts. Two options are then possible. In the first, the guarantor makes cash payment to the guaranteed as compensation for any losses incurred. In the second, 'new for old' model, the guarantor would seek out a party to replace the trade. This replacement would then be novated to the client.

[494] Or, better, in the client's account at a CSD over which the central margin custodian has a lien.

[495] While we would probably not want the guarantor to write contracts which were as a legal matter insurance, the analogy of the guarantor as a mutual insurer is a useful one. Guarantee fees are like insurance premiums, and the loss allocation mechanism corresponds to the members writing excess of loss reinsurance on the insurer's pool of risk.

[496] The literature on the difficulties of resolving regulatory choices via cost/benefit analysis is considerable. For instance, B. Hutter in *The Attractions of Risk-based Regulation: accounting for the emergence of risk ideas in regulation*, ESRC Centre for Analysis of Risk and Regulation Discussion Paper Number 33 (March 2005) available at webfirstlive.lse.ac.uk/researchAndExpertise/units/CARR/pdf/DPs/Disspaper33.pdf outlines issues in the quantification of indirect costs, data quality problems, the selection of utility functions and the subjectivity of risk assessments.

10

The Aftermath of Mandatory Central Clearing

Now vanish before the holy beams
the gloomy dismal shades of dark;
the first of days appears...
Affrighted fled hell's spirits black in throngs;
down they sink in the deep abyss to endless night.
Despairing cursing rage attends their rapid fall.
A new-created world springs up at God's command.
Libretto for Haydn's Creation

Introduction

Central clearing is transforming the OTC derivatives market and its risks. It will have an impact on end users, dealers, execution venues, and products. Some of the consequences of change are unequivocally good; some bad; and many mixed. Moreover, it is often not the fact that trades must be cleared that is important, but rather detailed design choices in how CCPs, supervisors and clearing members implement clearing that are determinative. We will review some of the impacts in this chapter, and look at their consequences for the post-mandatory clearing OTC derivatives market.

In order to frame the discussion, we begin with a summary of the advantages of central clearing of OTC derivatives, and some of the concomitant drawbacks. We then go on to examine the effects of mandatory clearing regulation, considering markets and market infrastructure; dealers; and end users. The book ends with a perspective on rule-making informed by post-crisis OTC derivatives regulation.

The benefits of central clearing, with their accompanying caveats, are:

• Central clearing facilitates multilateral netting	at the cost of splitting netting sets;
• It enforces margin discipline on CMs and clients	but creates procyclical liquidity risk;
• Losses above the defaulter's resources are mutualised	Reducing counterparty due diligence;
• Some segregation models facilitate client portability	These are more costly & have more liquidity risk;
• Product terms and counter-party documentation is standardised	By a private party who may not act in the market's best interests;
• Infrastructure is standardised	But it may be costly to connect to;
• Standardisation promotes liquidity	Vertical structures can localise liquidity in one silo;
• Counterparties become more fungible	Perhaps further reducing due diligence;
• Trade compression is facilitated;	
• Contracts continue[497] despite CM default	Provided that the CCP does not fail;
• CCPs default-manage net cleared portfolios	The adequacy of IM & DF is key to avoiding losses here;
• CCPs centralise loss allocation	This is potentially arbitrary, & non-defaulting CMs can be hit by losses from multiple CCPs;
• CM failures will be less systemic	Some CCPs are too big to fail.

10.1 Winners and Losers

An important question in the analysis of any matter of public policy is 'who benefits?' When dealing with questions of financial regulation, this is doubly true. One might imagine a very crude scorecard for the post-crisis OTC derivatives reforms which provides an answer[498].

Figure 10.1 summarises our view here.

Party	Outcome	Reasons
Leading G14 dealers	Mixed	Higher capital for bilaterals, higher costs & liquidity needs for clearing, but potential profits from reduced competition & collateral transformation
Smaller dealers	Lose	Too expensive & risky to be CMs so they have to be clients; this is costly & they will have a smaller piece[499] of a (perhaps) smaller pie
End users	Mostly lose	Higher costs & liquidity demands for both bilateral & cleared derivatives, but more pre-trade transparency
Supervisors	Mostly win	Seen to have responded to crisis, new rules create new jobs, and new risks
CCPs	Win	New profit stream created by the requirement to clear

Figure 10.1: Winners and losers in post-crisis financial reforms

This table is not presented censoriously: rather, we want to emphasise that any substantial regulatory change has different impacts on different parties, and that the character of the change is determined by these effects. This is certainly true of the post-crisis OTC derivatives reforms.

The impact created by these rules will change the shape of the future financial system. We will try to outline some of the features of the post-reform financial system in the next two sections. The market and its features are considered first, then end users are discussed.

10.2 The Future of OTC Derivatives Markets, Products & Participants

Financial markets are remarkably adaptive to change. It has long been recognised that, in the face of burdensome regulation, innovation occurs[500]. Some of this is unpredictable, but some can reasonably be foreseen, especially as the main forces for change are now palpable. A perspective on the shifts that we think are reasonably likely is given next.

10.2.1 The ownership of infrastructure

The activity mandated by regulators have made clearing houses attractive to investors. Their equity prices have grown in response to market expectations of future profits, and this has allowed them to make acquisitions[501]. Clearing houses are also targets, as the London Stock Exchange Group's acquisition of a majority stake in LCH.Clearnet indicates[502]. These trends are likely to continue.

Questions have been raised about the impact of current and likely future clearing house consolidation and market ownership of vertical CCPs. As we discussed in section 9.2.1, vertical structures give rise to competition issues, especially given that OTC derivatives clearing is a natural monopoly[503]. Certainly the optimal balance between the safety of clearing houses; attracting new capital to support financial risk; and costs for users is unclear and worthy of study. If competition authorities do intervene, this could have a profound effect on the risks and costs of central clearing.

10.2.2 Interoperability

The question of linkages between OTC derivatives CCPs is a difficult one. On the one hand, domestic CCPs linked to global champion clearers can provide some jurisdictions with control over clearing without excessive splitting of netting sets. On the other, links may create new channels for risk propagation[504]. Given the novelty and risks of interoperability for OTC derivatives clearing, the current best guess must be that it will not play a major part in the new landscape. Rather, we suspect that many jurisdictions will become comfortable with their local institutions' use of global CCPs, at least until supervisory cooperation is put under strain. If this judgement is right, a few large CCPs, perhaps no more than two or three per asset class, will come to dominate the market for OTC derivatives central clearing[505]. These clearing houses will of course be systemically important institutions.

10.2.3 Dealers

The very largest dealers will spend most of 2013 signing up clients to OTC derivatives clearing. They will be members of most, if not quite all clearing houses since they cannot afford not to be able to clear where their clients want them to. The improvements in infrastructure and the lower costs of electronic trading will benefit them.

For the next tier, things are less rosy. These players do not have enormous books of business so they benefit less from multilateral netting.

Moreover, they have lower client revenues to pay for new infrastructure. Some of them will decide either to withdraw from OTC derivatives, or to scale back their activities. Indeed, there is evidence that this is already happening[506].

10.2.4 Futurisation

A future is an exchange-traded derivative. Successful futures contracts refer to liquid underlyings. Benchmark interest rate swaps in a number of currencies are liquid, so it is perhaps no surprise that the idea of a swap future has been introduced. This is simply a future whose underlying is a standardised cleared swap. Swap futures are particularly attractive in the new regulatory environment as futures are treated more benignly than swaps. Specifically, the minimum MPOR in the US is only one day for a future. The impact of this smaller MPOR is, roughly speaking, to halve the margin required[507]. Moreover swap futures have certain advantages with regard to large trades[508], and create lower capital requirements.

The trend of replacing trading in an OTC derivative by that in a future on a related instrument is called 'futurisation'. It represents a regulatory arbitrage, in that swap futures have near-identical risk and economics to swaps, but a more benign margin and capital treatment[509].

Swap futures may be attractive to some market participants[510]: they can keep their exposure by rolling futures contracts, or let the futures contract run to maturity and take delivery of a cleared swap as desired[511]. Dealers could use swap futures to remove most of the interest rate risk of their portfolio, with cleared swaps, interest rate futures or other instruments (some of which will be uncleared) used to fine-tune the hedging.

10.2.5 Opportunities for new entrants

There are various opportunities for new entrants in OTC derivatives markets, infrastructure, and dealing. For instance, the regulations on execution venues may offer the opportunity for innovative new ventures. In this space listed derivatives exchanges will likely compete with platforms set up by inter-dealer brokers and by the dealers themselves[512]. The winners in this competition may well be decided by a combination of access to global CCPs and costs (including the costs of capital and margin requirements[513]).

10.2.6 Product standardisation

The combination of new capital requirements and clearing rules may well cleave the OTC derivatives market in two.

The split envisaged is:

* On the one hand, cleared plain vanilla transactions;
* On the other, customised uncleared trades tailored to meet end user needs.

Products in the first class will be highly liquid (at least at trade date), and will benefit from pre-trade transparency. Those in the second will be much less liquid and subject to higher capital requirements. However, these will be offset by substantial structuring fees[514]. Both of these types of product have a viable future: it is the middle ground of non-clearable products which are not profitable enough to pay for their capital requirements which will probably decline in use.

10.3 The Impact of Mandatory Clearing: End Users & The Economy

Futurisation is not an attractive trend for corporate end users. They may be faced with the unpalatable choice of a cheaper swap future that leaves them with significant basis risk[515], or a more expensive, less liquid swap that is a more precise hedge. It seems undesirable that one of the consequences of the clearing rules is to create issues like this for genuine end users. Moreover, this type of problem is not unique to futurisation. In this section we examine some more of the difficulties end users will face once clearing mandates and other associated regulations come into force[516]. First, though, a structural issue.

10.3.1 Who is responsible for the economic impact of financial regulation?

Regulators are responsible for financial stability. As such, they are naturally and rightly conservative in their prescriptions. Given the choice between enacting a measure that probably enhances financial stability and not enacting it, they tend to prefer action, despite the costs they impose on others. To a certain extent, this conservatism used to be countered by lobbying. However, this has (understandably) been less effective recently. One consequence of this has been that regulations have been less diluted than was sometimes the case pre-crisis, but another has been that few voices have been able to credibly oppose any supervisory over-reach[517]. It is reasonable to ask if the lack of a check on regulatory prudence sometimes creates excessive costs for the real economy[518].

10.3.2 Exemptions and bilateral capital

The major regulatory environments contain end user exemptions from mandatory clearing, as we reviewed in section 9.3.2. However, these typically contain some form of threshold or other qualifying criteria, and there are costs associated with monitoring these criteria[519]. Moreover, an exemption from clearing is not an exemption from increased costs: higher capital requirements for bilateral derivatives (likely combined with higher margin) mean that trading bilateral OTC derivatives will be more expensive for end users too.

10.3.3 Multiple clearing members

End users who are mandated to clear will have to seriously consider splitting their business between multiple clearing members. This is because they are unlikely to be able to port to a party they have no relationship with, so if they wish to take advantage of client portability, they will need multiple clearing members. This will split their netting set, and create at least two sets of documentation, liquidity requirements, and so on.

10.3.4 Liquidity risk and segregation options

The existence of multiple segregation options for clients poses a dilemma. Should they select higher levels of segregation, which cost more[520] and impose more liquidity risk but offer enhanced safety; or should they adopt a higher risk, lower cost approach? This is a business decision, and different end users will make different choices. However, it is likely that few clients will find the choice congenial: the net result may simply be less OTC derivatives trading, with more risk remaining on end user balance sheets.

Policy makers' unwillingness to impose initial and variation margin requirements on all corporate end users is understandable, given the impact. The exemption of sovereigns, para-statal and multi-lateral bodies is less obvious. Certainly if one wanted to reduce counterparty credit risk in the OTC derivatives system, then forcing all end users whose exposure was over some system-threatening amount to post variation margin would be a simple and effective solution[521]. The equivocation we have seen here suggests that counterparty credit risk reduction is not the only aim of the clearing rules. This begs the question of what is, something we return to in section 10.4.5 below.

10.3.5   Collateral financing and transformation

One of the benefits leading dealers see in the clearing rules is the imposition of CCP margin requirements on end users. Some end users do not have cash to meet these, and many cannot move money fast enough for clearing houses. Therefore there is an opportunity to provide collateral and to transfer it on a client's behalf: and of course to charge for this service. Many clients will require either:

* Short term collateral financing, whereby the CM funds and transfers margin on the client's behalf, with the client refunding the balance to the clearing member as its systems and processes allow; and/or

* Collateral transformation, whereby a provider swaps assets which are not accepted as collateral at the CCP for cash, which is.

The provider in the latter case may not be the clearing members: securities depositories see an opportunity here, too[522]. In any case, many commentators agree that there will be at least localised squeezes on collateral and possibly broader shortages. This has various causes:

* The Basel III liquidity rules (discussed in section 5.2.3);

* Ring-fencing requirements[523] and the growth of subsidiarisation at the expense of branching;

* The requirements for more collateral on bilateral OTC derivatives (as per the supervisors' proposal discussed in section 5.5.4);

* The decline of rehypothecation[524];

* The collapse in the interbank unsecured lending market (and hence the growth of collateralised borrowing by banks); and

* Mandatory clearing rules.

The various stake holders differ about the total impact of these factors, but even conservative estimates of the extra collateral required are in the trillions of dollars[525]. Inevitably this represents both a risk for some parties and an opportunity to others[526].

10.3.6   Timing

Mandatory clearing is coming, despite all of the above. It is likely that soon after this book is published in the summer of 2013, OTC derivatives CCPs in Europe will have been authorised and some users will have to clear some OTC derivatives at them. The United States timeline is similar.

Dealers are broadly prepared for this, but some end users are not[527]. This may lead to a fall in end user trading as the deadline approaches.

10.3.7 Uncertainty

The fees leading CMs, and leading CCPs will charge are uncertain. At the time of writing, for instance, many market participants will only commit to charges six months ahead. This is because there is significant uncertainty, much of it regulatory. The capital rules in some areas[528] are unknown at the time of writing, as is the scope of mandatory clearing. Until these questions are resolved, it will be difficult for some end users (and indeed some dealers) to finalise their OTC derivatives strategy. Many potential clients have a lot of decisions to make, including:

- Which CCP(s) they wish to use for each asset class and jurisdiction in which they are required (or may wish) to clear;

- Which clearing member(s) they wish to use, based on the available terms of client clearing;

- What the split of their business between their clearing members will be;

- Which level of segregation they wish to select at which CCPs, and what portability arrangements they wish to make;

- How they will move collateral and what forms of collateral they wish to use;

- Whether they wish to enter into any collateral financing and/or collateral transformation transactions and, if so, what the terms of these will be;

- How they will monitor their credit exposure to their clearing member(s), to CCP(s), and, if applicable, to any fourth party custodian or other parties involved;

- How they will address any unexpectedly large increases in margin, or decreases in their own credit quality, or both;

- How trade reporting requirements will be met; and

- How the economics and uncertainty of all of the above affects the risk/return profile of their hedging arrangements.

10.4 Post-crisis Ruling Making and its Consequences

New financial regulations are often the children of crises[529]. This has certainly been the case for the 2008+ credit crisis. Regulation was needed in many areas, and supervisors made ample provision. In this section we look at the process by which these rules were developed. This has consequences not just for the quality of the rules themselves, but also for the on-going legitimacy of financial regulation.

10.4.1 Many cooks, and much cooking...

New financial rules have been created at the global, international and national levels. For OTC derivatives alone, efforts from the Basel Committee, CPSS, FSB and IOSCO are relevant at the first level; the EU (as interpreted by ESMA) at the second; and a wide range of bodies at the third (including, to give a small sample, the BOE, CFTC, CSA, FED, FINMA, FSOC, JFSA, MAS, RBA, SEC and the UK FSA). This is understandable given that there was considerable political pressure for new regulation. However, the sometimes uncoordinated nature of the rule writing was unfortunate especially when applied to a global business such as OTC derivatives. Many authorities share the same broad policies, but the details vary substantially, and indeed both overlap and aggregate[530]. Some regulators have been accused of extra-territorial overreach[531], which could compound the problem as there can be multiple inconsistent rules in force for a given transaction.

One might wonder if the OTC market, with its modest single digit trillions of credit exposure and ten million odd transactions deserves all this attention. Undoubtedly change was needed, but the sheer volume of OTC derivatives regulation may be disproportionate, especially given the minor part OTC derivatives played in the crisis.

10.4.2 ...but little tasting

The lack of detailed quantitative analysis of the impact of the new regulations is another lacuna in the regulatory process[532]. Before mandatory OTC derivatives clearing rules were finalised, supervisors should have conducted a quantitative impact study broadly as follows:

+ A set of participating dealers are identified, ideally including all the G14;

+ Participants identify their portfolios with four categories of counterparty: (1) corporate end users; (2) other non-financial end users including sovereigns; (3) financial institutions who are not systemic and (4) global systemically important financial institutions (perhaps according to the Financial Stability Board definition[533]).

• The current state of affairs is summarised by quantifying for each counterparty various indicative parameters. These would include the current value of their portfolio, the amount of collateral held, the net current credit exposure, and the potential future exposure (based on some consistent definition thereof). Participants summarise the gross totals of each measure for each category.

• Participants also calculate margin and regulatory capital requirements using the new bilateral rules.

• Supervisors identify a number of clearing scenarios. For instance these could include:

  — A single global 'utility' CCP per asset class;

  — A single 'utility' CCP per asset class per jurisdiction;

  — Two or three competing CCPs in each asset class and jurisdiction.

• In each scenario, participants split their portfolios with each counterparty into a remaining bilateral piece then various cleared pieces[534].

• The various indicative parameters (margin, portfolio value, net current credit exposure, regulatory capital etc.) are then estimated in each scenario. A refinement would be to also calculate initial margin and variation margin in stressed conditions. This step might require some assumptions to be made about what is cleared where, the nature of client clearing and segregation arrangements, and so on.

• Finally, participants are invited to conjecture various future post-clearing portfolios, and to recalculate the parameters accordingly.

It would not be entirely trivial to conduct such a study, and there would be a good deal of judgement involved[535], but the results produced would nevertheless give insightful into the risks of different categories of participant in the OTC derivatives system in each scenario. For instance, we have made the case that the impact on financial system liquidity of CCP and compulsory bilateral initial margining could be profound. Such a study would provide evidence for or against this hypothesis.

10.4.3 The bilateral market may still deserve attention

One of the consequences of the rapid push for mandatory central clearing has been an increase in demand for derivatives experts. Banks, clearing houses and end users all need derivatives lawyers, operations specialists, technologists who can connect their systems to clearing infrastructures, and so on. The demands of clearing have slowed progress on bilateral infrastructure markedly. It is not entirely clear that given the choice between implementing central clearing six months faster and improving bilateral infrastructure[536], one would necessarily pick the former. By focusing on clearing, supervisors have limited the improvements that can be made to bilateral OTC derivatives market infrastructure.

10.4.4 Transparency

Some post-crisis financial rule making has been reasonably transparent. The CFTC, for instance, has made the laudable commitment to provide information on all meetings and correspondence that they have with outsiders regarding Dodd Frank Implementation[537]; it also provides full details of its senior staff, and it has an independent internal audit unit. However, many other rule writers, such as the Basel Committee, are more opaque[538]. It is important that the rule making process has broad legitimacy, so this lack of transparency is unfortunate.

10.4.5 Supervisory goals

Clearing houses perform a number of functions and central clearing has benefits, as we set out in section 9.5 and the introduction to this chapter. It is unclear which of these supervisors view as most important. Is it multilateral netting, contract continuity, default management, or something else? Are all the attributes of a centrally cleared market equally important, or are some peripheral? There is a suspicion, too, that some supervisors may simply wish to see less OTC derivatives trading for no very well-motivated reason[539]. This may not be true, but the fact that the doubt persists is evidence that sometimes supervisory goals are not clearly articulated. It would be substantially easier to assess regulations if regulators always stated their intent rather than just the means for achieving it.

10.4.6 Some clearly beneficial rules...

Some of the post-crisis regulations represent self-evident improvements in financial stability. It is difficult to argue with the requirement to report transactions to a trade repository, for instance, or to quibble with the disincentives to use ratings-trigger CSAs. Compulsory VM for inter-dealer portfolios also makes sense, although the bilateral market was close to this standard prior to regulatory intervention.

10.4.7 ...and some less evidently optimal ones

We have seen in the previous chapter that credible alternatives are available to the mandatory clearing of a fixed set of OTC derivatives. Without a clear understanding of supervisors' goals, or quantitative study, it is difficult to argue conclusively that these would be better than central clearing as mandated, but the strong suspicion must be that some of them are. The lack of discussion of these and other alternative approaches in the official community does not intimate that there is an urgent search for the best solution regardless of provenance. It rather seems as if the authorities' interpretation of how to implement the G-20 Pittsburgh declaration (discussed in section 5.5) has been taken as fixed, regardless of its costs and benefits, and regardless of the (sometimes arbitrary) choices that supervisors have made[540].

10.4.8 Responsibility

The post-crisis mandate for reform allowed rules to be made with less consultation than was commonplace hitherto[541], as we discussed earlier in this chapter. This, combined with the lack of a detailed impact study, leaves regulators with an uncomfortable dilemma. They are naturally reluctant to renege on the major post-crisis policy initiatives, but they do not know what the consequences of their rules will be. The financial system has been so decisively reshaped by regulation that substantial changes are highly likely. The responsibility for these changes, and for the behaviour of the new financial system, lies with the authorities: it cannot be otherwise, given that the post-crisis rules have largely been imposed by *fiat*. This is a substantial burden.

10.4.9 The legitimacy of regulatory arrangements

The current paradigm in financial regulation appears to be[542] techno-cratic. Politicians have vested authority in groups of experts. In some areas, transparency has not been required; nor are there always mechanisms to ensure accountability. It is only when the regulation is seen to fail dramatically, as it did in the crisis[543], that it receives wider attention.

This is understandable, given the complexity of the issues, and of the rules which seek to address them[544]. The average politically engaged individual will likely not care about the splitting of netting sets, procyclical liquidity risk, or the dangers of CCP stress. However they will be deeply perturbed if the failure of financial institutions yet again creates costs that they must bear. Moreover, they will also not tolerate minimal growth and tight credit forever.

Another vulnerability of the current paradigm is its global character. The major standards setting bodies are often global, as is the market; but this global consensus must be transposed into national legislation. If there are doubts about the legitimacy or efficacy of the bodies which produced the global rules[545], then national politics may intervene[546]. This may become likely if the post-crisis rule making does not yield the desired financial stability and growth. A retreat from global, consensus-based rule making would increase costs on many market participants without necessarily enhancing stability[547]. Therefore it is to be hoped that, despite their inchoate nature, the speed of their enactment, the lack of clarity over their goals, and the unquantified selection of arbitrary policy, the new regulations will enjoy a measure of success.

Concluding Remarks and Public Policy Perspectives

Financial regulation is clearly necessary. There was an overwhelming imperative for better rules after the crisis, and a widespread perception of urgency. In retrospect, though, it seems to this author that an opportunity for adopting a better, more evidence-based, less narrowly hegemonic approach to public policy may have been partially squandered. This would proceed thus:

- Politicians, perhaps in co-operation with supervisors, articulate a clear set of goals.

- The gap between the current regulatory environment and the desired end state or states is identified. A collection of metrics to measure the success or failure of new policies are identified[548].

- The metrics are put out to comment and revised if necessary[549].

- Various alternative proposals which may close the gap are selected. These may include 'club' approaches[550], such as were used in the FED letter process, as well as new regulations.

- Draft rules to implement the principal alternatives are proposed.

- These rules are put out for public comment and revisions are invited.

+ Public hearings are held.

+ All comments made and any lobbying received are disclosed. The minutes of all supervisory deliberations are published (perhaps with a delay).

+ A quantitative impact study is launched on the various alternatives.

+ A separate group is convened to analyse the potential costs, unintended consequences, and regulatory arbitrage potentially introduced by the proposed rules[551].

+ The comments and impact analysis are considered at an open hearing, and a 'winning' mix of proposals are selected.

+ Final rules are proposed. If the new rules are substantial or innovative, a second comment and analysis period may be required.

+ The impact of the rules is regularly reviewed. The selected metrics are recalculated, market changes are analysed, regulatory arbitrages are identified, and the results of the review are published. Recalibrations are made if required.

+ The participants in the process are held accountable for the success or failure of the regulations.

This would be a substantially more open and less sacerdotal model of public policy development than the one that has characterised the development of recent OTC derivatives regulation. There is, of course, the danger of subversion due to the substantial resources the industry has available to devote to the comment process. However, this danger is perhaps over-stated[552], and can anyway be mitigated by the inclusion of independent experts, academics, and other interested parties[553]. Critically, it includes objective measures of success. Any process of accountability would be contestable, but at least the articulation and measurement of key metrics would provide evidence in this dialogue.

The financial system is too complex, and its reaction to change too unpredictable, for anyone to be able to accurately predict the future. Even well-intentioned, thoughtful and knowledgeable groups of people will sometimes write regulations that have undesirable side effects. This is especially so when the changes are profound; the rules are inter-related; and when a single technique, such as the posting of collateral, is relied upon to reduce risk.

The unintended consequence of regulatory change is sometimes increased systemic risk, sometimes a reduction in economic growth; and sometimes both. This does not mean that public policy should not develop, but it does imply that there should be a degree of modesty in claims concerning the efficacy of regulation, a thorough process for identifying deleterious consequences, and a means of correcting them. The fix should not always be new rules either: it should be possible to subtract as well as add to the regulatory corpus.

The post-crisis rule making demonstrated some of the best of policy makers: firm actions were taken. However, some ill-considered, suboptimal rules were enacted too. We should not be afraid to admit this, and to try to produce a better framework. Society was not well-served by the pre-crisis financial system, and it does not deserve reforms that introduce substantial new costs and new risks, unless these represent clear, quantifiable improvements. OTC derivatives clearing as currently mandated may not be the optimum policy, for all the reasons set out in the preceding pages. It may not even unequivocally increase financial stability.

Therefore, despite regulatory fatigue, we hope that it is not too unreasonable to suggest that supervisors consider a little more change. Many modifications could be recommended, but most of them would require significant policy adjustments. We end, then with three wishes for OTC derivatives clearing rules which might be possible within the current framework:

1. Change the clearing mandate from one based on products to one based on a percentage of transactions, start slowly[554], and initially at least grant wide exemptions from mandatory clearing. It is also important here to make the changes required to the rules for bilateral derivatives needed to make these exemptions effective[555];

2. Enforce higher risk management, equity capital and financial resources requirements on systemically important OTC derivatives clearing houses[556], and enact legislation allowing them, when necessary, to have access to the central bank window;

3. Reduce liquidity risk by requiring CCPs to adopt margin practices which have low procyclicality, and do not require initial margin posting by non-systemic counterparties in the bilateral OTC derivatives market.

Notes

[497]One of the advantages of contract continuity, as W. Dudley points out in his speech *Reforming the OTC derivatives market* (19th March 2012, available at www.bis.org/review/r120323b.pdf), is not just that one party does not have to close out, but also that stressed parties who are close to failure do not suffer liquidity outflows caused by novations.

[498]As usual in such matters, these conclusions are debatable: for instance the judgement as to whether smaller dealers will benefit more or less than larger ones depends on the balance between communist and capitalist policies.

[499]The IMF suggests that the impact of mandatory clearing rules and the clearing membership bar could further concentrate the benefits of OTC derivatives trading in a small number of firms: see chapter 3 of the October 2012 Global Financial Stability Report available at www.imf.org/External/Pubs/FT/GFSR/2012/02/index.htm.

[500]See, for instance, E. Kane, *Interaction of Financial and Regulatory Innovation*, American Economic Review Volume 78 (1988).

[501]The IntercontinentalExchange's share price has more than doubled from its post-crisis lows at the time of writing. ICE recently acquired NYSE Euronext. Subsequently one of the motivations for the transaction – economies of scale in clearing – became clear when acquirer and acquiree announced that they have enacted a clearing services agreement under which ICE Clear Europe will provide clearing services to the London market of NYSE Liffe. See ICE's press release *IntercontinentalExchange and NYSE Euronext Enter Clearing Services Agreement; ICE Clear Europe to Clear NYSE Liffe's Derivatives Markets*, 20th December 2012 available at ir.theice.com/releasedetail.cfm?ReleaseID=728051.

[502]See LCH's press release *Closing of London Stock Exchange Group Plc's Offer for LCH.Clearnet*, 13th April 2012 available at www.lchclearnet.com/media_centre/press_releases/2012-04-13_3.asp.

[503]P. Norman in *Combining safety, efficiency and competition in Europe's post-trade market* (CSFI, October 2012) available at www.csfi.org/files/files/Combining_Safety_v10_WEB_VERSION_1MB.pdf suggests that the European Commission should launch a competition policy investigation into listed derivatives clearing houses. This should be extended to OTC derivatives central clearing too, especially given the increasing connectivity between listed and OTC markets caused by potential cleared OTC/future cross-margining and the futurisation discussed in the section 10.2.4. Perhaps the injection of competition considerations into this debate may ameliorate the understandable tendency of supervisors not to interfere with market structure unless there are stability concerns. Thus for instance the CPSS have commented that there is insufficient evidence to suggest that one model of clearing is less stable than another (*Market structure developments in the clearing industry: implications for financial stability*, November 2010): that may be, but questions of efficiency, moral hazard, and the extraction of monopoly rents are also important. As R. Seitia et al. point out in *Derivatives reform: Evolution, not revolution* (Barclays Research, June 2010), there is a

danger that CCPs become the new Government Sector Enterprises: they could easily become too big to fail, while functioning as quasi-monopolies run for private profit.

[504]This last phrase come from the CGFS's *The macrofinancial implications of alternative configurations for access to central counterparties in OTC derivatives markets*, Paper Number 46 (November 2011) available at www.bis.org/press/p111117.htm. This contains a longer discussion of the risks and benefits of interoperability.

[505]It is interesting that earlier drafts of EMIR contained strong access provisions which would have made vertical silos less likely: these were watered down in the final version. This may however not be enough to protect the franchises of new entrants to European OTC derivatives clearing.

[506]UBS's exit from trading most fixed income products is an example of this trend. For a wider perspective, see Citibank Research *Global Banks and Brokers Sizing Up "The Elephant in the Room" – Regulatory Paradigm Shift and the Impact on Fixed Income Trading*, 30 May 2012.

[507]The estimate that future-style margining (i.e. with a one day MPOR) will produce requirements that are approximately 50% lower than those needed for cleared interest rate swaps comes from CME: see *Deliverable Interest Rate Swap Futures* available at www.cmegroup.com/trading/interest-rates/deliverable-interest-rate-swap-futures.html.

[508]The Dodd Frank block trading requirements do not apply to futures.

[509]The replacement of swaps with swap futures potentially challenge a number of elements of the reform agenda in addition to margin and block trading requirements including dealer registration, execution competition and trade reporting to a single aggregating repository.

[510]It has already proved attractive in the energy market: see the Financial Times article *NYSE Liffe readies for OTC shake-up* 3rd December 2012.

[511]For more details on the contract, see the CME's *Deliverable Interest Rate Swap Futures* (December 2012) available at www.cmegroup.com/trading/interest-rates/files/dsf-overview.pdf.

[512]For a broader perspective on these issues, see the Morgan Stanley/Oliver Wyman report *The Future of Capital Markets Infrastructure*, 16th February 2011.

[513]This means that supervisors must be vigilant in monitoring (a) the 'chase to the bottom' in IM; and (b) cross margining benefits between OTC and listed products whose prudence depends on being able to liquidate OTC and listed portfolios simultaneously.

[514]McKinsey research, in *New regulation and its impact on capital-markets businesses: Day of reckoning?* (September 2011) has a further discussion of the need for banks to 'optimise' the product mix that they carry, reducing in particular their activities in products like bilateral OTC derivatives with high capital requirements.

[515]If the basis risk is sufficient to deny them hedge accounting then they may also have unwanted earnings volatility too.

[516]A further analysis of the impact of the US rules on end-users can be found in J. White et al., *Implications of New U.S. Derivatives Regulations on End-Users of*

Swaps, Cravath, Swaine & Moore (2012) available at www.cravath.com/files/Uploads/Documents/Publications/3387193_1.pdf.

[517]We discussed in section 6.2.4 the extension from the widely agreed 2008 position of developing a CCP for credit derivatives to nearly all classes of OTC derivatives (with FX being the special case). This decision, enacted without detailed study, could perhaps serve as an exemplar of policy set before its consequences were clear and never re-visited.

[518]This is a difficult area as there are few commentators without a vested interest. Regulators naturally and properly wish to demonstrate that their proposals enhance stability without creating a serious impediment to growth, while financial services institutions and end users wish to reduce costs and other burdens on them. The point here is that it is reasonable to ask whether the result of this dialogue is an optimal balance between cost and safety. Certainly, as David Lawton, Director of Markets at UK FSA said recently 'If derivatives hedging is no longer available to the real economy at a realistic price, this would be a significant problem' (Speech, November 2012 available at www.fsa.gov.uk/library/communication/speeches/2012/1122-dl.shtml).

[519]For instance, in the CFTC's proposed regime, a non-financial entity is exempt from clearing a swap if it uses that swap to hedge commercial risk, and the transaction is reported to a trade repository. Moreover, the terms 'financial entity' and 'commercial risk' are defined ones, and there will be a cost associated with monitoring these. See the Commodity Futures Trading Commission's *End-User Exception to the Clearing Requirement for Swaps; Final Rule*, Federal Register Volume 77, No. 139 (July 2012) available at www.cftc.gov/ucm/groups/public/@lrfederalregister/documents/file/2012-17291a.pdf.

[520]These higher costs are partly a result of the need to fund larger cash amounts, and partly due to the operational complexity of maintaining segregated accounts. For instance, full segregation of a large asset manager's cleared transactions could require tens of thousands of collateral accounts, each of which must be separately processed and reconciled.

[521]It has been anecdotally reported that the liquidity demands of dealing with one-ways CSAs, as required by many sovereigns and sovereign wealth funds, are a motivation for some second tier OTC derivatives dealers to consider withdrawing from the market.

[522]P. Norman, *op. cit.* discusses the investment by both Euroclear and Clearstream in European collateral businesses: these are just two examples of the rush to exploit the opportunities thrown up by collateral optimisation.

[523]Such as those proposed by the Vickers and Liikanen reports: these will increase bank liquidity requirements by forbidding some forms of inter-group funding and by imposing limits on exposures between group companies.

[524]This has been analysed by M. Singh, J, Aitken in *Deleveraging after Lehman–Evidence from Reduced Rehypothecation*, IMF Working paper WP/09/42 (March 2009).

[525]K. Meyer, T. Riesack, in *OTC Clearing Part 4: OTC Clearing and its Impact on Collateral Management*, DerivAlert article, 5th October 2012, available at www.derivalert.org/blog/

bid/82778/OTC-Clearing-Part-4-OTC-Clearing-and-its-Impact-on-Collateral-Management put the increase in required collateral from these effects at between $2T and $4T while reminding us that the International Monetary Fund (in their April 2012 Financial Stability Review) predict that sovereign downgrades will, by 2016, reduce the supply of high quality collateral by $9T. If even these comparatively conservative estimates are correct, then collateral optimisation may be as important a trend for banks in coming years as capital optimisation.

[526]It is worth noting that if a CM finances margin for a client, then the cost of that financing has to be paid by the client. This spread could remove some of the advantages of pre-trade transparency by adding an opaque factor into pricing.

[527]By June 2012 the ratio of cleared inter-dealer trades to cleared client trades was nearly three hundred to one: this is perhaps an indication of the lack of enthusiasm from clients for clearing.

[528]Such as that for bank default fund contributions.

[529]M. Power, in *The Invention of Operational Risk*, LSE ESRC Centre for Analysis of Risk and Regulation Discussion Paper No. 16 (June 2003), available at eprints.lse.ac.uk/21368/1/DP16.pdf says that regulation evolves 'in the shadow of crisis', a nicely evocative phrase given the deep abyss of endless night we began the chapter with.

[530]Supervisory concerns about counterparty credit risk have been addressed in Basel III with extra capital requirements, in Dodd Frank and EMIR by clearing, and in joint IOSCO/Basel work by margin requirements for bilateral transactions. These changes interact and potentially create a larger aggregate impact that their sum: such effects are worthy of study.

[531]For more on the issues around extra-territoriality see for instance Shearman and Sterling's two memos *OTC Derivatives Regulation and Extraterritoriality* and *OTC Derivatives Regulation and Extraterritoriality II* (respectively October 2011 and September 2012 and available via www.shearman.com).

[532]It should be noted that there is no requirement for supervisors to only enact rules which have no costs. In some jurisdictions at least they are however behoven to analyse costs before enactment. See for instance Judge Howell's opinion in the US District Court District of Columbia case *Investment Company Institute, et al. vs. United States Commodity Futures Trading Commission*, 12th December 2012.

[533]At the time of writing the FSB's list is given in their document *Update of group of global systemically important banks* (November 2012) available at www.financialstabilityboard.org/publications/r_121031ac.pdf.

[534]It may be too difficult to do this for every portfolio, so representative portfolios for each category of counterparty might have to be used, then some intelligent scaling applied. For instance, IM should scale roughly as short term PFE.

[535]Notably in the splitting of the client portfolios and in the hypothesis of the future balance of business.

[536]E.g. trade confirmation and reconciliation processes, daily valuation and collateral management processes; enhanced trade compression; or the development of a

market-wide process for determining the close out amount on a portfolio of bilateral derivatives: see the Third Report of the CRMPG, *Containing Systemic Risk: The Road to Reform* (August 2008) available at www.crmpolicygroup.org/docs/CRMPG-III.pdf for more details.

[537]The page www.cftc.gov/transparency/index.htm has more on the CFTC's commitment to transparency.

[538]As D. Held and K. Young put it, 'most institutions of financial governance have promulgated an exclusionary model for participation'. See *The world crisis: global financial governance: principles of reform*, LSE Research Online (May 2012) available via eprints.lse.ac.uk.

[539]See for instance S. Cecchetti's remarks *Making OTC derivatives less OTC* (June 2010) available at www.bis.org/speeches/sp100616.htm. This speech contains the suggestion that OTC derivatives dealers should be encouraged to create standardised exchange traded derivatives. It does not consider the costs to the real economy of the basis risks introduced by standardisation; it does not make the case for exchange-trading (as opposed to alternative execution models); and it confuses an absence of counterparty risk with exchange-trading and central clearing. As we have seen, counterparty credit risk arises whether a contract is cleared or not, and it can be mitigated in both bilateral and cleared markets. Would it be entirely unreasonable, then, for some readers to consider that this style of reasoning amounts to a non sequitur?

[540]See for instance the Financial Stability Board's *OTC Derivatives Market Reforms – Third Progress Report on Implementation* (15th June 2012) available at www.financialstabilityboard.org/publications/r_121031a.pdf. The discussion here is replete with reaffirmations of commitments and redoubled efforts; there is scant appraisal of whether better public policy choices could have been made. Moreover, and perhaps more importantly, policy has been made incrementally, with new initiatives built on old. There has been no review of the whole framework; no 'clean sheet of paper'. Thus for instance clearing has been mandated based on existing (mostly securities and listed derivatives) CCPs, without considering the potential for a new, global utility OTC derivatives clearer.

[541]The implementing rules, such as those produced by the CFTC or ESMA, were subject to public comment, but the primary legislation was not.

[542]T. Büthe and W. Mattli, in *The New Global Rulers: The Privatization of Regulation in the World Economy*, Princeton University Press 2012 say that the essence of global rule-making is political: despite the technocratic window dressing, there is much to commend this view.

[543]It should be noted that the asset class which Basel II treated most generously – residential mortgages – was also the asset class responsible for the largest financial crisis in two generations.

[544]The regulatory framework has come under increasing criticism for its complication: see for instance the Jackson Hole paper by A. Haldane, V. Madouros, *The dog and the frisbee* (Bank of England, 31st August 2012) available at www.bankofengland.co.

uk/publications/Documents/speeches/2012/speech596.pdf. The increasingly intricate (and arbitrageable) nature of the bank capital rules has caused many investors to lose confidence in them.

[545]For a rosy, pre-crisis view of the legitimacy of the Basel process, see M. Barr, G. Miller, *Global Administrative Law: The View from Basel*, European Journal of International Law, Volume 17, Issue 1 (February 2006), available at ejil.oxfordjournals.org/content/17/1/15.full.pdf. C. Bradley, in *Consultation and Legitimacy in Transnational Standard-Setting*, Minnesota Journal of International Law, Volume 20 (July 2011) available at www.minnjil.org/wp-content/uploads/2011/07/Bradley-Final-Version.pdf takes a more nuanced, post-crisis perspective.

[546]The beginnings of this process can perhaps be seen in features of national legislation such as the Collins Amendment to the Dodd Frank Act (limiting the benefit that US banks can obtain from internationally agreed changes to prior rules) or the EU's modification of the Basel III definition of capital.

[547]There is, though, one argument in favour of regulatory diversity. If global rules are destabilising, then the resulting crisis may affect the entire financial system. Local rules may do less damage. Moreover, they facilitate competition between rule sets which might in time lead to better rules everywhere. Against this, the potential for regulatory arbitrage in a setting with diverse regulatory frameworks is considerable.

[548]Metrics are vital to add accountability to the regulatory process. Without them, there is a real danger of a 'do this – there, we said it would work, and it did' model, whereby changes in regulations are never explained, failures are not admitted, and no responsibility is taken. This may serve to reduce the legitimacy of the regulatory framework, so mechanisms are needed to prevent it. For a much longer discussion of accountability and legitimacy in regulation, see J. Black, *Constructing and contesting legitimacy and accountability in polycentric regulatory regimes*, Regulation & Governance Volume 2 (2008), available via www.lse.ac.uk.

[549]Goodhart's law, whereby economic indicators lose their information content once they are used to target policy, should of course be borne in mind here.

[550]'Club good' techniques change shared infrastructure or documentation without the need for regulation, as discussed in endnote 4. Thus the FED achieved substantial reduction of operational risk in the OTC derivatives market by encouraging private actors to resolve their confirmation backlog. Many of the suggestions made in section 9.5 seek to establish or extend club goods.

[551]I first suggested that regulators consider including a regulatory arbitrage group in their rule-making process during Basel II. Subsequently, the suggestion of a Devil's Advocate has received wider coinage. It is for instance one of the mechanisms proposed for avoiding regulatory capital in D. Moss and D. Carpenter's chapter *Conclusion: A Focus on Evidence and Prevention* in *Preventing Regulatory Capture: Special Interest Influence and How to Limit it*, the Tobin Project (2013) available via tobinproject.org. Additional means of achieving this end include regulatory transparency, consumer empowerment, and the inclusion of diverse viewpoints and interests in the rule-making process.

[552] K. Young, in *Transnational Regulatory Capture? An Empirical Examination of Transnational Lobbying over the Basel Committee on Banking Supervision*, Review of International Political Economy, Volume 19, No. 4 (2012), discusses lobbying and regulatory capture. The issues are nuanced, with lobbying being rather less effective than feared (or hoped), and indeed sometimes decidedly counterproductive.

[553] For an impressive example of the ability of interested parties outside banks or trade associations to make meaningful comments on financial regulations, see Occupy the SEC's comment letter on the Volcker rule, available at www.sec.gov/comments/s7-41-11/s74111-230.pdf. A wider analysis of lobbying and regulatory capture is given in *The Making of Good Financial Regulation: Towards a Policy Response to Regulatory Capture*, S. Pagliari (Ed.), International Centre for Financial Regulation (2012) available via www.stefanopagliari.net.

[554] A slow start is a good idea not just because it will take market participants some time to smooth out operational and legal issues, but also because supervisors are still learning how to supervise OTC derivatives CCPs. There is a lot to do here, as the UK FSA's *FSA Review of Counterparty Credit Risk Management By Central Counterparties* (Finalised Guidance, January 2012, available at www.fsa.gov.uk/static/pubs/guidance/fg12-03.pdf) indicates, and this process should not be rushed.

[555] For instance, supervisors should exempt banks from the Basel III CVA charge on those parties who do not have to clear, and exempt all but the most systemic parties from compulsory initial margin posting. This would go some way to ensuring both safety and that the bilateral market was a viable alternative to clearing for end users.

[556] The CPSS/IOSCO principles (discussed in chapter 8) are a useful start, but they do not in my view go far enough when applied to systemically important OTC derivatives clearing houses.

Index

Printed and bound by CPI Group (UK) Ltd, Croydon, CR0 4YY